THE CHINESE TRAGEDY OF *KING LEAR*

The Chinese Tragedy of *King Lear*

Nan Z. Da

PRINCETON UNIVERSITY PRESS
PRINCETON & OXFORD

Published by Princeton University Press
41 William Street, Princeton, New Jersey 08540
99 Banbury Road, Oxford OX2 6JX

press.princeton.edu

GPSR Authorized Representative: Easy Access System Europe - Mustamäe tee 50, 10621 Tallinn, Estonia, gpsr.requests@easproject.com

ISBN: 9780691269160
ISBN (ebook): 9780691269177

Library of Congress Control Number: 2024047266 (print) | 2024047267 (ebook)

British Library Cataloging-in-Publication Data is available

Editorial: Anne Savarese and James Collier
Production Editorial: Natalie Baan
Jacket Design: Chris Ferrante
Production: Erin Suydam
Publicity: Carmen Jimenez and Alyssa Sanford
Copyeditor: Anne Cherry

Jacket image: DesignToonsy / Shutterstock

This book has been composed in Miller

Printed in the United States of America

10 9 8 7 6 5 4 3 2 1

For Wang Shiwei

CONTENTS

PREFACE

FOR MORE THAN SIX YEARS I have taught Shakespeare's *King Lear*, a piece of literature far outside my field, in a class that introduces students to the history and praxis of literary criticism. I usually take six classes to read the entire play out loud, together, asking at every turn: How did this happen? How did we get here? If you do not remember, why might you not remember?

I picked *Lear* because it fast-tracks students to the hardest parts of literature and literary criticism. It is in the discussion of *Lear* that the terms "data" and "critical data" come up for the first time in literary studies: "data" in an 1819 lecture by Samuel Coleridge and "critical data" in an influential essay by Stanley Cavell, published in 1987, called "The Avoidance of Love: A Reading of *King Lear*." These are not coincidences, as *Lear* places a great strain on interpretive validity, on accurate assessment and recall. The play gets to the very heart of literary criticism, and every critic must confront it at some point.

I also picked *Lear* for private reasons: *Lear* helped me understand a history that has followed me across two continents and over a still open-ended stretch of time. Something about it had felt familiar for too long. In my mind I was drawing a long and elaborate analogy.

Teachers of literature and criticism have to deal with bad analogies and allegoresis all the time. You suffocate something with a one-to-one connection, ironically by proving that any connection can be made. Nonetheless, here it is: *Lear*, China, China, *Lear*. I promised some people I loved I would tell a story and, being poor at storytelling, I resorted to a literary critic's gambit. If I can show you some things about *Lear*, a story that did not technically happen, then I can show you some things that did happen. If you had no interest in *Lear* but some interest in contemporary Chinese history, then you might change your mind about *Lear* after the comparison.

The tragedy of Maoist and post-Maoist China and Shakespeare's *Tragedy of King Lear* are uncannily similar: they reveal each other's most intricate inner workings and contextual circumstances. In a sense this book treats China's long twentieth-century history as a manifestation of the play and uses this history in turn to explain the design of *Lear*. The most "Chinese" of Shakespeare's plays, *Lear*'s comparability to China goes beyond themes of filial piety, ingratitude, scalar disharmony, and merit-blind redistribution. The two also share a logic of gaslighting, a pain rooted in real withholding, and other crimes and cruelties that come from the empty forms that pop up when the personal totally collapses into the political.

I begin with things one knows about *King Lear* from hearsay, the things you probably know about the play even if you have never read it or seen a stage production of it, and I begin with tales from my own childhood in late 1980s China. Even if you know only the basic outline of the play and this period of history, you've already encountered enough strange things that don't quite add up. You vaguely remember that King Lear asks his daughters to say how much they love him, and promises to divide his kingdom accordingly. He does not wait to hear every daughter's answer, however, before he makes his assignments. Instead, it's one answer, one third of the kingdom; another answer, another third. This fact, plain for all to see, is that we have here a pro forma ceremony, one in which the outcome is decided in advance and everyone is simply expected to go through the movements. The pro forma presages evil and discord and contains, as well, great, beseeching love. We'll learn later that that last third—the one reserved for the favorite daughter—is not like the other thirds, and that there are other unsolvable problems of authority, such as the debate over *Lear*'s different versions and the mysteries of its immediate circumstances. We can set that aside for now and begin as a beginner begins, with only the information that's been given. The same goes for Chinese history—there is a huge volume of it (most of it in the chapter titled History), but you enter it through tales.

This book is divided into Tales—the stuff you hear as a child—then History, Tragedy, Comedy, and Romance. The "Tales" chapter tells some simple stories from *King Lear* and twentieth-century China, hoping to reveal something about the tale as a form. I also say a little here about how *Lear* got to China each time it got to China.

The "History" chapter contains historical information—on Maoism but also on broader and deeper events in China—and reflects on the challenges of historiography, the genre into which *Lear* also falls, given its other title (in the Quarto version, *Lear* is *The History of King Lear*; in the Folio, *Tragedy of King Lear*) and its confounding relationship to British succession.

The "Tragedy" chapter takes up the nature of Learian tragedy and the link between tragedy and politics; surveys the tragic arts, including Jacobean plays and Peking opera; and includes a longish bit of personal/family tragedy.

The chapter called "Comedy" discusses the actually very funny parts of *Lear* and Maoism, the comedic work of restoration and repair, the role of the critic as fool, and the way comedy can precipitate tragedy. I ask what happened to Lear's Fool, and what befalls things that come as duplicates or in halves, or as critical other-selves.

The book ends with "Romance" because it's romantic to do so, and because I think *Lear* is about being deeply in love. If history repeats itself—and *Lear* gives you the reason it would do so—the first and last signs of that repetition tend to occur in romance and in love.

Note

This book uses the Conflated version of *Lear*. The 1608 Quarto edition of *The True Chronicle of the History of the Life and Death of King Lear*[1] has 285 lines not in the Folio *Tragedy of King Lear*, including an entire scene (scene 17). The Folio version, which scholars agree reflected a performed play, has 114 lines that do not appear in the Quarto. These and sundry other differences guarantee that readers, audiences, and commentators are never on the same page. The Conflated version presents its own troubles, ranging from the existence of discrepant conflated versions to the possibility that it does not sort out mistakes of printing and misjudgment on the part of through whose hands the play passed. My method of citation is minimalist: longer passages from the play will be marked with act, scene, and line number. Footnotes are few. Sources can be found in the chapter-by-chapter bibliography at the end.

1. The title page of the First Quarto advertises the play as "a true chronicle historie of the life and death of King Lear and his three daughters With the vnfortunate life of Edgar, sonee and heire to the Earle of Gloster, and his sullen and assumed humor of Tom of Bedlam: as it was played before the Kings Maiestie at Whitehall vpon S. Stephans night in Christmas hollidayes."

CHAPTER ONE

Tales

YOU THINK I won't do it?

Bluffing is one way to commit yourself to something. Of all the bluffs in literature, the most devastatingly childish one occurs at the beginning of *King Lear*.

A king wishes to engineer something complicated involving his domain, his retirement, and his daughters, each in their turn. He bounds onto the stage and without delay sets this into motion. He asks his daughters to publicly profess their love, promising to divvy up his land accordingly. The two older daughters answer with gross flattery, the youngest with reticence. What happens next is what happens when the worst human beings are simply handed the keys to the city.

Something is amiss in Lear's division of the kingdom. Leave aside the practicality of the redistribution itself and, still, something is not right. The eldest daughter, Goneril, goes first; Lear gives her a third of the land. Then his second daughter, Regan, receives the second third. Finally we get to his third daughter, Cordelia, who answers his request to speak with "Nothing, my lord." *Nothing?* he asks. *Nothing*, she responds. *Nothing will come of nothing*, he quips. Goneril and Regan digest the kingdom between them. Cordelia is exiled.

If Lear wished to base his rewards on their answers, he should have waited for everyone's response before making the assignments. Parceling out the kingdom one third at a time, rather than at the end, reveals the test to be an empty formality, a type of cheating. What tends to happen in these circumstances? What is the causal relationship between "the wish to obtain by one means what can only be had by another," as Blaise Pascal put it, and catastrophic, insatiable cruelty?[1] Within twenty-four hours, it seems, the kingdom is shoddily divided; his loyal servant, the Earl of Kent, exiled, his other servant, the Earl of Gloucester, tricked into grievous mistakes. Everything happens in what the King of France, a suitor for Cordelia and later her husband, calls "a trice of time." Lear had envisioned that in his retirement he would stay with Regan half the time, Goneril the other half. A few days later (certainly not much later) the two older daughters start to pare down his needs. Meanwhile, the Earl of Gloucester also wrongs his own child, Edgar, and effectively casts him into exile. It all happens in no time. Doors are closed on the elderly, leaving them exposed to the elements; the vulnerable become destitute and homeless; a faithful retainer is put in the stocks, his time there arbitrarily extended; an old man's eyes are clawed out, one after the other; a war is fought and quickly ended; a prisoner is spared too late, with no good reason for the delay. A few people devise some way to take someone down a peg, and keep going, because nothing intervenes.

The Romantic critic and poet Samuel Taylor Coleridge was the first to notice something wrong with the opening scene and put it in writing. We don't even need to get as far as the division of the kingdom! Just the first "four or five lines" of the play indicated that the division of the kingdom was "already determined and in all its particulars," a formality that had all of the subsequent tragedy coiled within it.

1. From *Pensées*, no. 151, trans. J. M. Cohen (Penguin Classics, 1961).

Even now I go over this knowledge talismanically, like the Chinese multiplication drills that I learned as a young child. Learning about *Lear*'s illogical setup marked the beginning of my literary-critical consciousness, and the beginning of my ability to process what had happened to my family and the grown-ups around me, the fact that something so large had happened at all. In paying just a little attention to the sequence of actions you could see what might be wrong.

People feel vindicated by the exposé of a pro forma. A test of worthiness has been conducted with the outcome determined in advance, a fait accompli that asks only for the ceremony of rubber-stamping. After all, you are calling bullshit when you say that the division of the kingdom is a done deal. Cordelia's refusal to play along speaks truth to one of the worst forms of power, a weak authority hiding a private purpose inside a public one. In Mandarin Chinese Cordelia's temperament might be called *zui ying*, "hard mouth," an image of an unbending will. In making the sounds *zui ying*, the palate is already preparing an invitation to cruelty.

Lear is bluffing, and when his bluff is called he has no choice but to follow through and bring about the worst possible outcome. If he can do it quickly and with force, he reduces the risk of losing face. And when face is still lost, he plays the only card he has left: *I'll make an example out of you. I'll make an example out of all of you.* Citizens of authoritarian regimes might accordingly identify with Cordelia's position. Indeed, who wouldn't identify with Cordelia? What could be more satisfying than to call such a bluff? This is tyrannical power that rewards the most mercenary and hyperbolic, power that puts a gag on those who would call it out. Silencing happens in many ways, but in *Lear* the gag is existential. For the two older daughters, the philosopher and critic Stanley Cavell observed, the task is simple enough; they need only pretend to love where they do not love. But Cordelia isn't simply being asked to say what's not true, what she does not feel. Cavell explains that it is actually worse than this. For Cordelia, "to *pretend* to love where you really *do* love, is not obviously possible."

Is reasoning possible here? Cordelia cannot quite play along, either because she cannot grasp unreason when it comes so quickly, or because she doesn't want to compromise her conscience, or because she doesn't think it would work. Lear's bald need is immature, as observed by the early-twentieth-century critic A. C. Bradley, who saw in Lear's "mere form" "a childish scheme." Cordelia so angers her father because she, as Bradley puts it, has "put him to open shame." Moreover, Cordelia couldn't take her own advice to "love, and be silent." Forced to speak, she sees a chance to gently correct his mistake. *Look*, Cordelia says, *the math doesn't check out*: "Why have my sisters husbands if they say they love you all? Haply when I shall wed that lord whose hand must take my plight shall carry half my love with him, half my care and duty."

Using elementary logic, Cordelia has denied the tyrant his preferred mode of human interaction: a show of love unmarred by dissent, an acceptance of unreason without any balking. She who does not flatter the sovereign is an ancient type that appears across all cultures. In the Chinese world order, truth-telling and governance overlap in harm. Chinese tales, romances, tragedies, philosophies, and histories all tell us that the only end for such a character is a fate worse than death.

In the end, the forthright person-child-statesman can speak only of their love. In Chinese poetics, one's country becomes the dearest of the dear, endangered by forces from without and within. One's sovereign becomes the dearest of the dear, a person's second heart. Around 290 BCE, near the end of the Warring States Period, a minister from Chu was banished to the North. The kingdom of Chu had survived three hundred years of warfare with neighboring states (in a region that would become the northeast portion of China), but it would soon be crushed by the Qin. This minister, Qu Yuan, had seen it coming. He had been banished once before, a victim of court politics, under the rule of King Huai. He returns from his exile to serve King Huai's son, King Qingxiang. Again, his advice is unheeded, and his reputation slandered. Qu Yuan lived to see King Qingxiang perish in a foreign land as a starving prisoner—one of the most humiliating ends that could befall a sovereign. Qu Yuan knew he was living in the last light of his kingdom. The aptly named "Spring and Autumn" period of history would also now end. Twilight immediately followed new beginnings. New beginnings tumbled straight into twilight.

In the premature twilight of Qu Yuan's life, the kingdom of Qin set neighboring states against one another, and thus began the first dynasty of imperial China. Empire was nigh. With Qin unification would come new forms of brutality, standardization, and human control, as well as new forms of beauty, intelligence, and resplendence. For Qu Yuan, however, it was the end. Sometime after receiving news that the capital city had fallen, Qu Yuan drowned himself in the Miluo River, clutching a heavy stone. In his poem "Beset by Sorrow," more popularly known as "Encountering Sorrow," the first Chinese long poem on civic injustice and civic love, he writes:

> The months and years wouldn't wait
> Spring and autumn kept trading places
> seeing plants and trees stripped bare
> I feared my fair one's time was short[2]

"Fair one" refers to many things: his king, his son, his country, himself. The king "saw not my heart / deceived by slander he spurned me," Qu Yuan laments. But the sovereign's misjudgment *still* does not cause total disillusionment. "Even dismembered," he

2. This translation of Qu Yuan's *Li Sao* is provided by Red Pine in *A Shaman's Lament: Two Poems by Qu Yuan* (Gray Dog Press, 2001).

writes, "I could not change / for how could I forsake my heart?" How could you pretend to love when you really do love? How could you forsake your heart?

When everything is excessively performative, even love has to overperform just to be able to see itself, even cruelty has to overperform just to be able to see itself.

Obeying some merciless law of physics, Lear's empty show balloons out and then caves inward. *You want to get real?* ask Goneril and Regan. *You want to get everything down to crude, quantifiable terms? Then let's get really real. Let's get really crude.* Lear has arranged to spend his retirement with these two, alternating between their estates. He thinks they've also agreed to the upkeep of a hundred soldiers for him. This retinue would help him pass the time but would also keep him from harm. Is that too much to ask? . . . Is it? For Lear it guarantees a modest amount of good company and protection. But one could also argue that a hundred people following you around to provide merriment, if nothing else, is just an empty form, a housekeeping burden. That's how Goneril and Regan see it. A hundred rabblerousers to have to attend to in an already unwelcome parental stay? "Men so disordered, so debauched and bold, / That this their court, infected with their manners, / Shows like a riotous inn," the daughters complain. A hundred people is too many, and so we wish "a little to disquantify your train," Goneril says to Lear after he's stayed with her awhile. Come to think of it, fifty people is too many. So is twenty-five. Come to think of it, what have you need of one? It is Regan who delivers this final blow. *You like empty form, my father?* Any last fig leaf of human dignity is just empty form. Being alive itself is just empty form.

⸙

What happened in China in the long twentieth century to millions, then to more than a billion people, resembled *Lear*'s imagined and actual worlds: a plague, a regime change, political paranoia, persecutions that were religious and theatrical in nature. These particular catastrophes begin in vicious formality and its multiplying effects.

In the course of the twentieth century, Mao Zedong, chairman of the Communist Party of China who led the People's Republic from its establishment in 1949 to his death in 1976, became increasingly paranoid about his own party cadres, and so intensified his internal purges by intensifying nationwide purges. Purges became increasingly theatrical over the three decades of Communist rule, culminating in the hysterically cathartic show trial of the Gang of Four, the Communist Party officials retroactively deemed most responsible for the horrors of the Cultural Revolution. Drop in here and you will find my paternal grandfather, a loyal party member who in the mid-1950s oversaw several units of his county's transportation bureau, a small job in an insignificant town. Because he was a hardworking bureaucrat and came from the "lower-middle peasant" class, this grandfather avoided most of the atrocities of the 1940s and '50s, except a touch of famine. In 1961, however, the party split into two factions. China enacted a new round of purges and the revolution came for him.

Even the nature of one's employment became creative inspiration for cruelty. Members of the transportation bureau, openly accused of fidelity to the state's persona non grata at the time, were denounced and then made to crawl along the newly tarred roads that they themselves had built only a few years after purging their previous higher-ups. My grandfather crawled from the entrance of the bureau office all the way to the East Gate of the old city wall. They crawled in a line for eight hours.

Later that year, my grandfather was directed to stand at the far side of the proscenium in a denunciation ceremony, a weekly ritual in which hundreds and sometimes thousands of people gathered to watch newly identified enemies of the party apologize and receive verbal and physical assaults. My grandfather stood almost offstage, and so missed the worst assaults because of an arbitrary stage direction. The official who stood at the center of the stage that day died from the proceedings, his body left onstage. Mao had set a number a decade earlier for how many people ought to die from these purges. It was rather poetic: it should be one in every thousand. In 1961 that meant 660,000 people.

I was born into the tail end of this history. In the early nineties, just before I immigrated with my family to the United States, the kindergarten teachers in the school I attended had devised a system of punishment and reward involving the production of red construction-paper socks. Each student had their own sock—there were around forty of us in the class—and altogether they took up an entire classroom wall. Props in a moral credit system, these socks were made to hold small, red tissue-paper flowers made by the students themselves. Visually, this system merged the "big red flowers" pinned to the chests of socialist heroes of the previous generation and, prior to that, to Chinese bridegrooms, with the novelty of Christmas and other European paraphernalia that Deng Xiaoping's economic reforms had brought to China. Our teachers allowed us to pin one flower to our sock every time we did something commendable or correct. It was always a joy to see one's sock spilling over with flowers.

Our social and moral credit system was a routine performed every few hours or so, and every child could keep track of every other child's status in the classroom. Demerits and capers deducted flowers from one's sock. My flowers got put up quickly, and they came down quickly. When they were plucked—and this was always an unbearable humiliation—the teacher would ask the class president to do it in front of everyone, dropping the flower ceremoniously into the rubbish bin.

By the time I left for the United States at the age of six and a half, I had been twice demoted—from class leader (*ban zhang*) to vice class leader (*fu ban zhang*) to nobody—my red stocking nearly empty despite several successful campaigns for status rehabilitation. My last memory of these efforts are from the celebrations the school held on June 1, 1992, International Children's Day. When the day arrived all the boys and girls in school lined up to be painted with the same makeup: a red dot on forehead, red cheeks and lips. Each child received a tambourine, fan, and waist drum. Officials from the Hangzhou traffic ministry visited our school and a male classmate and I were selected to present the "dear leaders" (*qin ai de lingdao*) with red tissue-paper flowers the size of our heads. Taught exactly what to say, we took turns, two phrases each, demonstratively shooting our palms up at each crescendo.

Two years later, in a faraway region of China, more than three hundred people, most of them young children, died in a school fire. Over a hundred more suffered various degrees of burns. Our family had already migrated to the United States and would learn this news many years later, thinking it happened much more recently than it did. In Xinjiang, the once semiautonomous Uighur-populated region of China, the elementary school students had gathered to welcome top-level officials from the party with song and dance. They performed in the Friendship Theater, a questionable Soviet construction whose auditorium was outfitted in unsafe flammable fabrics and plastic upholstery. When the thirteen curtains on the stage went up in flames, the auditorium swelled with the toxic fumes of melting synthetic fibers. Seats caught fire and melted skin off. As the fire wrapped around the theater the children were told to stay still in their seats to "allow leaders to exit first."

Things that were wrong happened at the same time, in the same space, as things that were very right and getting better by the minute. If anything, we sensed that 1990s China was rounding up great joys, just for us, and that such tragedies as school fires and construction failures would soon become a thing of the past. The country of my early childhood had gotten over Maoism, finally, and had not yet reached that point where a vast wealth gap created irreparably distorted realities. People gathered in a relative's apartment around a watermelon and a television program. We were so greatly attached to each other, so enamored of the way each person laughed, and we made mental notes never to forget it. I first encountered the tale of *Lear* at the seeming end of its possible relevance to my own life. China—cities like Hangzhou in particular—was restoring itself to order, slowly reversing the previous decades' descent into disorder, reversing the mechanisms by which cruelties compounded.

Tales come in handy when your frames of reference are shifting, as mine were. You know that injury is inevitable, and that complaining about everything achieves nothing. And yet, still—the child wants to be sure of right and wrong, and the right time to speak that knowledge and the right time to keep silent. She understands that things sometimes have to be done for form's sake, and concessions made for love's sake. She cannot be certain at any moment whether she lives in a perfect society or a terribly broken one. What's more, because large and severe human-made calamities in this society began in theater and ended in theater, she cannot be sure what is real and what is provisional, what is a short- or long-term act.

I've wondered since early childhood why communication, even between loved ones, looks like platitudinous pandering, deemed worthless by the parties involved unless it is performed in a public forum, where everybody can see. Phone in hand, kinfolk compete with each other for "likes" and ask others point blank why their likes have not come in. Hundreds of people in rows all clapping at the same time, bouquets and pictures with VIPs, accolades written out on red banners held by pretty children.

Why was empty speechifying and flattery—*pai ma pi* 拍马屁—a part of every event? How did we get here? What were the steps? Aren't you curious, reading *Lear*, why anyone would act this way, shooting themselves in the foot, guaranteeing that they won't be taken seriously by those they most adore?

Even without any literary-critical intervention, *Lear* will feel familiar to the average Chinese person. You have extreme loyalty contrasted with extreme treachery, a great risk for any literature that would wish to avoid the obviously good or obviously evil. You have a dry run at communism—a division of land and resources blind to merit—that is glitchy and soon becomes catastrophic. You have the gruesome collapse of law and order that happens when a wounded paternal authority doesn't give himself a face-saving exit.

You have the severance of the natural bonds between civil servants and their lieges, between kith and kin. You have the gendered burden of caring for aging parents that cannot be outsourced, and the magnification of the consequences of ungrateful children and irresponsible parents. How many times have Chinese children heard the Chinese equivalent of "How sharper than a serpent's tooth it is / To have a thankless child!," or versions of the even more severe curse that Lear brings on his daughters?

> If she [the thankless child] must teem, Create her child of spleen; that it may live, And be a thwart disnatured torment to her! Let it stamp wrinkles in her brow of youth; With cadent tears fret channels in her cheeks; Turn all her mother's pains and benefits, To laughter and contempt. (1.4.295–300)

Every day, amid joy and goodness, impotent anger and panic surged in the corridors of hospitals, schools, governmental facilities, and on the streets, in broad daylight. Almost every day I heard the Chinese equivalent of "That all the world shall—I will do such things,—What they are, yet I know not: but they shall be / The terrors of the earth." Children were struck dumb by the violent sounds made by family members, by the velocity of their spittle and tears. People making terrible scenes structured the rhythms of childhood.

In its vehemence, *Lear* gives us a modern and feudal dystopia more Taoist and Confucian than anything else I've read in the Western canon. Every circle of relations, from the personal to the cosmic, has been disordered. Things are wrong between husband and wife, sisters, brothers, fathers and daughters, fathers and sons, kings and courtiers, masters and servants, the people and the land, the land and the elements, words and the words right after them. *Lear* is the only Shakespeare tragedy to have a subplot, in the story of Gloucester and his sons, that mirrors the main plot so closely. The Earl of Gloucester, like Lear in age and rough size, has two sons, and he too cannot see correctly who is true, who is false. *Lear* gives you doppelgängers at the level of characters, phrases, and things even more abstract than these . . . and they are all wrong between and within themselves and can't even help each other. Gloucester's tale, for example, doesn't make Lear's any easier to understand or avoid.

Lear reads like a Christian allegory *and* a Confucian morality test: Christian allegory, in the sense that it is designed to make you learn what hope is, what despair is, and the basic characters and tropes that will appear on your way. The play does depict what can only seem like evidence of God's abandonment of humans, just as critics say, though I do not believe it ends in nihilism. Its human sacrifices straddle the primitive and the modern world, sacrifices like Christ's, whose point, whose effectiveness, is not easily comprehended. *Lear* scans like a Confucian morality test because it cares so much about the actual best and the actual worst, about right and wrong, true and false. A popular view of Confucianism, when it is not appearing in fortune cookies, is that it codifies fawning traditionalism and biological conservatism: husbands and wives must look like this, families must look like this, master and servant must look like this. I don't know if Confucianism is conservative or liberal, if it is a philosophy, religion, or a cultural tradition, but I do know that *Lear* offers a solid example of something that *activates* its spidey senses: we know that parents mistreat children and children mistreat parents and that things are bad when kings are bad . . . but where does one first notice that something is wrong, and that this is a wrong that is difficult to correct? How do you know something's wrong in the first place? Is it normal disorder or not? Sometimes it's hard to know things are wrong when your whole world is just starting to move into or out of disorder, and also just because there are so many confusing signals at any time.

I first came upon the story of *Lear* through a back channel. At the end of the nineteenth century, *Lear* arrived in China as a children's story in Charles and Mary Lamb's *Tales of Shakespeare*, translated in 1904 into classical Chinese by the scholar-poets Lin Shu and Wei Yi. The translators gave the Shakespeare plays intensely cryptic names, and *King Lear* was retitled *Nü Bian*, which might be translated as "A Regime Change Caused by Daughters/Women," "The Daughter's Coup," "The Mutability of Women," or, even more darkly, "Women Causing Things to Change, to Turn (Against)."

Like anything else, Shakespeare was altered when it arrived in China. The first Chinese *Lear* left out critical sequences, for example. Mary and Charles Lamb's abridgment still preserved the illogical division of the kingdom into equal thirds one third at the time, but Lin Shu and Wei Yi's did not. *Lear* had to wait almost forty years to appear in Chinese in a less condensed form. In 1941, poet-critic Sun Dayu made a capable and fastidious translation of the play that is still considered the gold standard. He would become one of the most famous "Rightists" targeted in the Anti-Rightist Campaign of 1957, one of many Maoist purges.

The vice president of Fudan University and fifteen other academics turned him in. Sun was sentenced to six years of imprisonment by the Shanghai People's Court.

Lear was also one of four Shakespeare plays translated by the scholar Zhu Shenghao in 1943, waiting out the war with Japan in his hometown of Jiaxing, his health rapidly deteriorating. Six years earlier Zhu narrowly escaped Japanese-occupied Shanghai with his Oxford edition of the *Complete Shakespeare*, determined to complete his translation of thirty plays amid the escalating atrocities by the Japanese imperial army.[3] Many of his translation drafts were lost in the bombardments, and he had to begin again from scratch. In the summer of 1944, Japanese forces destroyed the Suzhou-Jiaxing railway and pushed nearer his hometown. Zhu died in the winter of 1944 at the age of thirty-two in a besieged city.

But none of the earlier extant translations mattered to the general public in 1989. Whatever they added or left out, whatever they wished for and feared, these translations had not been available to most people for a very long time. The literary critic and scholar Liang Shiqiu had translated a fuller version of *Lear* as early as 1936, but its debut in China was delayed till 1996, four years after our family had already left the country. Tense relations between China and Taiwan, where Liang had emigrated, caused the final delay. Before that, for an inordinately long period of time, the country had sealed its borders, closed its doors, and nothing could be seen anymore, or seen for what it was.

In 1989, I was a child in a world that was just beginning to reintroduce foreign reading materials into anthologies that you could actually buy in a bookstore. These anthologies were expensive, not affordable to us. My mother earned eighty yuan

3. In 1954, thirty-one of his translated Shakespearean plays were published together by the People's Literature Publishing House (*Renmin wenxue chubanshe*); twenty-seven of them had been published elsewhere before the founding of the People's Republic of China. It was not until 1978 that Zhu's completed texts were finally published in Beijing.

a month. An eight-volume edition of *Children's World Classics* printed on cheap paper was still four hundred yuan. Prices made no sense. Earnings made no sense. Anyway, this is how I finally got hold of *Lear*:

I remember that year there was a citywide search for the most gifted child, the beginnings of marketing campaigns for educational programs. First prize was a life-size stuffed animal, which no one in China had seen before. Second prize was this set of *Children's World Classics*. My school nominated preschoolers and kindergarteners, and parents tried to see to it that the winner would be their child. Contest officials parsed hundreds of thousands of voices looking for a kind of "child's sound," or *tong shen*, that could shift the sound of the country from the agitprop of yesteryear to the new genre of "sweepstakes." My mother also worked hard to get me into the first round, worried I would be ineligible for things, like an older sibling in charge of a seemingly precocious, but in fact terribly slow, child. Bad things happened all the time in those days to those slow on the uptake, and opportunities were lost at the last minute because of some obscure disqualification that nothing could gainsay. People hardly went through the day without waiting to hear about some exception being made or the words "I'll see what I can do for you," caught up as we all were in an anxious economy of favors given and exceptions made by mere public functionaries. Energies were focused most intensely on getting children whose parents were once in political disfavor readmitted into schools; procuring television sets from relatives who were lucky enough to be assigned to work in the television factories; and devising various ways to outmaneuver the ironclad, USSR-inspired residence registration systems to transfer residencies from rural China, where many families had been sent, back to the cities.

After a month of dreaming and yearning, I found myself eliminated in the first round of the contest. A box of blocks was dumped on the table in front of me, with instructions to put the blocks back in the box. I thought they meant I had to arrange the blocks exactly as before, and ran out of time. *Lear* came to me anyway, because some uncle or uncle of an uncle knew someone in the educational publishing bureau, and my mother groveled or almost groveled. In any case, the books were mine. Stories in these volumes included "Bluebeard," "Aladdin and His Magic Lamp," and "The Little Mermaid," and I loved them so much, and read again and again how characters come to harm and get out of it. As a children's tale, *Lear* found good company with the many other good stories in my mother's repertoire: "Ali Baba and the Forty Thieves," "Rikki Tikki Tavvi," "Scholar Dong Guo and the Wolf," "The Orphan of Zhao." Many dealt in what Bradley called "tragic effects of ingratitude," a problem that stalks all storied versions of Chinese history, and it is unclear what kind of justice should be served except death.

Lear's fairy-tale formula begins with choosing among three things: three sisters need husbands, and one draws envy from the others for being judged wiser and fairer. Nested in the story of Cordelia's rescue by the King of France after her rejection by the Duke of Burgundy are all the daughters of children's tales who need to be married off. Cordelia gathers in herself all the modest true princesses who outshine their ugly sisters in her faithfulness to the father, and faithfulness in general. Driving each of these tropes is the ancient problem of daughters and what they will or won't do. Such a lesson comes across clearly in the anonymous play performed in the 1590s called *The True Chronicle History of King Leir, and his three daughters, Gonoril, Ragan, and Cordella,* published in the Stationer's Register shortly before Shakespeare's *Lear.* In this 1605 *Leir*, quite good in its own right, the division of the kingdom begins as a clear-cut stratagem meant to solve the problem of marrying off a choosy daughter.

Morphological readings of *Lear*—asking after the other fairy tales that are embedded in it—can reveal the practical harms involved in choosing among and for women. There are many such readings—*Lear* as a version of Cinderella, or of the Judgment of Paris, for example—but it was Sigmund Freud, taking this approach to *Lear*, who characteristically arrived at the most extreme conclusion. According to Freud, Lear steps into a time-honored tradition of choosing among three women. Only here, there is no choice at all. In choosing among them, Lear chooses death.

Freud's reading doesn't make sense at first, or at all, but one can appreciate his severity. In so many words he's telling us that the play is a blind alley. In his own way, Freud was treating the play as a study in false choice: What's the point of pretending that choosing matters? In choosing anything, Lear effectively chooses death. He needs to die—the rest is just details.

For a long time readers and audiences considered *Lear* one of Shakespeare's cruelest stories, unsuited to be staged. From the late seventeenth century to the mid-nineteenth century, only an adaptation of *Lear* by the Irish poet and dramatist Nahum Tate was performed in the United Kingdom, a version that revised almost every part of the play. In his version, Cordelia welcomes her disinheritance because she is secretly in love with Edgar, Gloucester's legitimate son, and she sticks around after the division of the kingdom to help and protect her father. The people of England are disgusted enough to move to depose Goneril and Regan and restore Lear as king. He heroically saves Cordelia from murder, makes her queen, and retires as a hoary elder. Something about Shakespeare's *Lear* so disturbed Tate that he felt he had to fundamentally alter the *tale*.

When do you first sense that something is off in *King Lear*? Once you've encountered the actual play, and not just the tale, look at how it really begins. Before anything else has happened we are in the wrong, already confused in our judgment about someone else's judgment, and other people's worth.

> KENT: I thought the King had more affected the Duke of Albany than Cornwall.
>
> GLOUCESTER: It did always seem to us, but now in the division of the kingdom it appears not which of the Dukes he values most; for qualities are so weighed that curiosity in neither can make choice of either's moiety. (1.1.1–6)[4]

Later we will learn how frightening it is that the courtiers cannot tell who the king favors more, Albany or Cornwall. As if they could be indistinguishable, Albany and Cornwall! Albany might be closer to a Cornwall than to a Kent, but that's still a handsome distance away. Evaluation is severely off in this kingdom, and we need to figure out why.

Lear begins not with the division of the kingdom, then, but with this little interlude of wronging and being wrong. We learn right away that Gloucester is the type to belittle a grown child in front of another person for the sake of a crude locker-room boast, one of those character weaknesses that children most despise in their parents. Even accounting for historical attitudes toward illegitimate children, his performance is despicable. "Is not this your son, my lord?" Kent asks when, just a second later, they run into Gloucester's illegitimate son, Edmund. Hearing Gloucester's immediately deprecating remarks about Edmund and not comprehending, Kent says, "I cannot conceive you." Gloucester thereupon immediately puns on "conceive" to boast about his whoring. "Do you smell a fault?" Gloucester asks at the end of his little riddle about Edmund's conception, smug in his cleverness.

It looks like Shakespeare is stalling—Get on with the business of the division of the kingdom, already!—but he is in fact

4. This is the gloss given in the Norton edition: "that careful scrutiny of both parts cannot determine which portion is preferable."

rushing. He needs to show you something, quickly, in a tempo that Coleridge described as "combin[ing] length with rapidity." Shakespeare is rushing and stalling at the same time.

Shakespeare wrote this play during one of many severe plagues and equally severe quarantines between the death of Queen Elizabeth and the accession of James I. The young were being picked off; London teemed and was barren. Plague is only directly referenced twice in *Lear*, but the plague's superstitious link to evil is relevant here. Literal contagion also helps formalize the law of guilt by association. Plague outbreaks practically consumed the first decade of the century (1603–4, 1606, and 1608–9). Ordinary people joined in the business of scientific monitoring, community organization, and innovative health policies, as well as paranoia, mutual recrimination, and abandonment.

England was also experiencing a kind of cultural revolution whose crucibles and depths are largely known to Americans only in the form of seventeenth-century witch hunts. Theaters in London were shuttered more than half the time, and when they reopened players and playwrights walked on eggshells. Other immediate prehistory includes the forced sanitizing of Shakespeare's and other playwrights' previous works, the persecution of Catholics, and the dragnetting of the conspirators behind the Gunpowder Plot. Sycophantic court masques were being rolled out every week for James I, and they competed with Shakespeare's works.

From this background Shakespeare made a selection for the opening of the play—the minimal amount of information you need to know to be sufficiently afraid of what comes next. Of all his tragedies, *Lear* has the scariest opening, more so even than the beginning of *Julius Caesar* in which the enforcement of a curfew presages totalitarianism ("Hence, home, you idle creatures, get you home! . . . Speak, what trade are thou?").

Shakespeare is cramming information into these first lines of *Lear*. He is trying to give you a *quick* glimpse of how misjudgment of character and boastful fun at your child's expense figures in the tragedy to come. You can *already* hear it in the idle chatter of the elites, its putative representatives, that something is really off in this realm.

My hometown, Hangzhou, and the nearby city of Suzhou are known all over China and the world as "paradise on earth," an epithet that predates any modern tourism marketing blitz. Night stalls were busy with commerce, and well-made folk crafts could still earn people a living, or at least allow them to scrape by. Lives were lived amid the scenic, much of which remained sequestered in secrecy despite the city's throngs of visitors from all over China.

You weren't inside a painting, exactly, but you weren't too far from it, either, and the thoroughfares of the traditional arts flourished and also let in a permissible amount of commercial items and fakery, because people had to live. Every few hours you received signs from your surroundings that you were in a wronged society, its priorities in the wrong order, but it was also so pleasurable to be alive.

I was born in the middle of a period in China called *Gai Ge Kai Fang* 改革开放, the "Reform and Opening-up." Eight years earlier, in 1977, college entrance examinations were restored, and Deng Xiaoping implemented *baluan fanzheng* 拨乱反正 ("to pull out the chaos and return things to order"). Economic liberalization hit breakneck speed. Meanwhile, most Chinese people still had Soviet hearts—a heartbreaking sensitivity to cruelty, the ability to inflict it en masse for conformity and for a cause. My mother used to sing Chinese versions of old Soviet and partisan songs like "Evenings in the Outskirts of Moscow" or "Ciao Bella," or hum the theme music from *Walter Saves Sarajevo* or *Here, the Dawn Is Quiet.* Other Soviet-era leftovers included grueling youth calisthenics classes and residual programs of rationing (commodities, then electronics). You could still feel the state apparatuses everywhere, in the assigned jobs, the struggles of the *hukou* system (residency quotas that acted as controls on mobility).

For a few years my mother and I lived in a housing complex called a *tongzilou* on Qingnian Lu, "the avenue of the youth." The perpetually waterlogged buildings were barracks-like constructions modeled on dormitories for factory workers, a step above tenement housing. Individual units opened onto a dark, narrow balcony which overlooked a concrete courtyard and doubled as the thoroughfare. From its ledge every family rigged their own drying systems, the bamboo poles subtending each other underneath the undergarments and bedspreads. You cooked your meals on the shared stove in this thoroughfare, worried your coal, butchered your small animals. Every once in a long while someone would bring back a soft-shelled turtle and make quick work of it. Everyone got to enjoy the delicious, savory smell for days, like something you could hold in your fist. In the stairwell someone kept chickens, even though it was against the rules, and we'd have chickens and sometimes eggs to eat, until a city ordinance against such practices legislated resentful neighbors to round up the birds in the courtyard, where they were beaten to death with canes.

China was developing rapidly, and this was a good-enough rhythm, a good-enough pace. We honestly didn't know what kind of a world this was. Were we a generation before the opening act of *King Lear*, or a generation after? How far were we in measured meters from the play's opening lines? One can use a simple measure. If a piece of world literature can come to a child in affordable codex form, that means that things are still okay.

The beginning of *Lear* tells you where to look for the first signs of wrongness in that kind of world, gives you a real taste of how hard it is to remember what is happening and what has happened. Tales stick to the most important parts, knowing that important details are left out. The tale of *King Lear* is scary, and it's scary in a particular way. What happens to Gloucester's eyes is scary, as is what happens to Lear and Cordelia, as is the Fool's final announcement to "go to bed at noon" after going with his master such a long way. But I mean that it is scary for the mind, too, a hard tale to remember. As the child moves from tale to the play, she realizes how many crucial details there are. Even seasoned readers have trouble with it. Who is Curan? Whose letter first brings news of trouble between Albany and Cornwall? The play refers to seven different letters: What is the content of those letters? How large *is* the French troop that allows Cordelia to be captured? Is it a very large contingent or a pathetic, dozen-man operation? How much co-plotting between Lear loyalists and France, the crime of which Gloucester is accused and that costs him his eyes, could there really have been? Everyone famously goes to Dover, but are they anywhere near Dover or does most of the action take place a league or even just a few furlongs out from the castles? Where are the sympathetic "well-armed friends" who live in Dover, or was that just an empty "boast," as Goneril's servant, Oswald, maliciously suggests? What does happen in this play? No matter how old the reader or playgoer, their memory of what has immediately happened seems to falter, then fail.

Lear triggers other difficulties with memory. My mother and I talk about memories, argue over just-happened events. Between us we have forgotten stretches of years. I have tried to go over it, step by step, but it's like dragging furniture through water. Viciousness and extreme love both cause senescence, and I take this to be the first of many kindly lessons in *King Lear*.

CHAPTER TWO

History

LEAR SOMETIMES CALLED itself a history, sometimes a tragedy. This could have been just the whim of playhouses—some nights it was billed as one, some nights it was the other—or the consolidation of time—first as history, finally as tragedy. A textual historian would caution against reading too much into the title. Still, we have to take the distinction seriously. Choosing one word over the other is a close call for *someone*.

The first close call has to do with plausibility. Could the story of *King Lear* have happened in real life? We learn later just how historical this play is: it makes use of immediate history—current events, even—in the landmark case around 1603 involving Brian Annesley, Lord of the Manor of Lee, and his three daughters, Grace, Christinna, and Cordell, and the matter of their inheritance. Grace and Christinna had tried to commit the father for insanity and contested Cordell's inheritance of the estate on those grounds. The play was directly speaking to this most modern historical problem: What to do with the elderly, and who gets to draw the legal line between sanity and insanity? With the story of *Leir*, Shakespeare also was joining many others in making a point about the current state of England and the question of the reunification of England, Scotland, and Wales, which had been experiencing something like a resurgence since the end of Elizabeth's reign. One could even argue that the changes made to the play since its first debut until Shakespeare's death are evidence of historical *strain*—that history is what hurts us and a text's integrity. We could say the play was commenting as closely and intensely on the historical present and the historical past as anyone really could.

Still, to an ordinary person, history seems absent on first and last encounter; the play feels like a tetherball whipping around its own pole. Dividing an entire kingdom to hear your favorite child declare their love in public is surely absurd, the stuff of fable rather than of history. Readers have faulted *Lear* for its too-muchness, its hyperbole. They complain that the play's premise is itself improbable. Coleridge himself called the play "wickedness in outrageous form," but added, "improbable as the conduct of Lear is, in the first scene, yet it was an old story, rooted in the popular faith—a thing taken for granted already, and consequently without any of the *effects* of improbability."

Bradley took a different angle for this problem of implausibility, calling *Lear* a "defective" play and explaining why it needed to be one. Something in the way it's made guarantees that when you try to remember what causes what, what necessitates what, you'll have remembered incorrectly. On this reasoning, the play is "defective" because it cannot back-engineer a scenario that could convince you its premise is possible. And yet, Bradley concedes, these things do happen, a conclusion echoed in Cavell's later description of *Lear* as "ordinary." "Ordinary" referred to the tenets of ordinary language philosophy, a principled return to the commonplace meaning of words, of which Cavell was a practitioner. But he also meant: this kind of thing happens to *everyone*. You don't think it happens, but it happens. It happens. It already happened in real time. It can happen anywhere.

For a long time, *Lear* was altered to accommodate the sensitivities of the eighteenth- and nineteenth-century theater-watching public. This kind of stuff happens, but no one wanted to see it. No one wanted to look in that direction. For this and other reasons, and because the thing itself sounded like an adapted fable, *King Lear* seemed to fall outside the realm of historical possibility.

Before we can understand the extent of *King Lear*'s experiment with history—its commitment to history writing—we have to accept the careworn historian's first and fundamentally ahistorical premise: something from the distant past is happening again. The writer who uses historical allusion to critique the present is counting on the real possibility of large-scale reenactment. He is counting on the fact that we needn't turn to the imagination to see *Lear* played out in real life—not just in pre-Arthurian or Elizabethan/Jacobean England but later, in our lifetime.

On July 1, 1947, the body of a literary scholar and journalist was thrown down a dry well in a remote part of China. He had been hacked to death. This execution happened somewhere between the city of Yan'an and the Jin Sui military area where he was being escorted as a political prisoner. A decade prior, this critic had translated Engels's *Revolution and Counter-Revolution in Germany* and Marx's *Value, Price and Profit* into Chinese, as well as Thomas Hardy's *The Return of the Native* and Alphonse Daudet's *Sappho*. In 1942 he wrote an essay called "Wild Lilies" and published it in the pages of the *Liberation Daily*. Lilies grew in the wild in that part of China where the Chinese Communist Party settled to regroup and strengthen after the disastrous but trumped-up Long March. Mao's Red Army had spent two years retreating from Nationalist forces during the Chinese Civil War, marching over nine thousand kilometers of mountainous terrain from southern China, through western China, ending in the northwest province of Shanxi. Eighty-six thousand people began the Long March; only eight thousand people came out at the end.

In the middle of the Second Sino-Japanese War, the party stationed itself in the city of Yan'an and dedicated three years to thought reform and attitude/atmosphere rectification. Someone spoke up. Wang's "Wild Lilies" pointed out some obvious hypocrisies: instead of equality in the party, "uniforms were divided into three colors; meals were divided into five classes."[1] His words directed righteous anger at the person behind Yan'an's alarming cult of personality, not realizing how much power that person already wielded. Mao had followed closely in the footsteps of Lenin, consolidating power by gathering yes-men in a psychologically—and actually—militarized party that had long ago lost checks and balances. Mao read Wang Shiwei's essay and declared that it was Wang Shiwei, and not Marx, who now ran the party. Wang refused to recant and apologize. Then he realized he could not even leave the convention, as the party did not allow him to withdraw his membership. In his "trial" he was persecuted by all the attendees at Yan'an but especially by the fellow writers and comrades he had known intimately for more than a decade. This group included Chen Boda and Ding Ling, the writer who had earlier denounced Wang in writing, who had retracted her own essay critiquing party leaders' abuse of the institution of divorce. It also included the writer Ai Qing, Ai Weiwei's father, who would one day be sentenced to hard labor cleaning communal toilets in a village in Xinjiang.

Mao had already given everyone fair warning in his 1926 "Analysis of the Classes in Chinese Society." That essay begins, "Who are our enemies? Who are our friends? This is a question of the first importance for the revolution." Mao's questions always functioned as threats. Less than a year later he would

1. The Chinese expression he used was: *Yi fen san se, shi fen wu deng* 衣分三色, 食分五等.

recommend the death penalty or life imprisonment for any counterrevolutionary activity. In his "Regulations for the Repression of Local Bullies and Bad Gentry," delivered in the Third Congress of the Communist Party in 1923, Mao had in effect declared martial law: "peaceful methods cannot suffice." He had also, in effect, given a killing quota. Anyone owning more than 4.5 acres of land—roughly 15 percent of the population—qualified as a counterrevolutionary and could be attacked with impunity. According to Mao's own boasting, three million would perish in the Land Reform Movement; 12.5 million would be sent to "reform through labor" in prison factories.

Wang Shiwei was early and late, witness to the youth and senescence of the party. His life was lived in *King Lear* and it ended in *King Lear*—a world of perverse love, gross flattery, silencing, schoolyard cruelty, and desolate deaths. During this Yan'an period, now fondly remembered in Chinese history, more than ten thousand people had been killed, and others saved from execution and torture only by confessing to outrageous political crimes and giving the names of others to denounce. And yet Wang Shiwei's death finds us still in the adolescence of the Chinese Communist Party. Already the elderly and the young do not look right. By 1930, Mao had already purged local Communist forces in Jiangxi, accusing them of spying for the Kuomintang (KMT), and the contingent in Futian that rebelled in response to these purges in Jiangxi. Chinese Trotskyites became the next target, Trotskyites being essentially anyone who still believed in communism but balked at Mao's replication and intensification of Stalinism. The battalion of two hundred Red Army soldiers that tried to defend those who were purged against accusations of Trotskyism were killed for mutiny—killed in an ambush execution in a theater, not before a tribunal. Between 1930 and 1946 the party would kill off 90 to 95 percent of its intellectuals. It was still early days.

In 1942, the same year that Wang Shiwei wrote "Wild Lilies," a sixty-three-year-old man died of a heart attack in the town of Jiangjin, Sichuan. He had once written under the pen name "Three Loves," referring to three of his favorite Chinese writers. In his early fifties he had been allowed to eke out an existence as a junior high school teacher in a stricken area far from Beijing, far from the corridors of Peking University, where he was once on the faculty and a dean. For his anti-Stalinism, for his critique of Mao's prescriptive essays about literature/sociality/China, and for his increasing vocal alarm at the actions of his party, Chen Duxiu, one of the four founding members of the Chinese Party of China (hereafter CPC), would be expelled by the party and allowed to *shan zhong* 善终 (die in peace) in war-torn China. During his expulsion Chen would lose two sons in the war against the Nationalist Party (the KMT, handed down from Sun Yat-sen to the tyrannical Chiang Kai-shek) and witness mounting atrocities committed on his former friends and countrymen by both parties. He served out five years (of a thirteen-year sentence) in KMT-ruled China, but was in fact exiled from both Chinas. Offered rehabilitation by the Nationalist Party, Chen said, "Chiang Kai-shek killed many of my comrades. He also killed my two sons. He and I are absolutely irreconcilable." He was also unwilling to renounce Trotskyism, Mao's new target, in exchange for his readmission into the CPC. Chen lived the remaining five years of his life in obscure poverty, unable to afford medicine, care, or even modest burial fees. He died after ingesting a tincture made from broad beans that had rotted, the cheapest homeopathic remedy he could afford to try to reduce his high blood pressure. His friends had to raise money for his burial. When Chen's son later transferred his coffin to his hometown, Anqing, he didn't even dare engrave his father's full name on the headstone, lest someone defile it. Instead it was only "Chen Xianshen"—Mr. or Teacher Chen—expressly avoiding the title "Comrade." Since Chen is one of the top five most common surnames in all of China—in 1942 as now—the grave might as well have been anonymous. It preserved only the essential details of a man's life, not so despairing of history as to forfeit all of his place in it. Chen Duxiu represented an entirely different kind of threat to the Communist Party. For more than thirty years, no one could sweep his grave, or pay their respects.

A critic is exiled but for some reason stays behind, perhaps because he is not allowed to leave, perhaps out of love for his country. An old man who once had authority is mistreated and the severity shocks us. History begins here. What happened up to this point? What will come now? *Lear* dramatizes this critical moment, wraps a story tight around it.

You must first close the doors. Then you must cut off nearly all communication with the outside except during zoo hours. Then you must raise the pitch of verbal violence inside the building. Then you must lower the volume of dissenting voices until they are nothing.

Lear is the trickiest of Shakespeare's histories, if we are to count it as a history. Leaving aside ancestry and lineage, what's the immediate, personal cause of this ugliness? Surely the arguments, empty threats, and unforgettable lessons that make up the play have had dry runs before. The characters must have entered this neck of the verbal woods a long time ago, and yet no personal explanation is given for this tragic need of Lear's, where it comes from, why it has been allowed to metastasize. The division of the kingdom into three may have recalled Brutus's legendary division of his kingdom around 1100 BC (by Monmouth's account) and would certainly have recalled the reunification of the kingdom under the rule of James I, but we are permitted no glimpses into the recent past within the play. There are no ugly remembrances in *Lear*, just as there are no fond ones.

We are given so little background information about Lear, the princesses, the mother, and the officials of the court. If the princes have mothers, they are held in contempt. Edgar's mother bears no mention; Edmund's mother is a nameless prostitute; and the only mention of the mother of Goneril, Regan, and Cordelia comes in that vituperative moment when, enraged by Regan's inhospitality, Lear swears to dig her out of her grave to retroactively nullify the marriage and make their children bastards. Dead, and her memory verboten, the queen is either a calumniated wife and mother, or the cause of many of these sins.

Even as a moment from British dynastic history, the play walls itself in. Where is everyone in *Lear*? Have you ever seen a less populated play about dynastic succession and war? For all the pomp and ceremony of the division of the kingdom, Lear himself has almost no audience. And the number of people who *have to* attend to him are dwindling.

In these historyless moments we see an elimination game between the dearest of the dear. As soon as the foolish division of the kingdom concludes, Lear's prime minister, the Earl of Gloucester, falls for a stupid trick devised by Edmund, his bad son, designed to turn him against Edgar, his good son. Lear learns from his daughters Goneril and Regan that they will reduce his train to nothing, and he storms out into the rain. Lear, the Fool, and Lear's loyal servant Kent (in disguise) end up in a hovel to shelter from the rain, and there they find Edgar (also in disguise, as Tom O'Bedlam, an insane vagrant beggar). They are joined by a conscience-stricken Gloucester, come to offer warning and help: Get you all to Dover, he says; there you will be met with "welcome and protection." Gloucester has made the mistake, however, of relaying all of this to Edmund, who conspires with Regan and Cornwall to have his father arrested as soon as he returns to his castle.

Meanwhile Cordelia brings an army back to England, a righteous coup that is supposed to restore Lear to the throne. But this war seems a rather puny effort. We imagine that an entire French army arrives, with Cordelia at its head, to rescue Lear and restore the kingdom, but we soon learn that the King of France has "suddenly gone back," leaving the Marshal of France,

Monsieur La Far, to finish the job. Back in his castle, Gloucester is accused of treason (aiding France against England), is bound, and has his eyes put out by Regan's own hands. He stumbles toward Dover, blind, until he runs into Edgar, who manages to save him from suicide and kill off the assassin Oswald, but who soon leaves his father to get back to more urgent business. Lear and Gloucester reunite, briefly. Cordelia's scouting party finds Lear, though their reunion is also brief: the two are soon captured by English forces with seemingly little effort, a bizarre outcome considering how much was made of the French intervention. (After all, Gloucester lost his eyes for the "confederacy" he supposedly had "with the traitors late-footed in the kingdom.") Edgar, meanwhile, has returned to the main scene of action, this time as himself. He and Albany, Goneril's husband, both confront Edmund, who has not only been sleeping with both Goneril and Regan but who has, with Goneril, plotted to kill Albany and take over England himself. Cornwall is out of the picture at this point, dead from the wound inflicted by his servant, who had tried to stop Gloucester's torture. So, too, are the evil sisters: Goneril has killed herself after poisoning Regan, perhaps out of guilt but more likely because she senses imminent defeat. Edgar challenges Edmund to trial by combat and kills him, but not before Edmund orders the assassination of Lear and Cordelia. Cordelia is hanged, even though Edmund rescinds the order. Lear dies heartbroken, and Kent leaves, promising to soon end his own life. The Fool disappeared a while ago. The King of France, Cordelia's husband, is still nowhere to be found. Edgar, or sometimes Albany, depending on the version of the play, gives a speech indicating that he will take over the throne.

Lear feels even less populated than the two plays to which it is most often compared, *Hamlet* and *Macbeth*, both of which briefly inflate with the arrival of the players or a banquet or a small phalanx of people dressed as bushes. In contrast, it is empty, empty, empty in *Lear*. People and action are missing even from the war, represented only as a capture and two military executions. Death brings underpopulation, naturally, but the ending of *King Lear* is too silent and empty for the deaths of heads of state.

We know roughly which period of dynastic British history *Lear* dramatizes: the eighth century BCE, in the last years of the male line of Brutus of Troy, a descendant of Aeneas who founded Britain. In this quasi-mythological history, Aeneas flees the sacking of Troy and settles in Italy; his son Ascanius later founds Alba Longa, a precursor of Rome; either Ascanius, his brother Silvius, or Ascanius's son, Silvius, fathers Brutus. The boy Brutus inadvertently kills his parents as prophesied—his mother in childbirth, his father in a shooting accident—and is exiled from Italy. Brutus wends his way to the island of Albion (Britain) through Gaul and, in one version, liberates a group of enslaved Trojans in Greece and takes a Greek princess as ransom for the life of the Greek king Pandrasus. Brutus and his followers battle the giants of Albion, win, and settle on the banks of the Thames, establishing a New Troy, Troia Nova, whose name is slowly corrupted into Trinovantum, and then, eventually, London. Brutus would divide his kingdom among his three sons, and the kingdom of the son named Locrinus would be taken over by his father-in-law, Corineus, founder of Cornwall. Roughly nine generations after Corineus we have Leir, whose father, Bladud, had supposedly cured himself of leprosy, communicated with dead spirts, and affixed wings on himself and plummeted to his death. Leir would be followed by Cordelia (variants include Cordell, Cordilla, Cordella), and so on. The end of the Brutus dynasty is the effective end of Britain's Bronze Age and the beginning of the Iron Age. What happens here presages what will happen an epoch later, at the end of the Iron Age, marked in history by the invasion of Great Britain by the Romans. *Lear* is said to epitomize the end of feudalism, dynastic rule, Britishness as a category of identity, and pagan-Christian civilization. It catches the end of something very ancient. It also catches the very beginning of something whose full novelty and cause for apprehensiveness is not yet known.

Lear is a composite king of Britain, one perennially bedeviled by succession, by the thirds of Britain, by France, and by the absence of male heirs. From Brutus to Leir a syncretic British history comes into being. In fact, Brutus's own name would come to signify a chronicle of British history—the *brut*. All this history and yet *Lear* feels far more devoid of actual history than even the historical legends, more historyless than the other adapted *Leir*s. *Lear* comes like a bat out of time to those without a sense of British history, watching or reading it without context. What happens before it? What happens after it? Who knows? Who cares? But here is what living inside history looks like if the history looked like this.

In the sources Shakespeare drew upon, the legend goes more or less like this: Leir errs in similar ways, and the kingdom is similarly ruined. Leir becomes more quickly disillusioned with his two older daughters. At this point he either flees to France, where he is taken in by Cordila and her husband, King Aganippus of the Franks, or he is rescued by Cordila, who never left England at all. They invade Britain and trigger civil war. Cordila's army ousts her sisters and their husbands, restores Leir to the throne, and establishes the new seat of the monarchy in Leicester. Leir rules for three years and is succeeded by Cordila as regent. Then we learn that, years later, after the death of her husband, Cordila is overthrown in a coup by her nephews Marganus and Cunedagius, Goneril and Regan's sons.

If we go to *Lear*'s historical and legendary counterparts we find something even worse than what happens in *Lear*. In Monmouth's *Historia Regum Britanniae* Cordelia had "a peaceful possession of the government for five years." And then: "After a general waste of her countries, and several battles fought, they at last took [Cordelia] and put her in prison, where for grief at the loss of her kingdom she killed herself." This grisly and desolate outcome at the hands of her nephews is more or less shared among Shakespeare's inspirations, including John Higgins's tale in *Mirrors for Magistrates*, William Warner's *Albions England*, Raphael Holinshed's *Chronicles of England, Scotlande, Irelande*, and even Edmund Spenser's *The Fairie Queen*. In these versions Cordelia's calamity would come *after* her triumphant overthrow of her sisters. Peace is restored for five years and the historical saga continues: after Leir dies and Cordila dies at the hands of her nephews, we get the story of Regan's son, Gorbudoc; his frightful wife, Judon; and their warring children, Porrex and Ferrex. Porrex kills Ferrex, and is then killed by Judon, who is then killed by the nobility and elites, who then wage civil war with the lower classes of society. It's familial brutality and anarchy, again, but with a different twist. The story of Leir shows the accursedness of pre-Christian British dynastic rule when left to its own devices. At its center is Leicester, a city in the east midlands that Leir is said to have founded and the seat of government where Cordila—the historical person—establishes her government. It would continue to be associated with beheaded sovereigns in British history.

Which is more merciless: Shakespeare's version of these events or the historical versions of these events? Which makes you more afraid: the reign of Goneril and Regan and their respective husbands, or of Goneril and Regan's sons and their respective wives? Is it better to have a tragedy drawn that cuts off at some point, or to end with the deaths or disappearances of all the major players save one?[2]

2. At least *Lear* unfolds at the pace preferred by allegory. It is mercifully fast. Stretch out cruelty toward a parent into the glacial pace of living in history, and you get Prince Hal's treatment of Falstaff in *Henry IV*, Parts 1 and 2. You get to witness Falstaff's death by a thousand cuts, from casual fat shaming to petty thievery to open repudiation. All of this is hard to watch, because it moves at the

A history—

I am thirty-nine years old. My parents left China for the United States at this age. My father was only marginally involved in the student demonstrations of 1989, but he and my mother were relieved that we were able to leave the country, first my father, then my mother and I, in the next few years. Just as we were leaving, some Chinese expats were coming back to help, not knowing what kind of situation would await them.

In the city of Hangzhou, where we lived, about two hundred kilometers south of Shanghai, people hung banners on newly constructed urban skyways. Propaganda slogans and the "Big Character Posters" from the Mao years were now for an antigovernment message: Blood Evidence of a Massacred City! Blood for Blood Vengeance! Protestors around the country explicitly invoked *Lear*, comparing the massacres to Cordelia's execution, and figuring China as a no-man's-land for the critic who loves her country (see figure 1).

Most people would say that Deng Xiaoping, the man who succeeded Mao and truly ended the Cultural Revolution, had done the best he humanly could before and after 1976 to leach the poison out of Maoist totalitarianism, restore peace, and stabilize the country. It's hard for Westerners to appreciate the ambivalence of even the most liberal Chinese thinkers concerning the viability of student-led democratic movements, and democracy as such. In 1980 China had a population of 980 million people, all emerging from the psychological and infrastructural devastations of the past century. Even today, people who were jailed and tortured for their involvement in the student uprisings cannot be sure that student-led democratic movements wouldn't have destroyed China. This ambivalence and

pace of history, almost just as you would experience it, and it is unbearably slow. To my mind, this is more difficult to watch than *Lear*.

FIGURE 1. Banners made by artists in reaction to the events of June Fourth, photographed June 7–8, 1989, in Hangzhou, China. Source: UC San Diego. Visual Arts Legacy Collection, Artstor, JSTOR. Accessed July 29, 2024.

uncertainty can be found even among people who, like student activist Zhang Ming, were jailed after the June Fourth Incidents in factories that were labor camps where common criminals often devised and carried out the punishments of political prisoners or prisoners of conscience.[3]

It's an ambivalence that sometimes feels like acquiescence to the fate of an entire people. The thinking goes like this: In giving the orders to quash the student uprisings through violent means, Deng Xiaoping did what he had to do in a broken and impoverished world that was just getting on its feet. The gunning down of students at Tiananmen Square just meant that things had gotten out of hand. In the late 1980s American historians and reporters traveled from Yunnan to Harbin, asking people they met what they thought of democracy and its viability in China, and who they believed would make a good president. Some of the villagers recommended their neighborhood elders—"What about Old Liu who lives down the street? Give him a chance!" Some had not even heard of Deng Xiaoping. It was, honestly, confusing. If the democracy movements were associated with anything *concrete* it was: further removal of Maoism, rule of law and a partial free market, cleaner separation of powers between executive and judicial bodies. People were justly fearful of mass mobilization, its worst atrocities having ended just a few years prior, and representative government, since they had just seen how everywhere people elected the wrong spokesperson—the hall monitor, the neighborhood committee, the student assembly committee member, the leader of the people. Representative leaders didn't inherently mean anything. Even the educated classes, making up for lost time, faced an existential crisis over the form of government the Chinese people really needed and deserved. Throughout the

3. Zhang Ming was jailed in the Lingyuan Prison Production Complex in Liaoning. "Lingyuan" was also a manufacturing plant and had an "enterprise name." Most prisons in China were and are still named like this.

late 1970s in China, many small democratic reform movements were stamped out, by not just the machinery of the party but people's own mistrust of people.

Still, you can't help but feel that Deng could have exerted a little more effort during the 1980s to avoid repeating the past, to reset and repair completely. He might have worked harder to avoid language that preserved Maoist corruption and totalitarianism for a later date. After all, he had ample reason to seek vengeance and the complete restoration of justice. His son Deng Pufang ended up paralyzed for life after a long period of physical and psychological abuse at the hands of the Red Guards, the paramilitary student usurpers who became Mao's new army. Deng Pufang was either pushed out of a window at Peking University or jumped out himself. We know that he was turned away from every hospital after his fall. In early 1976 Mao brought a campaign—which is to say, mobilized all of China—against Deng Xiaoping. It was called, rather straightforwardly, the Criticize Deng and Oppose the Rehabilitation of Right-leaning Elements campaign. After the incidents of 1976, during which people used the funeral of the beloved premier, Zhou Enlai, to protest the abuses of the state, the horrors began to visit Deng Xiaoping's family. Like millions of other people, Deng was physically humiliated and brutalized in methods that combined Stalinism with more traditional Chinese forms of torture and the games of schoolyard bullies.

Deng Xiaoping inherited the rage of a people that, by 1976, had victimized one another for more than three decades. A sizable part of the Cultural Revolution's atrocities was simply revenge for the Anti-Rightist campaigns of the previous decade. Anti-Rightist campaigns and the Cultural Revolution were themselves just larger duplicates of the Zhengfeng exercises, also known as the Yan'an Rectification Movement, in the early 1940s, which was a duplicate of the Futian Purge of 1930, which was a duplicate of Stalinist techniques, which were a duplicate of Lenin's techniques. Mao was Regan to Lenin's Goneril and Stalin's

Cornwall. Regan "has no ideas of her own," as Cavell says: "her special vileness is always to increase the measure of pain that others are prepared to inflict; her mind itself is a lynch mob."

The end of the Cultural Revolution had become truly grotesque: there had been campaign after campaign after campaign; those doling out punishments had gotten more and more creative. To deal a final blow to the young female student Lin Zhao, one of the better-known dissenters of that time, the government asked her parents to pay for her executioner's bullet. It is a Cordelia-like tragedy, but this young girl had herself orchestrated the executions of "landlords" in the previous years. Like the rest of her countrymen, Lin Zhao had faithfully carried out Mao Zedong Thought and his calls to open killing. Deng Xiaoping was the same, and Zhou Enlai, the most fondly remembered leader next to Mao, was even worse, having directed over 50 percent of the most violent struggles in a 1971 purge of around 130,000 people called Investigation into the May 16 Counterrevolutionary Clique. Deng saw the worst happen to his own family at the end of the Cultural Revolution. He had often carried out such campaigns himself, perhaps with no choice, perhaps with zeal. Ironically, just as his daughters, and especially the one called Deng Nan, became actual zealots during the last days of the Cultural Revolution, Deng himself was denounced by all Chinese adults and children as a daily exercise. Deng knew how much he needed to make it finally end.

On June 27, 1981, a document was passed in the Eleventh Central Committee of the Chinese Communist Party called "Resolution on Certain Questions in the History of Our Party Since the Founding of Our Country." This document determined how the calamities of the Mao era officially would be told. Like the show trial of the Gang of Four, it served as a faux truth commission. Here is what the resolution resolved: that the Cultural Revolution was largely a great success that was blemished by an internal crisis toward the end, a crisis instigated by "counterrevolutionary" contingents with the party—the various cliques, the Gang of Four. Deng Xiaoping had left a problem in the Four Cardinal Principles in a statement given in March of 1979. (The Four Cardinal Principles were: 1) uphold the path of socialism, 2) uphold the people's democratic dictatorship, 3) uphold the legitimacy of the Chinese Communist Party, 4) uphold Mao Zedong Thought and Marxist-Leninism.) Twenty years prior, while Mao was still very much alive, Deng had supported removing all references to "Mao Zedong Thought" from the party statutes at the 8th National Congress of the Communist Party of China. After Mao's death in 1976, he could do no such thing: national sentiment ran too high. Deng Xiaoping was a survivalist, someone who decided to terminate his relationship with his father and mother over his Bolshevik sympathies as early as the 1920s. Biding one's time is an equivocal virtue because it feels sly. In a speech he made in December of 1990, Deng Xiaoping gave this counsel for China's foreign relations: *taoguang yanghui* 韬光养晦, that is, keep a low profile, don't draw attention to yourself. Like Edgar, he understood the principle of *ying xing mai ming*隐姓埋名, *zhuang feng mai sha*装疯卖傻: literally, to go incognito and bury one's name, and feign madness and idiocy, to survive. Like Albany, Deng Xiaoping became visibly good at determining the right place and the right time and saying the right words. The country would go to him. *Lear* is helplessly equivocal on who inherits the kingdom, but neither seems like the type of man who can prevent a similar tragedy.

More than a testament to the pitch of democratic fervor in China, or the rectitude of the students, or the tragedy of revolution, the student uprisings of the late 1980s evinced China's wish for reform and the party's ability to whitewash in real time. What frightened people watching on the ground were the speed and extremism of these measures. Overnight the party decided on the narrative. Every piece of reporting villainized the protestors. The party couldn't bear to be examined or questioned even a little. Fundamentally, the party did not trust its own people to look at a controversial situation and make a fair judgment. If it didn't cover up a complex incident entirely, inflict near-total amnesia, and silence all voices that said otherwise, it wouldn't be judged fairly at all. It would simply be impugned without trial—sentenced to death.

Less than a year after the June Fourth Incidents, President Jiang Zemin was interviewed by Barbara Walters for *ABC News* and dismissed the talk about Tiananmen as "much ado about nothing." Alluding obviously to Shakespeare's romantic comedy, Jiang Zemin had inadvertently brought the dangers of wordplay into his interview. "Much ado about nothing" was as easily a critique of the West's exaggeration in reporting on harm seen as the party's own exaggeration in inflicting it. "Much ado about nothing" introduced a bleak frame of reference—for *King Lear* is also arguably much ado about a "nothing." Maoism, too, was much ado about a nothing. Jiang Zemin was also exhibiting an old form of cockiness: it's nothing, it's frivolous, nothing to see here. Chinese deaths have to number in the order of hundreds and thousands to be "something." What was Tiananmen compared to the stability of a nation of 1 billion people? Compared to the kinds of things Jiang Zemin had seen, the deaths of the student protestors really was "much ado about nothing."

Chinese history hides its own magnitude—the magnitude of its achievements and mistakes, the magnitude of difficulty in governing a country with a population that large, the magnitude of its sufferings. Take, for example, the mid-nineteenth-century Taiping Rebellion, which until fairly recently was unknown even to serious students of history. A man who sincerely believed himself to be the brother of Jesus Christ, and who subscribed to a militant utopianism, inspired Hakka and Han ethnic peoples to attempt to overthrow their Manchu rulers and topple the Qing dynasty. The sectarian violence that ensued, taking more than 20 million lives, created a blueprint for Chinese Han ultranationalism and large-scale civil wars.

Jiang Zemin adopted a Learian perspective, having lived a freakish history teeming with life and death. In 1949 China had half a billion people in it; by 1979 it had twice as many. China's population grew by 20 million people between 1971 and 1972, another 20 million in 1973, another 20 million in 1974. Mao had asked everyone to *Grow the size of the population* to serve the needs of the state soon after 1949, the establishment of the People's Republic of China. Overpopulation was achieved through propaganda and policy; women were eventually denied all access to contraception. My father is one of five children; my mother, one of nine. It should be puzzling how *anyone* can double the population of a country to that size, all during significant involvement in the Korean and Vietnam wars, constant trouble, famine, and state-sanctioned mass death. Compared to keeping 1 billion people alive, what is any number smaller than half a billion, really? Why bring up any number that's less than a quarter of a billion? Why bring up tens or ones? Even 58 million lives—the consensus between a former party member's history and the most critical "foreigner's" histories for total death count in Mao's China—can be lost to the wind.

Still, ashamed of itself like a parent who lifted their hand to their child and inflicted real harm, the state erased its own culpability in the last hours of this 1980s reform revolution, just as it erased its own culpability in everything up to the last hours of Mao's revolution. A small "lobby" for justice formed, called the Mothers of Tiananmen. They pursued the facts of the insurrection: Exactly how many were buried under thin dirt outside the school at the intersection of Chang'an and Zhongnanhai Avenues, and whose corpses began to rot in the open air? At what exact time did Deng Xiaoping give his orders? Details mattered because in them hung the balance of truth and love, state responsibility and personal responsibility. China had done them a great wrong, but they did not wish to *kuazhang* 夸张—histrionically exaggerate or confabulate. The party threw together a truth commission only two months after the June Fourth Incidents and published a book a month later called *The Truth about Beijing Turmoil*, edited by the Editorial Board of

The Truth about the Beijing Turmoil, and published by the (in-house) Beijing Publishing House. That did not inspire trust. The state was trying to be so honest, naming things straight, and yet the way it went about matters just invited more skepticism and, invariably, cynicism among thinking people.

Human rights violations became rampant in the immediate aftermath of June Fourth. On June 6, the literary critic turned scholar-activist Liu Xiaobo was arrested and taken to the maximum-security Qincheng Prison, in a northern district of Beijing. Qincheng Prison, like other prison-industrial complexes, is a jurisdictional no-man's-land, a place where political prisoners and dissidents are disappeared. A sizable number of people blamed for the June Fourth protests simply reentered what never were actually dismantled: the prison-industrial complexes—the labor camps—of Mao's state terror. People's Liberation Army soldiers, including students-in-training, had continued their raids on "counterrevolutionaries" and the ideologically untamable in the entire decade before 1989. Those jailed did not number in the hundreds of thousands, as in the previous decade, when nearly every jail in the country held political prisoners, prisoners of conscience, common criminals, and dangerous criminals. For the June Fourth protests, the number was only dozens, no more than two hundred. Still, the more that people, especially foreigners, investigated, the more the government cracked down. Liu Xiaobo was jailed for inciting counterrevolutionary insurrection—"counterrevolutionary" because the party and the state were de jure "revolutionary"—and remained in prison or under house arrest until he died in 2017, living exactly long enough to see that the time from the 1980s to the 1990s, which many people regarded as a promise-filled transition period, was actually only a brief pause. (Deng Xiaoping was appropriately named, it seemed; Xiaoping means "small peace," or "gentle smoothing over.") The behemoth machinery of propaganda and censorship only had to wait out living memory, to wait for those who knew better to die.

A centralized state power that has divided its power symbolically leaves itself with those who will say only flattering things until the day they are licensed to say and do what the state most fears. The state understands this dynamic too well. The Chinese Communist Party is like the suffering, maligned parent who never gets remembered for anything good, of which there are countless examples, only the bad (and, of the bad, only the most nightmarish). Foreigners and nationals exaggerate the numbers dead, and oversimplify cause and effect, in any Chinese catastrophe, or else commit the sin of underreporting. Westerners have fetishized Tiananmen for their pet causes, believing that China should remold itself as a capitalist liberal democracy, pursue rabid consumerism and identitarian, symbolic politics. But this is what happens to a political regime built on revisionism, on willed forgetting. It becomes fully vulnerable to anyone wishing to rubberneck, to make self-congratulating commentary, to draw ludicrous analogies. Made deeply curious by what the writer Yan Lianke calls the "state-sponsored sport" of whitewashing, many observers—even those who witnessed it—have endeavored to understand how history was nearly wiped out in a single lifetime.

This kind of state does not trust its own people to know what's in its heart, what good it genuinely intends, since what it did prior to making amends is so unconscionable that it cannot actually come to terms with the shame of it. Nothing can take away that shame. And so the state overcompensates, then denies, then kills again. The state's love of its people turns into bitter overwork turns into angry misunderstandings turns into parental violence turns into the behavior of selfish, brutish children.

You learn history ahistorically, in the gruesome things that happen to something small which you hold dear. A small animal, say. Something you wish to keep as a pet to keep it from harm. A pet is not "dearer than eye-sight, space, and liberty—beyond what can be valued, rich, or rare," to use Cordelia's words, but it is dear. You cannot part with it, and it can be taken away in an instant.

You're given glimpses, as a child, of a past that appears cartoonishly evil. When the pet golden retriever of one of our American friends died shortly after her owner, my mother said that the creature was doing exactly what her *san dashu*'s monkey had done. *San dashu*, or third uncle on her mother's side, had a pet monkey that had been taken away from him during the second of many Anti-Rightist campaigns. The monkey was "jailed" and, separated from its owner, starved to death. Prior to that, in the spring of 1966, my mother's family's Pekingese had been culled. Like the palace Pekingese of old, this dog had loved commotion, thrived on the sound of interesting and joyful young adults. By 1966, however, servants had long been let go; children had already been sent away; visitors were few and far between. Confused by the absence of commodiousness, the dog was now adrift in its own Learian world. Dogs and cats, wild and domesticated, were rounded up and killed in the streets. The more exotic animals that Chinese people had kept as pets were also killed or sent to zoos, where most died of negligence.

One of my father's earliest memories is of a man crawling out of the local governor's compound. When the inner courtyards of this compound had been left untended for an entire summer, the youngest schoolchildren went in. It had spread by word of mouth—that the seat of the county government, once the seat of the Nationalist government, had been ransacked by the "rebel" faction. Children poured out of the elementary schools that afternoon. Seeking ways to afford the simple pancakes, called *shaobing* 烧饼, sold on street corners, they pried the brass hooks and eyes from the windows of the compound, the last valuables left on the estate. They then took turns at the chairs that miraculously sank when you sat in them. At the beginning of the summer, members of the party had already ransacked the estate.

When they were done, the county governor crawled out of his residence, his legs broken at the shins.

In 1961 meat-filled *shaobing* cost ten cents apiece. No one my father knew had tasted meat in a year, and this caused people to employ strategies of supplementation and adulteration. People starved to death all the time—it had become commonplace by then. Dried sweet potatoes that had shriveled into horns could be slowly boiled until they released their purple starch. School cafeterias served preserved brown mustard leaves, but even this was done with stinginess. What the canteen servers shoveled around the tin trays was over 80 percent salt. Blossoms of salt would crystallize on the leaves between the serving and the eating.

In the late 1960s through the mid-1970s, many young people whose parents had been subjected to ideological reeducation were themselves assigned to remote regions to learn the hardship endured by peasants and make themselves useful. Students were invited (and then coerced) into staying, marrying the locals. Many were sent to build roads and fix infrastructure but often, in the end, were conscripted to enact large-scale environmental and cultural destruction. Schools were closed, universities shuttered. Some were assigned to nearby villages where they would be sheltered as cadre elites, some to remote areas that they quickly found ways to escape. For children of people deemed political enemies, their mandatory deployments took them to places like Daxing'anling Prefecture, some of the most Learian landscapes on earth.

At least in the region of Jiangnan, where my father was stationed, the years between 1957 and 1959 saw good agricultural harvest. That meant that the officials could immediately turn their attention to iron production, leaving cotton bolls and wheat to rot in the fields. My father recollects that, during his sent-down years, a textile mill was relocated to his town from another city. This was considered a great boon to their town, not on account of the mill itself but for the workers' biological waste, which was collected in wells outside the mill to be used as fertilizer. In no time at all worker units nominated youths to collect the excrement, drawing it up in heaping buckets. Eventually, students were lowered down into the mill well to scoop up the very last of the feces with ladles.

There was an elderly teacher from the next village, my father tells me, who used to come around all the time, like a straggler from another world, hoping very much to converse with some of the educated youth from the cities. Not a single person would talk to him, on account of his political status.

I don't understand why this happened. Can you please explain? I learned as a student of English to not begin sentences with "Because." "Because . . . Because . . . Because . . ." is almost as bad as "But . . . But . . . But." It triggers the ire of parents and teachers listening to a long-winded, poorly conceived excuse. *Complete your sentences on the front end, dammit.* But the child can barely catch her breath. An explanation can be given but she is not equipped to give it. To identify the antecedent is to rehearse a long, incoherent sequence of events that the listener won't want to hear. She has History to speak, but she can't get it out of her mouth.

Don't let's bring up the past anymore. This is how Cordelia consoles Lear in act 4, scene 7, when they're finally reunited. He has been abused, which she knew would happen all along. She has brought back an army to rescue him, and for a minute it seems like they succeeded. Lear wakes up in her army camp, a doctor already attending to him, Cordelia and Kent nearby. "I know you do not love me," Lear says to her, still faintly the cry-bully. "For your sisters have, as I do remember, done me wrong. You have some cause; they have not." "No cause, no cause" is her reply.

Lear is remorseful. He is getting more forgetful. These statements are heartfelt. Still, he's buried a pointless accusation in his words ("I know you do not love me, but . . ."). Still, he cannot really be reasoned with, and so Cordelia says the kindest and most sensible thing she can, under the circumstances. As the deeply bullied child knows, of course there is cause. Of course a very precise string of actions and consequences got us to where we are. For that child, a set of actions was set in motion, a set of character traits that determined the present. Of course it matters who was at fault, but we no longer live in a world overseen by anyone who cares. Cordelia's "no cause" stops this line of inquiry. More commonly known as forgiveness, this is a gesture that halts retroactive blame. It draws the line between history and tragedy.

"No cause, no cause." You can hear a shushing in the epizeuxis, the tender repetition. She's turning down the lights, tucking in an anxious child. "No cause, no cause," like her gentle "nothing" in the first act, causes us to think about cause.

No cause, no cause. This is the premise of tales and children's songs. Broadside ballads of *Lear* were sung in the early 1700s, and they begin the story with Lear's mistake, not its cause. The jauntiest of these ballads was written by Richard Jonson and printed in London sometime in the mid-1700s:

King Lear once ruled in this land,
With princely pride and peace:
And had all things with content
That might his joys increase:

Amongst those things that nature gave,
Three daughters fair had he,
So princely seeming beautiful,
As fairer could not be.

So on a time it pleas'd the king,
A question thus to move:
Which of his daughters to his grace
Could show the dearest love.

"So on a time it pleas'd the king, A question thus to move." Out of the blue, something wrong happens. The idea just dropped into his head. You needn't concern yourself with why. History is what hurts, as Fredric Jameson famously said, and we'll do anything to avoid a gratuitous hurt.

Clobbered by Chinese history, your life might open in a Learian world, but you can't remember how you got here. But of course you did not just arrive here without cause.

What was happening in Shakespeare's world that it came to this? *Lear* is a Jacobean play, not an Elizabethan play. It was written during a particularly harrowing round of the plague and a particularly harrowing regime change. *Lear* comments on its own historical present in the most subversive way, perhaps, by reflecting back to it a pessimistic historical double. Shakespeare was cutting it close with a play that expressed criticism of things of which King James I stood accused: excessive pageantry, abuse of office, and overzealous prosecution of treason and sedition. In the play, Regan and Cornwall accuse Gloucester of collusion with France—that's the alleged crime—but they are themselves the ones who spy on Gloucester and plot the takeover of their castle and estate. Shakespeare was cutting it close in his choice to depict royal spies, power grabs, spectacles of inquisitorial torture, the absence of due process (Gloucester is accused and right away bound in his chair for his punishment). *Lear* was bold in looking back to Brutus's division of the kingdom, ahead to the disunification and absolutism of Charles I and Cromwell, and, finally, directly at the present, a situation richly described in James Shapiro's account of these Learian years as a period of intense equivocation by abusers and abused alike.

It's a tricky historical commentary. Half of the English population might have taken *Lear* as a jubilantly optimistic historical double. The Quarto gives Albany the final lines; the Folio swaps him out with Edgar, perhaps under political pressure, perhaps to pander to the king, perhaps to make a correction, or perhaps for some other reason we cannot imagine. Wasn't James I just like Edgar, the survivor and poet-scientist-visionary-theater kid come back to restore sanity, peace, and juridical and philosophical soundness to the land? James I was also Duke of Albany when *Lear* was first performed, a title later passed on to this son (who would become Charles I). The play reflected James I's and the Stuart dynasty's ambitions for the union of the crown—the three parts of Britain: England, Scotland, and Ireland—into Magna Brittania, and the reunification of Christianity—that is, Catholicism reconciled with Protestantism into a mainstream Anglicanism. The play reflected the predicament of heirlessness in English succession, particularly felt when the Tudor dynasty ended with Queen Elizabeth's death in 1603. Arguably, Shakespeare's decision to jam the story of the king of Paphlagonia and his two sons from Philip Sidney's *Arcadia* (a text as inconclusive as *Lear*) into what otherwise still counts as history, reflected this impasse. From a story of dead daughters we pivot to a story of two sons, who, flawed as they are, guarantee that the country will go on. As soon as news arrived that Elizabeth had died, James I, who up to that point had been James VI of Scotland, made his way back to London from Edinburgh to claim the crown. Most of the country welcomed him with open arms.

It soon became clear, however, that this king might not be the right king. Things got off on the wrong foot. Blood was already bad, as James's mother had been put to death by Elizabeth, a fact that deeply influenced his treatment of the statesmen and nobility carried over from her rule. James would later exhume Elizabeth from Henry VII's tomb, where she had asked to be buried, and rebury her with Mary Queen of Scots, perversely binding them together in death to emphasize, among other things, their relegation to the past. The plague severely delayed the coronation of James I at Westminster Abbey, the delay taken by the English and Scottish Parliament to be a bad omen. The two Parliaments would work against his plans for unification for the rest of his rule. There were other bad omens: people spread word that James had discovered a pickpocket who had followed his retinue and immediately executed him on the spot, flouting common law's guarantee of the right to a trial. James I's religious tolerance and genuine hopes for reconciliation between churches and factions were always undercut by his own religious superstitiousness and paranoia. Catholic and Puritan conspirators alike set their sights on him, and he had to escalate what he already believed to be true: *quod principi placuit legis habet vigorem*—"that which pleased the prince had the force of law."

The Gloucester side-plot in *Lear*, and the flimsiness of the incriminating letters particularly, recall the way in which the Gunpowder Plot was exposed and the frenzy of purges that followed. The plot to murder the king by blowing up Parliament with thirty-six kegs of gunpowder was very much real, and foiled by a letter (the one warning Lord Monteagle, a Catholic, not to attend the opening of Parliament). Catching the plot in time just stoked the king's paranoia. Someone was always guilty of sedition.

To take the most Learian example, Sir Walter Raleigh, the most romantic, witty, and adventurous figure of the Elizabethan court, was arrested soon after James I's accession, accused of collusion with the Spanish in one of many plots to kill the king. Raleigh, just past the age of fifty, had already been demoted, his life made difficult. He had been put under the surveillance of the royal spies James I had sent to Durham House, where Raleigh lived. A confession was later extracted out of his friend Henry Brooke, baron of Cobham, that Raleigh was guilty of collusion with the Spanish and participation in the Main Plot (there were also the Bye Plot and many other side plots on the king's life). In one of the biggest show trials and miscarriages of justice in English history, Raleigh was repeatedly denied the right to evidence and the right to cross-examine his accuser. He was locked up in the Tower of London for another thirteen years before his release to go on an expedition that would, in a cruel geopolitical twist of fate, lead to his beheading back home, in 1618, this time to appease the Spanish. Raleigh worked on a book in prison, a history of the world that was intended as a guide for kings. James I read it and concluded it was "too sawcie [saucy] in censuring Princes." Not only was he not moved to pardon; he saw the book as a further offense.

Raleigh's life is Learian in so many ways. It is known, for example, that the baron of Cobham soon recanted his incriminating confession against Raleigh, but that recantation was not acted upon by Raleigh's prosecutor, Sir Edward Coke, the English jurist known to history (justly) as an architect of modern English law. Coke's own career expressed *Lear*'s hope, if a play may be said to have a hope, that the divine right of kings can be tempered by the rule of law, that justice and fairness will not invariably conflict with basic human needs and interests, including those involving kings, nobility, and heredity. And yet, in Raleigh's own words, Coke "crucified [him] with a thousand torments." The English exceptionalism that grounded Coke's principles also made him farcically prejudiced, racist, and quick to punish. Pure self-interest also played a part. Coke was someone who had done exceedingly well in the transition from Elizabeth to James—from attorney general for England and Wales to chief justice of England by 1613—and was able to live to a natural old age in very turbulent times. Such a smooth transition may have required the sacking of his political doppelganger, Raleigh. Coke's significant achievements for universal law were also tied to the fact that the chief justice of England had incentive to limit the power of kings. How much power could be wrested from kings, and through what legal invention, is a Learian lesson that would not be fully learned until the second generation of Stuarts. In 1603, it was clear to bystanders that Raleigh would be convicted and killed someday, no matter what, and that the rule of law would be suspended for some time.

Whatever faith there is in the divine right of kings, it is immediately thrown into question when the king exhibits ruinous favoritism and produces unimpressive heirs. This drumbeat in *Lear* could not help but sound in James's court. James's rule was almost immediately blemished by his inexplicable acts of largesse to those others perceived as undeserving, and by his unaccountable stringency and meanness toward privy counselors. The king oscillated wildly between a modern-feeling clemency and ancient-feeling ruthlessness, between advanced understanding of science and regressive superstition, between willingness to uphold the trifold division of power among king, representative body, and the people, and the active sabotage of that principle. James I fostered a pathological environment. He developed a system for rewarding personages who had no previous aristocratic ties with extraordinary power, sometimes out of love and fancy, as with George Villiers, and others out of practical calculation: these new titles had to be paid for by the title-bearers themselves, thus bringing in money to pay for the king's extravagance and to relieve him of financial dependence on Parliament. Rampant corruption and malfeasance carried over from late-Elizabethan excesses, as reflected in *Measure for Measure*, the first of Shakespeare's play to be shown to James after his ascension. Misdistribution in turn created resentment, inspired machination, and, in the final analysis, provoked superstition. In 1612 James lost his favored son, Prince Henry. When James died in 1625, he passed on the problems he had with Parliament, finances, foreign wars, and religious antipathy to his other son, Charles, a child he had always deemed not fit to serve. Charles's reign ended in the English Civil War and his own beheading, the first regicide of its kind.

Meanwhile, waves and waves of pestilence swept through the South and East of England between the 1580s and early 1600s. *Lear* was written during the shuttering of the theaters, decreed in part to contain the spread and in part to blame the plague on the burgeoning theater culture. Before the shuttering, 5 percent of the population of London was in a theater every single night. In a 1578 sermon the Puritan minister Thomas White railed that "the cause of plagues is sin, and the cause of sin is plays." *Lear*'s quarantine was nothing new, as Shakespeare wrote his first narrative poems, "Venus and Adonis" and "The Rape of Lucrece," during the plague of 1594, and *Measure for Measure* during the plague of 1603–4, when theaters were often shuttered, and blamed. But readiness to scapegoat and control the theater sharpened with each bout of plague, and severe control and cruelty were perpetrated in the name of health and safety. His livelihood now somewhat endangered, Shakespeare wrote about the plague's effects in the inner sanctums of the state. His plays responded to the confusion of cause and effect, scale and severity, isolation and overcrowding caused by pestilence and in the name of eliminating pestilence. With plague came state terror in the form of confinements, and religious terror in the form of exorcism. People came up with stranger and stranger folk remedies and pleaded, often hysterically, for supernatural assistance. They also invoked the plague in their curses.

Plagues, whether real or manufactured, overstated or understated, all have an inward turn, and thus are closely associated with sin. Plagues strain the bonds of society, and genuine fear can manifest in a plague as instruments of persecution. Plagues naturally justify authoritarian intervention, just as they encourage the conflation of hygiene with purity. In early-seventeenth-century England, animals believed to be carriers of the disease were rounded up and killed. As documented in the notebooks of an occult herbalist named Simon Forman, these small atrocities soon led to bigger ones: the shunning of those with treatable illnesses, sealing up entire families inside their houses if some showed symptoms. Meanwhile the actual plague, roaring on, began to inspire the notion that disease can be excised and exorcized for good. Superstition and scapegoating found new expressive possibilities.

Pestilence connects death and the cause of death in the shortest fashion, and examples of direct causality inspire human beings to try their hands at the same, applying this directness to everything else. Thrilled by the sense that proper blame can finally be traced, the men and women of plague times slide into an effective dark age—dark on every continent, in every civilization, and at any moment in history.

Modern English witch hunts were soon under way in Shakespeare's world. In 1604, the deliberation of cases of witchcraft was transferred from the clergy back to the common court. This restored witchcraft as a felony and expanded the kinds of punishable offenses. While it is not certain that James introduced the Witchcraft Act of 1604 to the House of Lords, his obsessive interest in demonology had already inspired waves of Scottish witch hunts in the previous decade, with deaths numbering in the thousands. In 1597, James published a dissertation on witchcraft, its detection, and its proper punishments. His obsession inspired new spectacles of extreme testing. Fathers began enacting the tale of the "Miller's Daughter," bringing in their own children for the demonstration of astonishingly sadistic and masochistic feats. Instead of being shut in a room and forced to spin straw into gold so that their fathers could appease the king, as in the tale, daughters were asked to demonstrate their ability to bear extraordinary pain—ingesting pins or sticking them into their flesh. The plague and bizarre natural calamities acted as cover for superstition, or the willful collapsing of longer, more complex chains of cause and effect. Kent puts it aptly in act 2, scene 1: "things that love night / Love not such nights as these."

After Edgar is forced to flee and adopts the persona of Tom O'Bedlam, he begins to refer to contemporary events, describing demons that "possess chambermaids and waiting-women." Edmund's name in *Lear* might also be a reference to "Father Edmund," the alias of a Jesuit priest who performed and instigated spectacular exorcisms in the 1580s in a traveling show of sorts called "Father Edmund's Devil Theater." These events are described in Archbishop of York Samuel Harsnett's diatribe against exorcism, a text whose language appears directly in *Lear*. Harsnett's pamphlet, *A Declaration of Egregious Popish Impostures, to with-draw the harts of her Maiesties Subiects from their allegeance, and from the truth of Christian Religion professed in England, under the pretence of casting out deuils*, exposed the logic of exorcism and its political opportunism. Decrying the scripted nature of such acts and its regression into wanton cruelty, Harsnett tried to show repeatedly that exorcisms were fraudulent, a black box that only proved the malintent of the exorcist. Shakespeare's heavy-handed borrowing from *A Declaration* was therefore pointed. Edgar acts possessed as Tom O'Bedlam, but he is not really possessed. Performance for theater is one thing; the performative theater of forced conversion and confession is another. *Lear* also expresses the same concerns about gullibility and malice, especially in the Gloucester-Edmund story, the violence of incriminations lodged by fakers and scammers. Accordingly, in *Lear*, as in *A Declaration*, there is no demonic possession among the persecuted except *hysterica passio*: human desperation and anguish at injustice and the open victimization of scapegoating. Severe scapegoating, plagues, and regime upheavals seem to go hand in hand.

In Chinese, there is a saying: *Tian zai ren huo* 天灾人祸. *Tian zai* means calamities from heaven or natural catastrophes, *ren huo* means the wrongdoings of man. In the expression, as you can see, *tian zai* and *ren huo* are set beside each other. No obvious grammatical relationship exists between them. Misery loves company, and natural disasters bring evil, and so human wrongdoing always comes with environmental calamities. Or, environmental calamities bring about human wrongdoing. When one is here, the other is never far away. Or, as my grandfather used to say, there is no *tian zai*, only *ren huo*.

Plagues are where histories have to start, because in plagues we have a primal confusion of cause and effect. History is most muddled in a plague; the most ruthlessly ambitious often see their opportunity here.

Soon after the defeat of the KMT (the Nationalist Party) and its last holdouts in the Civil War in 1949, the Communist Party, now the leaders of the People's Republic of China, turned to the management of public health. Mao's mass mobilization focused on two animals—snails and sparrows.[4] Grassroots efforts also surged to prevent the disease known as snail fever. That year Mao launched a campaign to deworm hundreds of millions of the rural population, an effort widely praised until the 1980s, when its wildly exaggerated successes were, like much else, brought to light and shown to have been falsified. Some snail fever was controlled, but the more important story is that it enabled the government to set up the apparatus for social control and invasive health management in every county.

Disease prevention campaigns were the primary mechanism of state power. One year before the end of the war that in China is called The Great Movement to Resist America and Assist Korea (1950–53), China accused the United States of waging bacteriological warfare on Chinese and North Korean troops. Allegedly, the US Army had dropped voles, fleas, clams, and other vermin carrying anthrax, meningitis, cholera, encephalitis, and bubonic plague out of the sky, an act of biological war that was said to echo Japan's hair-raising biological warfare against China in Korea and Manchuria in the previous decade. The army began a mass disinfection campaign in the county of Gannan, in the northeasternmost part of China. The rest of the country soon followed suit.

An eminent plague specialist named Dr. Wu Lien-teh (Wu Liande) decried this "long string of unfounded accusations,"

4. Incidentally, the two animals the Fool invokes in his chidings of Lear.

as these diseases were endemic to the region, unmatched to the supposed carriers, and, anyway, unviable in the deep winter when this campaign supposedly took place. Nevertheless, the allegations stuck. Quarantines and delousing methods started in the area bordering North Korea, which was renamed the "emergency prevention zone." Household pets were exterminated. People doused themselves with DDT solutions. Mao then extended pandemic prevention measures past the end of the Korean War, making use of the People's Volunteer Army to enforce sanitation and public health campaigns, including a large-scale vaccination program subsidized by the Soviet Union. The Central Epidemic Prevention Committee was renamed the Committee of Patriotic Health Movement, and the Four Pests campaign began. The "four pests" referred to four biological enemies, dubbed "vectors" of disease: rats, fleas, mosquitoes, and, bizarrely, sparrows. Daily life was organized around their elimination. Perhaps even more damaging than the ecological experiment was the popularization of sloganeering and the call to mobilization using the number four—a tic that would wend its way into "the Four Olds" during the Cultural Revolution as well as the "Four Cardinal Principles" from Deng Xiaoping's remarks in 1979 that would become enshrined in the People's Constitution in 1982.

Children and the elderly, party officials, and indeed, everyone in China began in earnest to kill flies for sport, sometimes getting up at 4 a.m. and not resting until dusk. Piles of insects and pests were compared across municipalities. To deflect attention from these ongoing human-made natural catastrophes, the government enlisted every level of society in the "prevention campaign." Brightly colored public health posters mixed Chinese folk art and Peking opera iconography with the style and formatting of Soviet propaganda.

Official reports of sparrows stealing grain started to come in when the Great Leap Forward was launched in 1958. Mao's centralized planned economy, modeled on that of the Soviet Union, promised to extract unprecedented volumes of grain and steel from the countryside—from the labor of peasants and primitive industrialization. Farmers in China were told that the rice had to be planted in March, instead of May, to increase the yield twofold, threefold, or fourfold to keep on schedule. Most of the time was spent on revolutionary activities and struggle sessions. When the party realized they needed immediately to rationalize expected low crop yields, they preemptively identified a scapegoat. Sparrows represented capitalism (by lowering the yield and sabotaging the five-year plan of the Great Leap Forward) and the folk superstition that was supposed to be eradicated (as it was long considered bad luck to destroy bird eggs). Sparrows were to be tortured by incessant noise until they fell dead out of the sky. The young and the old all joined in, finding sparrow corpses more measurable than the other three pests. Killing sparrows meant killing these class enemies, which allowed people to discharge the rage of not being able to kill the birds for food, as they were once able to do. By the close of 1958, a little over 2 million sparrows had been killed, wreaking havoc on the environment. With fewer avian predators to counter them, swarming locusts descended on the crops; people resorted to eating the insects themselves. Caterpillars fattened themselves on leafy vegetables, further damaging the nation's already diminished agricultural output.

Did anyone speak up? Yes and no. One senses the impossibility of truth-telling in the memo put forward by the party secretary of the Chinese Academy of Science in 1959: "In general, scientists think that the benefits and downsides of sparrows vary depending on the location and times of the year. Some scientists are lenient towards eliminating the damages caused by the sparrows but not all sparrows."

The officials sensed that something had gone very wrong and soon enough were accepting donations of sparrows from the Soviet Union to deal with the ecological crisis. For a while it seemed as though things would be okay for those who publicly raised an eyebrow at the madness. A few years later, however, in a different campaign, the scientists who had spoken up against the Four Pests campaign of 1958 were punished by the state. Ornithologist Tso-hsin Cheng (Zheng Zuoxin) was publicly humiliated and sent to clean toilets. Another scientist who had cagily spoken out against the slaughter of sparrows was driven to his death in 1962, then dug up by the Red Guards and subjected to "corpse humiliation," a form of punishment happening with alarming frequency.[5] The critic is never forgotten, and presents an affront even after death.

Class struggle, or *jieji douzheng* 阶级斗争—literally "fighting on the steps" in Mandarin—found perfect expression in preexisting demon-exorcizing tales and cultural traditions. Chen Boda, one of the "intellectuals" who had participated in the persecution of the literary critic Wang Shiwei and countless others, wrote an editorial in the 1966 issue of the *People's Daily*, the organ of the Chinese Communist party: "Sweep Away All Cow Demons and Snake Spirits." Chinese exorcism now exceeded the absurdity of Christian exorcism. Class enemies were called "white boned demons" after a character from *Journey to the West*. Fantastical elements once relegated to legend and poetry were now everyday words; people who were classified as "cow demons" were imprisoned in terrifying makeshift spaces called "cowsheds." Staged forced confessions were extracted amid the frenzy of true believers. Harrowing scenes could be found in every single work unit, every single day, in every single corner of the country. People who had never lived a day under capitalism were called "capitalist roaders," the final enemies of the revolution. But "capitalist roaders" was merely one label among many for class enemies, which were just evildoers. As a violent

5. In 1966, Sun Yat-sen's widow, Song Ching-lin, suffered confiscation of her property, the ransacking of her home, and the disinterment of her parents by the Red Guards, who left their bodies exposed for days. Song Ching-lin famously broke off with the Nationalist Party of her husband's family and of her sister, Song Mei-lin, the wife of Chiang Kai-shek, to devote herself to the Communist Party throughout the 1950s and 1960s.

regime communism tapped into preexisting extremes in Chinese pedagogy, and its relentless drive to disambiguate motives and causes, especially among the class of people who saw themselves as *qing guan* 清官 ("virtuous administrators"). People competed with one another to make do with less, and then covered up the inevitable hypocrisies and inconsistencies.

In the "people's communes," or *renmin gongshe* 人民公社, the largest collective units in Communist China, resistors to the planned economy were trussed up and confessions of fidelity to capitalism beaten out of them. Peasants who petitioned to withdraw from the system were rounded up by their nemeses as counterrevolutionaries. Land Reform Movement plans from 1946 to 1953 often came with a special quota for the number of people—at first landowners but soon anyone who dissented—who had to be publicly humiliated and then mobbed to death, quotas that were satisfied by work teams. "Landlords," most of whom were just slightly better-off peasants, were killed in the millions, often by neighbors who were only slightly less well off. Savagery spread across the countryside, peasants killing those nearly as poor as they were. People liked filling quotas, as well as adding simpler multipliers. In 1950 Mao rolled out the infamous "one in every thousand" killing quota; people did that times three. It was in the countryside, among the poorest of the poor, that modern totalitarianism combined with the chaos and ignorance of Chinese folk practices.

In 2019 I saw Sam Gold's Broadway production of *King Lear*, starring Dame Glenda Jackson as Lear. Besides the decision to play Lear queer and to cast a deaf-mute actor as Cornwall, one directorial choice really stuck with me. During the intermission the stage was altered so that everything thereafter happened in a trash heap. Goneril and Edmund fucked in this trash heap, Gloucester leapt from the cliffs of Dover in this trash heap.

By stripping away all of the structures, Gold could convey the nastiness of the material disorder that follows coercive authority. You see the immensity of waste and physical dereliction. There is no way, even now, to tally the extent of environmental and material damage, the ruining of natural, public, and civic spaces in China. This world was trashed. Literal trash tells it like it is, doing away with pretenses. By the end of *Lear*, almost all pretenses have been dropped. It is infinite tenderness and utter vileness.

Inasmuch as any staging of *Lear* slyly indicts existing autocratic governments, *Lear* is frequently interpreted as an allegory of fascist totalitarianism or monarchic authoritarianism. Look across *Lear*'s filmic and stage adaptations and you see an England that looks like Thatcherite England, Weimar Republic, Nazi Germany. Edgar (or Albany)'s final injunction to "Speak what we feel, not what we ought to say" was a message that resounded in the traumatic aftermath of two world wars in Europe.[6]

I believe *Lear* anticipates totalitarianism, Left and Right, East and West. Like its twin, *Coriolanus*, written around the same time, *Lear* knows that if you look and listen for duplicative assent among adults you will know what kind of world you live

6. In the Soviet Union, theater and film director Grigori Kozintsev became obsessed with *Lear*. He staged productions of the play for the Bolshoi Drama Theater in 1941. In 1970 he released a film adaptation of *King Lear*. His chronicle of making this film, *King Lear: The Space of Tragedy*, was published shortly after he died in 1973. Kozintsev was a People's Artist of the USSR. Still having to tiptoe through the Brezhnev years, he found in *Lear* a perfect screen. In his *Shakespeare, Time, and Conscience*, Kozintsev writes: "In order to bring contemporary processes into full relief, the shadow of another epoch was cast on the principals and on the course of events." When speaking truth to a very severe and bizarre power, one needs to become Shakespearean. From tsarist Russia to the Bolshevik Revolution, the Terror of the 1930s, and beyond, to the "division of the kingdom" in the Molotov-Ribbentrop Pact of 1939: *Lear* resonates anywhere that has been gouged from without and within, subjected to violence and starvation, and of course, as always, the pro forma in overdrive. Kozintsev's *Lear* also echoes Stalinist terror, by no means over, even by the 1970s.

in.[7] Totalitarianism exists in copies, in everyone who wishes to be an extension of the totalitarian state. You're in a play that, like its worst characters, turns resolutely against extraneous human lives. Lear's kingdom is such an empty place, and yet almost everyone is a spare. Spare evil sister (Regan), spare male heir (Edmund), spare foolish father (Gloucester), spare object of affection (Cordelia/Fool), spare villain (Oswald), spare servants, spare gentlemen. Of course they have differentiable actions and motivations, but, in state-endorsed anarchism, they are all spares. As Edmund says about the evil sisters, "Neither can be enjoyed / If both remain alive."

I had a remarkable freshman student who intuitively understood the modality of totalitarianism, and how it might be represented in literary form. In class she made the offhand comment that in *Lear*, frivolous and deadly serious skirmishes follow upon one another without hierarchy or temporal markers. She said that chronological sense has to be removed to show that power, in the absence of sovereignty, exists primarily as pure bravado and as pure harm.

Look in on almost any moment in *Lear* and you cannot quite see how bad the situation is. This is what struck me, reading it years later. A historian's warning: it's hard to see history as it is

7. In *Coriolanus*, reduplicatives expose mob-led, single-voiced prosecutions. The play begins this way:

> FIRST CITIZEN: Before we proceed any further, hear me speak.
> ALL: Speak, speak.
> FIRST CITIZEN: You are all resolv'd rather to die than to famish?
> ALL: Resolv'd. Resolv'd.
> FIRST CITIZEN: First, you know Caius Marcius is chief enemy to the people.
> ALL: We know't, we know't.
> FIRST CITIZEN: Let us kill him, and we'll have corn at our own price. Is 't a verdict?
> ALL: No more talking on't, let it be done. Away, away. (1.1.1–12)

happening. Albany barely understands Lear's nasty tussles with his daughters. It's just an ordinary day with the in-laws; how did things get so bad? Kent has shown up at Gloucester's castle and runs into Goneril's steward/henchman, Oswald. No one knows it's Kent because he is disguised as a fellow named Caius in order to stay on as Lear's servant and bodyguard and because Kent answers to Oswald as a member of Gloucester's household. We soon learn that Kent is too direct to be an effective hero and has other less-nameable flaws that disqualify him for the job of the bodyguard and messenger. Regan and Cornwall, who happen to be guests at Gloucester's castle, do not recognize that it's Kent who has gotten into a tussle with Oswald, but the disguise hardly helps him. Oswald blinks uncomprehendingly at Kent's anger toward him. *I don't know you, stranger!* he cries, *why are you insulting me and delivering blows?*

For these offenses Kent is put in the stocks. Does that seem unreasonable? *Lear*'s audiences often do not realize how bad Kent's situation is, even when Regan arbitrarily extends Kent's punishment. *We'll keep him like this till noon*, says Cornwall. "Till noon?—till night, my lord, and all night too," his wife replies. You hear, now, how eroticism and sadism share the same flippancy toward added time. It is a commonplace cruelty, like cats and dogs getting tied to a post somewhere and forgotten. And there Kent stays until . . . it's hard to say.

From the director and producer's standpoint, it's not easy to convey how cruel this detention in the stocks really is. Kent can often just look foolish onstage, sitting there idling. It's not torture, exactly. No screws are being applied. It's the Fool who finally describes what we're seeing, with reference to the spectacle of bear-baiting, then one of the most gruesome sports in Shakespeare's England:

> Look, ha, he wears cruel garters. Horses are tied by the
> head, dogs and bears by th' neck, monkeys by th' loins, and
> men by the legs. (2.4.10–12)

An arbitrary extension of immobility is hard to see. People can also be overstoical in their sufferings, as Kent was. "Mak'st thou this shame thy pastime?" Lear asks Kent, still in the stocks. "No, my lord," he replies. When he finally explains why he is where he is, the explanation sounds wordy, bizarre. I delivered your letters, and then another guy delivered letters, and then I was called forth, and he was too saucy. . . . *And then this small dumb thing happened, and then that small dumb thing happened, and then* "your son and daughter found this trespass worth / The shame which here it suffers."

The same problem occurs when Lear is locked out of Gloucester's castle just as the weather turns bad. We're still at Gloucester's castle, where several unbelievable crimes happen. Kent being put in the stocks was just a foretaste, which Lear himself understood. *You put my man in the stocks, and in someone else's house? What will soon happen to me?* Gloucester himself will soon experience the cruelty that Regan and Cornwall are capable of. In between Kent and Gloucester's torture we are shown a crime of negligence for which it is hard to determine fault. In this famous scene, Lear storms out after his bitter quarrel with his two daughters and their husbands, his train reduced to nothing, as no one will pay for the soldiers anymore. Perhaps twenty or thirty have trailed along, but they're nowhere to be seen. Lo and behold, it starts to storm. None of his children or in-laws go after him. Gloucester also does not go after him, despite many misgivings. It's a bit of schoolyard cruelty on the children's part: Father wants to be petulant? Well, he must be taught a lesson! "O, sir," Regan says to Gloucester's weak entreaty that they cannot send an old man out into this kind of weather, "to willful men / The injuries that they themselves procure / Must be their schoolmasters. Shut up your doors." Lear was not locked out, then. Rather, he leaves, and no one cares. "My Lord," says Goneril to Gloucester, "entreat him by no means to stay." Gloucester, a weak man, cannot decide what to do. "Shut up your doors," he is sweetly commanded a second time, this time by Cornwall, "Come out of the storm."

In Sonnet 29, "When, in disgrace with fortune and men's eyes," Shakespeare would seem to write another set of Lear's lines: "I all alone beweep my outcast state, and trouble deaf heaven with my bootless cries. . . ." It's a hard genre, asking for sympathy. Alone Lear beweeps his outcast state. Does that really constitute . . . exile? The audience and reader's moral judgment is being tested in this very moment: What am I looking at? Is this a small thing or a serious matter? Is this a just response to the petulant hysterical parent or is sending an elderly person into the rain an effective death knell? But you sound ridiculous saying that ("death knell").

Lear's characters never see the horrible thing coming because they're always reacting to being newly deprived or somehow in trouble. It all happens so quickly, and the effects are felt so slowly. It's stupidly slow, blindingly fast. The King of France shakes his head in disbelief at the precipitousness of the turn at the beginning of the play. "It is most strange," he remarks, that Cordelia—so good and so clearly favored—can "in this trice of time . . . dismantle so many folds of disfavor." In the blink of an eye she has incurred . . . such hatred?

There's a horrible play on words in the plucking of Gloucester's eyes—*I never saw it coming*—a truly shocking moment in *Lear* that always has to be handled delicately on the stage. It's so extreme. Gloucester did not see that coming. We did not see that coming because we do not believe people capable of such things; but, even more so, it does not seem like things had been building up to this point, though of course they had. From putting someone in the stocks to gouging out an old man's eyes, one after the other? Regan and Cornwall's capacity will seem out of the blue. But . . . *you were my guests*, cries Gloucester, finding himself bound in his own chair in his own hall. How could such a thing be possible? Though you know they are cruel, you really can't guess what Regan and Goneril are capable of until you see what they do. Only the last step confirms your suspicions about the first steps.

In a Learian world, what people are capable of in the last instance can be glimpsed in the first instance, but you'd be hard pressed to recognize the first instance. Excessive flattery of a doting father—who could prosecute this? Copying one's sister in excessive flattery of an irascible and needy father—on what charges can you arraign this individual, even in the private courts of human conversation?

Shakespeare made the title character someone who, like all fundamentally good people, never sees it coming. Lear is surprised by how it is that things can come to be this way, how people can do what they do, every single time, just as they're surprised by his extremes, every single time. "Let them anatomize Regan," he says, "see what breeds about her heart. Is there any cause in nature that makes this hardness?" He just doesn't get it, though it may largely be his fault.

"I thought the King had more affected the Duke of Albany than Cornwall"—this is how the play begins, remember?—in Kent's confusion over his misplaced certainty in Lear's judgment of character. He's confused, the way people are confused when the bad are rewarded and the good punished, or when something really not right is happening. Having to speak to Gloucester and Edmund, the bad and the worse, Kent is confused from the get-go that some comment or conspiracy seems expected of him. He remains kind and fair. It takes him a second to understand the fact that Edmund is an illegitimate child, but he is kind when he reacts; "I cannot wish the fault undone, the issue of it being so proper." Even disguised as Caius, Kent is recognizably Kent. He is someone who strategizes for the good but can only ever react to wickedness. He is always, to some extent, surprised by sin.

You didn't see it coming. In this trice of time you cannot ascertain the timing and execution of the prosecution of personal slip-ups. You're always surprised by the phrase "patterns of misconduct." This is because tyranny always catches you by surprise. The possibilities of what can be spoken have shifted away from you, and you find yourself muzzled, made dumb. You could never have seen it coming, because you could never have anticipated such changes to the rules of discourse.

Here is my grandfather, quickly sketching the atmosphere of 1958 in his memoir:

> I didn't wish to fall behind in this political atmosphere. Every day I was full of readiness to work, going to committee meetings and education sessions, writing and directing little performances, performing onstage, even while having to perform "Three Red Flags" in the streets. I worked day and night, sleeping four or five hours a day, and didn't feel fatigue.
>
> At that time the newspapers daily reported the "satellite news": "crop yield is twenty thousand kilograms"; "crop yield is thirty-six thousand kilograms"; "crop yield is one hundred twenty thousand kilograms." The front-page news printed a photograph of a young child atop a hill of grain, making no dent in it at all, so you can appreciate the volume. The party reports in this way, who would dare to disbelieve. And in any case, at that time, everyone had become a poet. Frictionlessly, the words leapt from mouths and spread through the land: "However brave man is, that's how much the land will yield!" You "inflated," he "inflated," everyone became an exaggerator, and we all lived out meaningless lives amid this hot air.[8]

8. Original text: "我在这样的政治气氛下、也不甘落后、每天干劲十足、一面开会学习、一面还要编小演唱；一面在舞台上演出、一面还要走上街头演出歌颂"三面红旗"的小戏。我日日夜夜拼搏、一天睡四五个小时、也不觉得累。

当时的报纸天天放"卫星"："亩产一万斤"，"亩产一万八千斤"，"亩产六万斤"...... 报上头版头条赫然登着一张照片：一个小孩子坐在田里稻谷上、沉不下去、可见稻谷产量之高。党报如此宣传、谁能不信！再说、那时候、人人都变成诗人、顺口溜满天下："人有多大胆、地有多大产!" 大家你吹我吹、人人都吹、人们似乎都在"吹"中混日子." Song Baoluo 宋宝罗, *Yihai Chengfu* 《艺海沉浮：宋保罗回忆录》, ed. Ren

Visceral fear of the ever-changing rules and punishments made people give up on description and causality. Language helped to keep the frogs in the pan, and it worked by exaggeration and underdescription, by making too much out of nothing, and describing monumental wrongs as a trifling matter. Being sent down into the countryside didn't seem all that bad, and still doesn't to those who conjure images of cheerful lakeside camps. Up to the Mountains, Down to the Countryside Movement: it's almost romantic. Even today anyone hearing about this period of history can just say, "What's so bad about hard farm labor for a few years?" What could be so wrong about an extended, nonsimulated look at the reality of the laboring poor? Indeed, even to me that sounds like a good idea. Mao knew how to name things. Land Reform Movement. Great Leap Forward. Cultural Revolution. Three-Years Natural Disaster. Hundred Flowers Campaign. They sound like earnest, progressive movements punctuated by a small climate disaster. At most they sound like euphemisms for bland events, a talking up of small accomplishments.

Point your camera anywhere in China, as did photographer Marc Riboud traveling in China in the 1950s and '60s, and you might not see anything amiss. Things seem strange—there are too many people doing the same thing, as in figures 2 and 3—but still well within the range of normal historical and cultural activity. How do you make sure you're not overreacting or underreacting? Westerners and even Chinese people themselves couldn't gauge the severity of Maoist pranks. *Being doused in ink and being made to wear a dunce cap? Is that a very big deal?* (figure 4). I think about photographs from the Cultural Revolution that show the mass bullying of teachers and elders, corky arms bound and lifted behind corky bodies. The bodies are obviously uncomfortable but not under obvious torture. *So what—they had some ink thrown on them? It's just paint.*

Mingyao 任明耀 (Zhejiang Arts and Culture Publishing House [*Zhejiang wenyi chubanshe*], 1999), 182.

FIGURE 2. Young pioneers drilling in the streets of Shanshing, Manchuria, with homemade wooden guns, 1965. Photo by Marc Riboud / Fonds Marc Riboud au MNAAG / Magnum Photos.

FIGURE 3. Antique-shop window in Liulichang Street, Beijing, 1965. Photo by Marc Riboud / Fonds Marc Riboud au MNAAG / Magnum Photos.

FIGURE 4. A Communist Party secretary and the wife of another official are denounced and splattered with ink at a 1966 stadium rally in Harbin, China. Photo by Li Zhensheng. © Li Zhensheng/Contact Press Images from the book *Red-Color News Soldier* (New York: Phaidon Press, 2003).

Mao had also fully grasped the natural suitability of photographic and filmic media for the broadcasting and cognitive technologies of totalitarianism. Posters and footage of bountiful plenty could be seen everywhere across a land that was actually ravaged by violent campaigns and manufactured famine. Photography also enabled the precursor of the "deep fake." A 1958 photograph of Chairman Mao taking part in volunteer labor at the construction site of the Ming Tombs Reservoir shows Secretary Peng Zeng by his side. By 1978, when this image was republished in one of Mao's many hagiographies, Peng Zeng had disappeared. In every layer of this world and its self-reporting you have falsification and distortion, done out of malice and real love.

Westerners looking in also compounded the problem. At the official invitation of the People's Republic of China, Italian filmmaker Michelangelo Antonioni produced a documentary called *Chung Kuo/Cina* (Zhong guo/China). *Chung Kuo* hardly scratched the surface of what had happened in China up to 1972, when the film was made, as Antonioni had purposely avoided anything negative, at the behest of the Party.[9] Almost no one knew what was happening to Westerners trapped inside China. In 1968 a Jewish Dutch woman named Selma Vos was persecuted to death along with her husband, Cao Richang, an eminent psychologist who had helped found the Institute of Psychology of the Chinese Academy of Sciences. Cao Richang had been assigned to hard cleaning work two years prior after

9. *Chung Kuo/Cina* was as rosy as a foreign documentary of life in Mao's China could be. And yet, even a filmmaker sympathetic to Maoism, someone who believed that it put "one billion protagonists on the world scene," could not help making a "problematic" film. Antonioni would pay a price for making *Chung Kuo/Cina*. Argument over the negative details in the film fueled factional violence in the CPC. The faction that won declared a Chinese-style fatwa on Antonioni, getting his film banned at the Venice Biennale and then siccing Italian Maoists on him. The writer Simon Leys learned this, too, in the 1970s, his career and life forever damaged by his intervention. Leys was one of the first to expose the crimes of Mao's China to the West and push back against Maoist enthusiasm abroad.

the couple had been spied on and turned in by other foreigners in China, including a writer and scholar named Sidney Rittenberg, the second foreigner to join the CPC. (In 1968 Rittenberg, who had helped the party victimize many, was himself subjected to ten years of solitary confinement). Selma Vos's story is particularly Learian. Her mother and other family members had been killed in the Sobibor extermination camp in German-occupied Poland. She and her father survived the Holocaust by hiding, like Anne Frank, in the attic of neighbors. How could she have anticipated such a second act? Vos even returned to the Netherlands briefly in 1966 and came back *as a Chinese national*, and therefore was unable to leave or seek amnesty during her incarceration, in part believing that things could not possibly come to that.

The crimes of the state, and of the people on the people, were drawn out, out in the open, socially normalized. Wang Bing's 2018 *Dead Souls*, an eight-hour documentary of the prison-factories in Gansu that ran from the 1950s to the present, is protracted to make you feel the slowness of the terror. State officials are coming for a visit, pictures are taken, the labor camp's demolition of human lives carries on in the background. Frightened protests are made to sound outlandish. There's no time to think, and yet time passes so slowly.

Although people labeled "reactionaries" were certainly soon against the revolution, "reactionary" itself was a terrible misnomer for most of the people who were targeted for killing, dispossession, and humiliation. Intellectuals, merchants, artists, teachers, writers, and students killed or persecuted to oblivion were themselves liberal-progressive by mid- and early-twentieth-century Chinese standards and even by today's standards. They had fought for a uniquely Chinese but also globally inspired anti-Learian outcome for their country: an equal and fair society in which all women, and not just ladies of the bower or favored children, would have equal access to education and resources; a clear separation of power in Chinese government;

a society in which the disabled and the elderly would thrive and contribute and be treated kindly, criminals would be given a fair chance, and the burden of social infrastructures would be shared by all. Ironically, "reactionary" became a perfect description of their predicaments. In Mao's era they could, in fact, only ever react.

How much do you know about your kingdom and conditions on the ground? This Learian lesson resonates with one of the oldest tropes in Chinese literature and theater: a sovereign must be downtrodden and not-who-he-is to see his country as it really is. That is the paramount lesson of the Chinese genre of *xishuo* 戏说: a "theatrical" rendition of historical drama. In these dramas, which are based on historical tales, the emperor or king or high-ranking courtier puts on a disguise and travels across his empire. Greatly endangering his own life, the sovereign learns how his people live and where injustice really occurs. The sovereign cannot learn this by hearsay and reporting because communication about the state of the country is in practice deeply inefficient. Corruption, injustice, and abuses of the public purse—these crimes spike during natural catastrophes like flood, drought, and pestilence, and yet are never accurately reported. In this world order, the wise sovereign knows that gossip travels fast, while the necessary information has a hard time ever getting out. He must make himself abject in order to learn what cannot be learned without direct experience.

Such abjection happens in *Lear*, but, like all else, it's too little, too late. Upon entering the hovel where he is to shelter, Lear expresses pity for his subjects living on the margins of society:

> Poor naked wretches, wheresoe'er you are,
> That bide the pelting of this pitiless storm,
> How shall your houseless heads and unfed sides,

Your loop'd and window'd raggedness, defend you
From seasons such as these? O, I have ta'en
Too little care of this! Take physic, pomp;
Expose thyself to feel what wretches feel,
That thou mayst shake the superflux to them
And show the heavens more just.

"Expose thyself to what wretches feel." "Take physic, pomp." Still a bit pompous, King Lear is admitting to shirking parental and kingly labor. "I have ta'en too little care of this," he concedes. He and those around him have not had anything to eat for a long time, nor will they get a meal anytime soon. In this country, as Cordelia tells us later, the fields have long grown rank with weeds.

Who else is to blame for such abject misery? Gloucester? Kent? Albany? Cornwall? How wide was the discrepancy between how the king thought his people lived and how they actually lived? Everyone is on a starvation diet, and they are as wretched as he is. Even though there is no direct evidence that his and Gloucester's castles feel shabby, far from their heyday, the England of *Lear* feels poor and mean.

Back in China, the sovereigns of the state did end up suffering just as the people did, but only because they had neglected to look and report correctly the first time around. By the time the Great Leap Forward began, officials and sovereigns were tasting their own folly. Mao, Zhou Enlai, Liu Shaoqi, and all major functionaries had made repeated sovereign excursions to the "countryside." But, just as in *Lear*, no one had been paying real attention to the lives of actual people for a long time now, out of fear that accurate reports would bring wrath.

When the rice withered and died during the Great Leap Forward, local officials lied about the yields to save their skins.

Communes were penalized (in rice) for failing to meet quotas, and after whatever meager harvest there was had been shipped abroad to prove that collectivized farming was a great success. What came next was inevitable. In preparation for the encroaching misery, farmers made a gruel from a glutinous variety of corn that, if husked, cooked up like rice. People huddled indoors as much as possible, using sesame twigs as fuel. People found that they could eat freshly fallen elm leaves if they were sautéed with cornmeal. By 1961, people were sweeping up the dead and rotting leaves as well, washing them off, and cooking them, too. My father remembers seeing the straw mats spread on the field outside his local school. Children played burial games, pretending to be paid mourners, acting out selling a daughter to pay for the burial of the father, an image from old China frequently conjured under the new dispensation.

Magical thinking was underwritten by the Politburo and the Central Committee, and almost every last party official. To distract from miserable yields and open starvation, the CPC began an industrialization program overnight. Across China hoes, pickaxes, doorknobs, and pots were thrown into "backyard steel furnaces," taking the last useful things from people who already had nothing. My mother and father both remember prying off locks and door hinges and rounding up any scrap of metal for smelting, which produced only a useless and toxic pig iron.

There are two schools of thought on whether Mao knew about all of this. Mass starvation strategies were hardly new in the mid-1950s. In the People's Liberation (from Chiang Kai-shek's KMT), the touted golden age of the Communist Party, Mao and his top cadres had already perfected a starvation tactic that would be repeated every three to five years for the next twenty years or so. The tactic that the Red Army adopted in the overthrow of the Nationalists and their urban strongholds combined an ancient method—starving out cities of millions—with tactics used in modern warfare. In the city of Shenyang alone, more than 4 million people were blockaded for nearly a year in 1947.

Like Changchun and many others, Shenyang, which had already been devastated by Soviet troops the year before, was turned into a city of death. Mao's modern siege warfare worked particularly well because it had two steps, both protracted. First, it transformed the city and its inhabitants into a totalitarian state, and then it closed the doors, forbidding any starving inhabitants from leaving.

Starvation became so severe during the Great Leap Forward in the less-developed provinces that people resorted to cannibalizing their own family members. Such places—far from wealthy cities like Shanghai, Hangzhou, Nanjing, Beijing—were a hell within a hell, another secret level with its own secret levers. A veteran of the Communist Party would later write: "In the Dawan production team of Longyang Commune's Zhoudian production brigade, Zhang Siwa clubbed his own twelve-year-old daughter to death and cooked her. Even so, no one from the four-member family survived the famine."[10] At the same time that human beings were eating bark, belts, mud, political prisoners, common criminals, and family members, one of the largest political theaters ever known to man was being enacted across China. When Mao visited counties and villages, peasants dug up crops and moved them closer to the train station. Officials made sure that the dining halls in people's communes overflowed with food. Also on tour was the Museum of the Chinese Revolution, a rolling exhibition of the bounties of harvests from nearby communes and fawning peasants who, like Liu Jiemei of Hubei Province, at first opposed collectivization but then came around to see the error of their ways.

In a "rapidly industrializing" modern state you were forced to believe in environmental, agricultural, and cognitive miracles. In 1960, the *People's Daily* announced, "Over the past two years,

10. Yang Jisheng, *Tombstone: The Great Chinese Famine, 1958–1962*, trans. Stacy Mosher and Guo Jian, ed. Edward Friedman (Farrar, Straus and Giroux, 2013), 143.

regions throughout China have suffered the serious effects of a natural calamity." "Natural calamity" became the official euphemism of the Communist Party for what happened during those past two years, and well before and after them. Meteorological data collected from weather stations across the country in those years showed no aberrant patterns in rainfall. Nothing supernatural caused the Great Famine, only the wrongdoing of man.

In his 1949 speech "On the Bankruptcy of the Idealist Concept of History," denouncing the notion that China's problem is its population, Mao writes: "Of all things in the world, people are the most precious. Under the leadership of the Communist Party, as long as there are people, every kind of miracle can be performed." People strived to perform such miracles. A commune member in Chairman Mao's Projection Team in Qinling reported this after a screening of a Great Leap Forward propaganda film: "Earning only 20 cents a day, I used to think, how can we build socialism in these poor mountains and deep forests? Now that I've watched *Mountain Agricultural Cooperative Prospective Blueprint* and *Great Leap Forward in the Countryside*, my eyes have grown bright, and I will work all my life to turn these mountains into paradise." This eyewitness testament to the possibility of miracles took place in 1959, in the middle of the Great Famine. Xue Muqiao, former head of the national statistics bureau, put it very simply: "we give whatever figures the upper-level wants." This applied to hectares of land affected by natural disaster, the grain yield, and the death count.

Of the many historians who have tackled the Great Famine, one stands out in the Learianness of his own story. In 2008, journalist, writer, and former senior party member Yang Jisheng, who supplied the earlier detail about cannibalism, published a 1,200-page work called *Tombstone*. His father starved to death in 1959, one of the 36 million victims that Yang would set about tallying in the 1990s. Yang had not realized that something was wrong until the Cultural Revolution. He confesses in *Tombstone*:

> During the Anti-Rightist Campaign in 1957, I believed the party when it declared Rightists to be bad elements. I was a student activist in 1958, and a poem I wrote eulogizing the Great Leap Forward was sent to the Huanggang Regional Education Exhibition Center. . . . At the beginning of 1959, I composed a "New Year's Message" for the newspaper in which I passionately extolled the Great Leap Forward. During the school's New Year assembly, the principal read out my essay as his congratulatory message to the school's teachers and students without changing a single word.[11]

Tombstone is a petition, an act of retributive justice, and a bid at redemption. Sharper than a serpent's tooth is the child who works with the totalitarian state to nudge you to your grave and then helps cover up the crime by contributing his ignorance and his amnesia in the form of propaganda. Yang Jisheng tells us that his *Tombstone* serves as a tombstone for his father, the dead, and himself.

Hannah Arendt captured the crescendo of this grisly form of governance—in which the personal truly overlaps with the political, in which citizens don't just listen to the state but actively mobilize against one another and replicate the state in every aspect of their lives—as "the mass organization of atomized, isolated individuals."

Arendt assessed Maoism cagily, unable to decide whether it was totalitarian-leaning or not. Her classic, *The Origins of Totalitarianism*, was finished in the autumn of 1949, right around the national birthday of the People's Republic of China, Mao's victory in the Civil War. Who could have made the call? Arendt wrote in this assessment that "We witness now the first nationwide

11. *Tombstone*, 7.

party purge in China and open threats of massacres" and that the specter of totalitarianism in China is "frighteningly likely."

Arendt's misgivings were right. In the 1930s and '40s Mao's theories of literature and society—and then, after a while, anything he wrote—were anthologized and mass-produced. Intelligent people would commit all of Mao's quotations to memory so that they could save themselves in time of need by outciting their accusers. Living entirely in the elementary linguistic world of Mao Zedong Thought, even subversively, they grew to love its thickets and its dales, its recitatives and its crescendos. The *Little Red Book* that soon became obligatory reading material was compiled by Lin Biao, the vice chairman of the Communist Party, a general who had starved out cities of millions during the Civil War, who played the sycophant in order to survive Maoism. He did not succeed. Lin Biao's kill orders during the Cultural Revolution were spoken loudly by all—"smash those persons in power who are traveling the capitalist road, the bourgeois reactionary authorities, and all royalists of the bourgeoisie, and . . . forcibly destroy the 'Four Olds': old culture, old ideas, old customs, and old habits." People recited passages from the *Little Red Book* as therapy, as creed, as total submission in the face of tyrannical patriarchal and matriarchal love.

In the year my mother was born, 1956, Mao again put out a very convincing call to writers and artists to freely express their opinions and criticisms. The speech, called "Let One Hundred Flowers Bloom," was in fact Mao's final reply to the critic Wang Shiwei and his essay "Wild Lilies." Mao had to have the last word, even though fifteen years had passed since the murder of his colleague and intellectual peer. *You want wild lilies? Let one hundred flowers bloom.* "Let One Hundred Flowers Bloom" drew out millions of forthright people who, like Wang Shiwei, were gullible in that they fundamentally believed in the persuasive power of language. Those who missed the first round of punishments in the Yan'an Rectification Movement of the late 1930s were right on time for the second round. Mao's ploy worked.

Most of the "hundred flowers" who spoke up were disgraced, stripped of their positions, and sent to prison for labor reeducation. By the end of 1957, 300,000 to half a million people had been labeled Rightists. Commissions after 1979 report the death count of this particular purge at half a million.

In her memoir and testimony, historian and writer Zhang Yihe describes how her father, Zhang Bojun, the cofounder of the China Democratic League, had been duped by Mao's rhetoric, and how things were shifted to the realm of "close reading." Close reading a "politically problematic" text, then quickly dismantling "folds of favor," to borrow Shakespeare's language, when an indication of defiance was found, was a method established early on but seen most clearly at the Lushan Conference of 1959, when Mao circulated a letter by the defense minister Peng Dehuai for everyone to study. For this critique of the Great Leap Forward's "winds of exaggeration," Peng Dehuai was branded a Rightist, a label that exposed him to abuse and humiliation during the Cultural Revolution. Like many top party members, Peng Dehui would die in ignominy in the 1970s.

Totalitarianism makes nothing out of somethings, turns somethings into nothings.[12] You hear it in the volume of identical assents, of wasted words. "Big-character Posters," used since the very beginning of the regime, reached psychotic levels by mid-century. Buildings were pasted over with slogans upon slogans, exclamatory denunciations upon exclamatory denunciations (see figure 5).

Mao was referred to as "our mother and father," someone who made one's own parents redundant. And it was an all-consuming love. In his name, the youth abused their elders, many of whom had themselves grown used to severe abusiveness in their youth,

12. On June 15. 1957, *The New York Times* noted several revisionisms in Mao's February 27 speech to the Supreme State Conference: "Criticisms of Stalin's policy in the Soviet Union and of Communist policy in Hungary, included in earlier versions of the address, were deleted. A reference to the liquidation of 800,000 foes of the Communist regime in China was also deleted."

FIGURE 5. A building covered with *dazibao* (posters with large characters) at Canton (Kwangchow) during the Cultural Revolution, c. 1966. The neon sign reads, “Long Live Marxism and Leninism.” Photo by Richard Harrington / Getty Images.

when traditional attitudes mixed with fascist tendencies in Chiang Kai-shek’s China. Parents and their children, people and the state, were locked in a Learian feedback loop: *You won’t admit how horrible you’ve been to me*; you *won’t admit how horrible you’ve been to* me. *You’ll see the error of your ways. No,* you’ll *see the error of* your *ways. Do you not see what pains I’ve taken for you*, the parent asks? The youth chanted Edmund’s refrain: “The younger rises when the old doth fall” (act 3, scene 1).

Like all dictators, beloved by all but his enemies and truest critics, Mao feared what would happen to him if he ever stepped down even one rung of leadership. His rageful fear sought new avenues for pomp and revolutionary fervor. Forcefully extending the literal and figurative party, Mao in his old age wished to be youthful, for the Revolution, which had grown tired and shoddy, to be returned to its youth. This wish engulfed the 1970s, and turned to younger and younger blood.

Working psychic terrorism into slow-moving physical terrorism, Mao's China eventually reached the point where children turned in their parents, neighbors their neighbors, and artistic, pedagogical, and scholarly life collapsed entirely. Historian Jie Li writes that the Cultural Revolution (1966–76) simply represents the moment that the "revolution" came for everyone. For intimate tensions and private disputes, there were no longer local authorities to judge your case. Your case could only receive judgment at the level of the state. But what was the state? Although the Communist state had uncountable layers of bureaucracy, uncountable committees and subcommittees, and was the engine of propaganda itself, the state was not actually an authoritative body. It had forfeited its authority to do anything but harm. All of these roles created the appearance of division of power, separation of party and state, but were in fact all extras, duplicates. The state's authority rested in someone whose authority solely rested in the populace and their agitations. And so the state just became the organized disciplinary apparatus of the intimate tensions and private disputations of people. The country "perforce prey[ed] on itself, / Like monsters of the deep" (act 4, scene 2).

Exiled historian Song Yongyi divided the Cultural Revolution into four different periods of killing: "The Red Terror" (August–December 1966), "All-round Civil War" in China (January–December 1967), Killing for and by the New Organs of Power (1968–71), Endless Killing (1972–77).[13] A housekeeper working

13. "1) mass terror or mass dictatorship encouraged by the government—victims were humiliated and then killed by mobs or forced to commit suicide on streets or other public places; 2) direct killing of unarmed civilians by armed forces; 3) pogroms against traditional "class enemies" by government-led perpetrators such as local security officers, militias and mass; 4) killings as part of political witch-hunts (a huge number of suspects of alleged conspiratorial

for the Ministry of Railways in Beijing withdrew her CPC membership in silent protest over the party's degeneracy. In 1970, two years after her arrest, she was paraded through the streets and strangled by guards, who were given orders to keep her silent before her execution. Comedian and storyteller Shan Tianfang had all of his teeth pulled out in public.

Parts of this world left *Lear* and moved straight to *Titus Andronicus*. In the city of Shanghai, a grandmother and her son were buried alive. This is truly beyond the pale, a Chinese-on-Chinese reenactment of atrocities committed by the Japanese during their occupation, the fullest extent of which the CPC, Japan, and the United States had all conspired to cover up. In the depths of the Cultural Revolution, Chinese people used Japanese fascist techniques on neighbors, teachers, and school or work rivals—any personal enemy that you were now licensed to find ways to label as an enemy of the state. A young man named Bo Xilai, jailed at seventeen years old, had kicked his father, Bo Yibo, in the ribs during the latter's public denunciation, breaking them. This ruthlessness was taken as a sign by his father that his son would eventually do great things. My maternal grandparents, like hundreds of thousands of other "Rightists," "reactionaries," and "class enemies," were lined up in the street under the hot sun, so that anyone who happened along could spit on them, urinate on them, or deliver a casual blow.

---

groups were tortured to death during investigations); and 5) summary execution of captives, that is, disarmed prisoners from factional armed conflicts. The most frequent forms of massacres were the first four types, which were all state-sponsored killings. The degree of brutality in the mass killings of the Cultural Revolution was very high. Usually, the victims perished only after first being humiliated, struggled and then imprisoned for a long period of time." Song Yongyi, "Chronology of Mass Killings during the Chinese Cultural Revolution (1966–1976)," *Mass Violence and Resistance* (SciencesPo), August 25, 2011.

During all of this, women had more and more children to meet Mao's implicit command. Women tried to outperform each other as "*guangrong mama* 光荣妈妈"—the honored and lauded mothers of the revolution. The biological social nightmare that ensued created mothers who were vicious and insane. In one of these cases, a man named Zhang Hongbing made a very public confession of matricide forty-four years after the fact. In the depths of the Cultural Revolution he, together with his father, turned his mother in for persecution they knew would be followed by execution. In his public atonement, Zhang attributed his crime to his zealousness for Mao. Young people loved Mao as one loved a bullied mother and would die for Mao, which the Red Guards literally did in the cerebrospinal epidemic that killed more than 160,000 youths. It is also possible that Zhang Hongbing and others like him could not deal with their mothers and fathers anymore and asked the state to kill them on their behalf. His mother had already been driven at least partially insane by the early Mao years, losing her father to political persecution and her daughter (Zhang Hongbing's sister) to the aforementioned meningitis. Her husband, Zhang's father, was subjected to eighteen rounds of persecution in the One Strike-Three Anti campaign. This woman became impossible to live with and no arbitrative body was left to which the child Zhang Hongbing could turn. Existentially unjust as it was, he turned his mother in. He did it unprovoked, by the authorities at least. He needed the parent to die.

Breaking one of the most serious social taboos in China, Zhang Hongbing aired their family's dirtiest laundry. In his blogpost he describes how his mother was tied up like a *zongzi*, a triangular rice cake. Netizens reading this told him that the only thing to do at this point was to kill himself. Some part of Zhang Hongbing must have known that the way to truly make the personal political is to kill—in this case, to make a final example out of himself and his family. Zhang broadens his own terrible case to comment on history itself: "[It] was a catastrophe suffered by the Chinese nation. We must remember this painful historical lesson and never let it happen again."[14]

In the Mao era, Shakespeare would slowly and perversely become weaponized for class struggle. Theaters in big cities rendered Shakespeare's plays as dramas of the collapse of the feudal order. *Lear*, along with the rest of Shakespeare, was "interpreted" along the lines Mao set forth, with little deviance. Those who tried the hardest managed to keep Shakespeare barely on the right side of "counterrevolutionary," at least until the mid-1960s, when even their efforts collapsed.

Shakespearean performance, on the other hand, underwent a marvelous transformation. Through cultural exchange with the Soviet Union, including instruction from Soviet directors like Yevgeniya Konstantinovna Lipkovskaya, the Stanislavski method of acting was introduced to China, its socialist realism blended with traditional Chinese storytelling. Actors, playwrights, and scholars studied at the Moscow Art Theatre, refining Chinese acting into a hybrid form. As soon as the Cultural Revolution ended, the Soviet/Brechtian/Shakespearean arts that had been developing in China would emerge with an almost blinding vitality. It was socialist realism, but with wit, irony, and humanity. Catch a moment between killing campaigns even during the Cultural Revolution and you can see Chinese people and foreigners engaged in real cultural exchange, doing the very best they can. You're witnessing a small Renaissance. Theaters in large cities, especially Shanghai, produced extraordinary performances of Shakespeare's

14. Zhang's story first appeared in news sources in the West in 2013. In 2016, he spoke out again. Zhang's petition to the government to reclassify his mother's tomb as a cultural relic is, as far as I know, ongoing.

plays, with *Romeo and Juliet* a perennial favorite. Shanghai and other big cities also enjoyed screenings of foreign cinematic adaptations of Shakespeare—including Sergei Yutkevitch's *Othello* and Laurence Olivier's *Hamlet* (dubbed and retitled *The Prince's Revenge*).

Until the mid-1960s, Mao had actively praised and endorsed politically correct renditions of Shakespeare's plays. In this sense Shakespeare was positively thriving in China throughout the 1940s, '50s, and early '60s, and in this sense Shakespeare made it even more difficult to see how bad things had become for the arts during this period. People can always point to the volume of Shakespeare in Mao's China as proof of its taste, liberality, and mirth.

As Shakespeare knew well, the dramatic arts can dodge censorship for a long time. When the hammer finally drops, it drops with the pent-up anger toward all that was dodged. Historical playwrights in dramatic arts, and especially Peking opera, were corralled into the most sadistic corners of Maoism, a place where existing cruelties of the art form and resentment toward harsh instructors and the harsh realities of a life in the theater found expression in violence toward the elderly and the traditional.

A denunciation appeared in the January 5, 1966, issue of the state-owned Shanghai newspaper, *Liberation Daily*: "Old Shakespeare would be ashamed of what he had written; to suppose that Shakespeare is some sort of god who cannot be surpassed is to lose direction and proceed contrary to the spirit of this epoch and our people." Because some playhouses still didn't heed this warning, *Liberation Daily* published another one on January 21: "Anyone who kneels before the shrine of . . . Shakespeare or other artists and writers is guilty of favoring moribund capitalism."

During this cultural cavalcade, theater students at Nanjing University were encouraged by their professor to go ahead with their scheduled performance of a montage of scenes from *Lear*, *Merchant of Venice*, *Hamlet*, and *Julius Caesar* in celebration of Shakespeare's four hundredth birthday. All four plays were too dangerous for such an environment, but *Lear* and *Julius Caesar* seemed, even now, exceptionally bold. The troupe's professor, Chen Jia, was a Shakespeare scholar who had long ago restricted himself to exclusively Maoist readings. In the late 1950s and early '60s he was defending Shakespeare against accusations of bourgeois apathy toward the working classes. Even this could not pass through the Cultural Revolution without harm. For his decision to go on with the show, Chen Jia would be publicly tormented and humiliated by student-secretaries from his university. His contemporary Bian Zhilin, another famed scholar of Chinese literature and Shakespeare of Mao's era, would be sent for three years to the May Seventh Cadre School in Henan, one of the many labor reeducation camps established in 1968 for urban "bourgeois" cadres. He had already been demoted two years prior; a former colleague and writer named Gao Qiufu caught Bian sweeping the floors and was told by others not to talk to him. At the May Seventh Cadre School—these schools had become insane asylums and theaters of elite political and personal revenge—Bian was anonymously accused of being a secret agent who colluded with counterrevolutionaries. Nothing else is written on this period of his life, only that he came out of it greatly changed in appearance. Bian would go on to finish his translations of Shakespeare's tragedies, which he began in 1954 with *Hamlet*, bringing out *Lear* in 1984.

In the year after the effective banning of Shakespeare, violent attacks began on historical playwrights. On November 10, 1965, in the pages of the Shanghai *Wen Huibao* (anglicized as the *Wenhui Daily*), a man named Yao Wenyuan implicated Wu Han, a civil servant who took on many roles—historian, playwright, and deputy mayor of Beijing. His crime was a play he had written in 1961 called *Hai Rui Dismissed from Office*, a play that some might say catalyzed the Cultural Revolution. Hai Rui was a Ming-dynasty official who contrived to bring before the emperor the cases of severe injustices suffered by the people, and who also attempted to open the emperor's eyes to the corruption of his magistrates.

Mao himself had applauded Wu Han's adaptation of this historical anecdote for Peking opera. But the winds soon changed. What looked like an updating of Ming-dynasty values to include bigger themes of humanitarianism soon became a liability, an invitation to willful politicized misreading. People were encouraged to whisper: Was this play actually an echo of General Peng Dehuai's criticism of Mao's handling of the Great Leap Forward, delivered at the Lushan Conference? And so, in 1965, Mao dismissed Wu Han from office and began to use this play to whip his perceived political rival, Liu Shaoqi.

In his public condemnation, Yao Wenyuan alleged that Wu Han's play was subversive, employing the time-honored method of using historical allusion to indirectly criticize his contemporaries—namely, Mao. Peasants were also wrongly depicted in this play, Yao alleged. Was Wu Han, the playwright, patronizing the peasants? They seemed overly dependent on a fair and noncorrupt officialdom. At the end of the play their lands were "restored" to them, and yet how could this be if, technically, the peasantry owned all the land? And what about this business of injustice? By Yao's lights, Wu Han's play suggested that much effort had to go into the overturning of an unjust situation. Is this supposed to be pertinent in any way in Mao's China, where the proletariat was master and all injustice had been abolished? And if it's not meant to be educational—if you could not imitate this Ming official due to his previous disqualifications—then the play could only be insulting.

Wu Han published a craven piece of self-criticism, walking back any meaning he had intended in the play. He thanked his critics for their "scientific criticism" and promised to rectify his own thinking. A month later, however, Wu Han published a *second* self-criticism, one that on first glance looks to be just as craven as the first; but a closer reading reveals a voice far less willing to cede intellectual ground. And so the revolution finally came for Wu Han. Every single person who defended him came to a grisly end. Peking University professor Jian Bozhan—another historian who held political and administrative positions—was singled out for three years of victimization. At the end of it Jian Bozhan died by suicide with his wife, Dai Shuwan.

One of the most severely punished intellectuals in the Anti-Rightist Campaign was Sun Dayu, the first Chinese scholar to translate *Lear* in its entirety. Imprisoned in Tilanqiao, a prison/labor camp/insane asylum, Sun spent six years earning "remission points" through nonstop thought reform, and through the compulsory reforming of others. Thought reform included the production of adulatory poems for Mao and "copying Chairman Mao's works every day." Fellow inmates at Tilanqiao included the legal scholar Yang Zhaolong and the girl martyr Lin Zhao, previously mentioned. In 1967 the guards and prisoners at Tilanqiao came under the administration of revolutionary committees headed by Mao's Rebels, which unlocked a new level of abusiveness: sixty-two police officers were killed in Shanghai alone; guards and prisoners were driven to vicious insanity. Meals were cut in answer to Mao's call to "practice thrift and wage Revolution"; family visits were discontinued. A report made on December 5, 1966, details Lin Zhao's acts and accusations made against her: that the socialist system was "a bloody totalitarian system," that the prisons had committed "many hair-raising savage acts of illegal torture," and that she had "brazenly dug out the head of the chairman's portrait and hung it upside down on the iron door of her cell."

There are other Chinese Shakespeareans who disappeared during the Cultural Revolution. Sometimes I see them in citations, their names shown with their birth and death dates. Many of them died in the late 1960s and early '70s. They were in their fifties and sixties, and so you cannot even make the call: Was it murder or natural death, natural death or crime of negligence?

I am not the first to write or teach the Chinese *History of King Lear* as a form of petitioning and a form of reckoning. Others arrived long before me. Around the same time (mid-2010s) that famed playwright and director Li Liuyi ran a star-studded *Lear* at the National Centre for the Performing Arts in Beijing, a former professor, Chen Hongguo, was recorded giving lectures on *King Lear* to very large crowds of people in the city of Xi'an. He had been harassed out of his position at the Northwest University of Politics and Law, where he lectured on constitutionalism, often through literary and philosophical examples. In these public lectures Chen perhaps distilled *Lear* down to its most obvious lesson: the plight of the critic. "King Lear had three daughters," he explained to the crowd. "Two told him what he wanted to hear. They weren't being honest. He didn't listen to the other one. The problem with King Lear? He didn't listen to his honest daughter. He didn't have to. Absolute power: this is a political problem that Lear faced, but he didn't recognize it." Alluding to Gloucester's famous cliff scene, Chen compared a system of government that looks like this to "the blind leading the blind."

Simple as it is, the lesson is inherently subversive. All of China was implicated in this allusion to the past to criticize the present (*jie gu feng jin* 借古讽今) and in the effective disappearance of Professor Chen, whose blog and Weibo channel have both since become defunct. We have come a long way from the first *pointed* use of the story of Leir and Cordella. When Shakespeare drew from John Higgins's 1578 contribution to *Mirror for Magistrates*, he was also drawing on the spirit of the entire collection, begun decades earlier by printers, stationery suppliers, poets, clergymen, lawyers, and parliamentarians in the most oppressive hours of the Marian regime (1553–58), a collection that had to await the death of Queen Mary I for publication. He was drawing from the efforts of the first contributors, William Baldwin and George Ferrers, to write British history in a way that got within close range of sovereigns and princes who criticized themselves and the wrongs they left in place, speaking even from hell, so that you would never be "first in line." If he also reworked the story of *Leir* from Raphael Holinshed's *Chronicles*, he was entering a pact to write progressive liberal history, one that believed in the possibility of reform and that drew clear lines from Britain's "ancient constitutionalism" to the balance of powers represented by the Parliament, one that was ready to critique and point out the latter's dereliction of duty. Shakespeare's *Lear* clearly wished to say arch things that can only be said in the genre of history and used sources that had already taken on this responsibility. He and others in Renaissance England made Leir and Cordella the ground zero of the modern citizen-subject.

Chinese authorities shutting down Professor Chen's talks also knew this in their hearts even if they never bothered to find out anything about *Lear*, or how oddly it subverts as a subversive play. *Lear* attracts those who pity the pitiful, who balk at cruelty, and who think about parrhesia—about truth-telling as gentle criticism, as the application of the past to the present, as unavoidable self-endangerment.

CHAPTER THREE

Tragedy

MY DEAREST OF the dear, why go there? The History of King Lear *is tragic enough. Why get into the* Tragedy of King Lear?

A. C. Bradley knew that one had to get into it when he set out to define Shakespearean tragedy at the beginning of the last century. One had to isolate tragedy's essential features to see what it precisely involves. In tragedy the timing must be bad and those who are noble must die. Evil must be shown to be costly. Because it is "merely destructive" in *Lear*—poorly planned, haphazardly bombastic, and self-sabotaging—evil destroys itself. Look at how Edmund, Goneril, Regan, and Cornwall end up. Consider what passes for villainous strategy and criminality in this country. Evil may be recklessly stupid, but its "expulsion," Bradley wrote, will require a tremendous "waste of the good." Because the evil in this play is not the cleverest, it is also the most costly.

You have to be so very good to tangle so closely with such evil. This, along with evil's inherent selfishness, means that evil will kill off all of the essentially good, intelligent, eloquent, and loving people in this play as it retires its own personnel. Good and evil are so close to each other here; that's why it hurts so much and why justice cannot be administered without sacrificing something terribly dear.

The afternoon light in our classroom has shifted into dusk. My students and I have just finished screening the 2018 *King Lear* directed by Richard Eyre and starring Anthony Hopkins, our first time seeing the play performed since the class began. We've arrived at the verge of tears.

Cavell believed that everyone reading or seeing *Lear* has in their minds their own Gloucester, their own Lear, their own Cordelia. Literary critics have been taught to be disdainful of the pathetic fallacy, of overidentifying with a text, so they forget how it works when it works well. When Bradley said that parts of *Lear* have to be purely imagined, that they really cannot be "acted out," he was referring to that which you supply from your own life. *Welcome. There's room in this hovel—room for all the whining and wronged, present and absent.* If you've ever been within earshot of an actual Learian predicament, *Lear* will make you so terribly sad, as if it were speaking directly to you. It hits so close to home.

Once upon a time and in different lands, tragedy was a political and cultural institution. Citizens and subjects would gather regularly to see the most pitiable people on earth slowly abandoned by everyone, including the gods. Nothing could help them, and no one wanted to. Such storylines were afforded the solemnity of state funerals, or the artistic splendor of large folk festivals. People had been taught by customs and society to be periodically assailed by the unbearable. Collectively, they writhed in horror and sympathy and wept. When public performances of tragedy do not look right, or if the exemplary ones cannot be shown any longer, then you know something is truly rotten in the state. Tragedy's integrity and public visibility is a barometer for the country and its collective human life. And so political theory always turns to tragedy.

My mother is the end of a line of Peking opera performers, people who have long participated in tragedy as a political institution. My maternal grandfather was a Peking opera singer who began his career as a child actor. He traveled with his parents and their *bangzi* 梆子 opera troupe from port city to port city. In Mandarin, such a life was called *pao matou* 跑码头, "running between docks." His mother played the role of Fool; his father played dual martial/civic roles (*wen-wu laosheng* 文武老生). China had only recently adopted the Julian calendar. Before its use became widespread, the country had already descended into warlordism. My grandfather was born in 1916, at the end of Yuan Shikai's rule, an imperial presidency called the Beifa Government that had forced the abdication of Emperor Xuantong, last ruling sovereign of the Qing dynasty. Mad with splendor and brutality, Peking opera flourished in northern China at the end of this dynasty.

My grandfather was considered a child prodigy. At the age of seven he had sung in Xuantong's (aka Emperor Puyi's) court during the emperor's brief restoration from 1924 to 1925. He had crammed dozens of long libretti into his mind by the age of eight in the same way the country crammed political change, neologisms, and modernity into the span of a few years. All through the twentieth century, in Peking opera's own late Renaissance, my grandfather put on performances for state leaders like Yuan Shikai, Chiang Kai-shek, and Mao Zedong. He witnessed the collapse of many worlds and states in one lifetime.

The rise and fall of dynasties and empires: this is the marrow of Peking opera. Though many people do not like the sound of it, the art form will persist, having survived the end of the Qing dynasty, the Republic of China, the Warlord Era, the Civil War, Mao's Era, the Reform and Opening-up, and Xi Jinping's China Dream. Like Shakespeare, Peking opera outlasts the demise of civilizations. Its extinction is not nigh. It has been abundantly revived to express national sentiments, cultural capital, and actual capital. It has adapted to every popular form, absorbing even hip-hop and rap. Its adaptation to socialist causes during the Cultural Revolution was Madame Mao's most successful propaganda campaign.

Peking opera makes you feel alive because you're at the end of the end of something, and everyone onstage and in the audience seems like the last of their kind. In this art form, the male actors who play both beautiful and plain women, or elderly women, as my grandfather did, are not regarded as the riffraff of society. Their mannerisms are copied, their styles imitated. The famous Chinese opera stars of the twentieth century, such as Mei Lanfang, were treated as dignitaries of state. In Peking opera, the aged are not ushered out of their lives by those next in the succession. Or, if they are—by exile, imprisonment, or execution—you know you're witnessing the tragic end of a dynasty. Private catastrophe links up with civilizational catastrophe, and private splendor always reflects back on civilizational splendor.

Like ancient Western dramas, Chinese opera, or *xi*, frequently enacts the human cost of speaking truth to power. Somewhat like Western tragedy, Chinese opera has fixed vocal/dramaturgical roles—Fool, Lady, Gentleman, Elder Lady, Warrior, etc.—stock roles into which are slotted a vast human typology. Unlike Western tragedy, it compresses thousands of years of dynastic and imperial unification and dissolution among a largely unified ethnic base (that is, the Han majority, if we account for the Sinicization of the Mongols and the Manchu). Unlike Greek and Shakespearean tragedy, it stops just shy of airing truly dirty family laundry. You need both kinds of tragedy to tell the Chinese story.

My grandfather took on the roles of a number of tragic historical figures in his opera career. They were adapted from the *Romance of the Three Kingdoms*, *Water Margins*, and other classics of Chinese literature, as well as well-known stories from history.

FIGURE 6. Song Baoluo as Han xian di 汉献帝 in *The Emperor Xian of Han*. Private collection.

He played military strategists, generals, and folk heroes, balancing virtue with ruthlessness, loyalty with skepticism. These historical worthies—for example, the Three Kingdoms adviser Zhu Geliang or the Eastern Han court physician Hua Tuo—delivered sought-after solutions under threat of great personal harm. He also played their less-artful historical counterparts, those who could not speak truth to power without harming themselves.

One of my grandfather's most famous roles was Emperor Xian, forced by the warlord Cao Cao and his heirs to abdicate the throne and thereby end the Eastern Han dynasty. He had in his repertoire two arias as Emperor Xian: "The Xiaoyao Ford" and "Shoushan Altar" (figure 6). Both lament the extermination of the virtuous and their wholesale replacement by the ruthless.

In the first aria, the deposed and humiliated emperor recounts the warlord Cao Cao's treasonous crimes against the imperial family—killing his consorts, his empress, and his children—and Cao Cao's treasonous crimes against the state. Emperor Xian is petitioning the last sentient jury—you, or the heavens, or the gods, or anyone who will listen—to heed and witness. In the second aria, Emperor Xian confronts and insults his usurpers—in his mind, that is. He has just been forced by Cao Cao's son, Cao Pi, to perform a ceremonial abdication. In this darker aria, the emperor lays a curse on posterity: he asks that his abdication altar be preserved so that Cao Cao's heirs might undergo the same deposition ceremony. Audiences know that he is vindicated by history: Cao Cao's heirs are deposed in a coup d'état by Cao Cao's longtime administrator and military strategist, Sima Yi. Biding his time, Sima Yi had served Cao Cao and his sons all his life and his family had acted as regents for Cao Cao's grandsons. Sima Yi's heirs would usurp the usurper, replacing the short-lived dynasty of Wei with the dynasty of Jin.

Chinese opera stages petitioning from all walks of life: anyone could do it, from the lowest of the low to those pulling the levers of dynastic power. Throughout Chinese opera's librettos and historical reenactments, you hear about corruption and injustices so extreme that no sovereign power could rectify them.

Show us proof that an extreme injustice has occurred. When proof does not come, the victims of tragedy call for a reversal of nature: let some forward-running course run backward. In *Snow in Midsummer*, a Yuan-dynasty play that was adapted into a folk opera, a woman named Dou E is wronged—wronged as a woman and wronged as a subject of the state. Dou E is a commoner, one of the *pinming baixing* 貧民百姓. As such, she enjoys no special privileges or protections and depends entirely on the sagacity of the sovereign. This class of subjects suffered at the whim of a justice system that worked only intermittently throughout a vast empire. Wrongly convicted, Dou E is sentenced to death. Before her execution, she calls for three miracles to posthumously prove her innocence. One, that her blood would not spill to the ground. Two, that snow would fall in June soon after her death. And three, that the region would undergo three years of drought. All three prophecies come true. Her blood stains her garments but does not touch the ground. And in the *sanfu* season of that year, the hottest period in the calendar, a freak snowfall blankets the city of Chuzhou, whereupon the crops cease to grow.

Miracles like these are invoked in order to demonstrate the severity of the crime and its cover-up. But since snow never falls in June, Chinese operagoers had to contemplate the same frightful prospect as Shakespeare's early-seventeenth-century audiences, that the laws of nature might bend to prove that severe injustice exists, but it would only mean that Nature had it in her to arrange such wrongs.[1]

Tragedy blossoms in biological disharmony, thrives on things being all wrong. Chinese tragedy is at least honest about this, as is *Lear*. What I mean is that they both understand wrongness as deep as wrongness goes, forward and backward in time. Gloucester has two sons, Lear has three daughters. There are no mothers. No one these days will blink an eye at these familial arrangements, but they are, by traditional standards, less than ideal. To begin with, there are problems of inheritance and patrilineal descent for both. *Lear* is suggesting, as much as Chinese tragedy suggests, that this "less than ideal" is enough to do it, enough to jam everyone in the spokes of tragedy's wheels.

1. Shakespeare's playgoers were beginning to question the justice of natural law. New scientific discoveries, such as the way beetles hatched inside other animals, delivered instances of natural usurpation and mind-boggling cruelty; this in turn unmoored the idea that natural law aligns with what's right, and other tenets of legal positivism, the idea that justice is what the law is. See Devin Byker's essay cited in the bibliography.

I don't think the play ever gives in to a prejudicial biological determinism, but I do think it knows that wrongness is good at linking up wrong things with wrongful things, the wronging with the wronged. In Gloucester's assessment of Lear's woes, he observes that "the king falls from bias of nature." Gloucester is in the middle of being duped at the time he says this. Still, having the rightness of broken clocks, Gloucester pronounces that it is in the nature of Nature to thrive and then devolve,

> scourged by the sequent effects: love cools, friendship falls off, brothers divide: in cities, mutinies; in countries, discord; in palaces, treason; and the bond cracked 'twixt son and father. This villain of mine comes under the prediction; there's son against father: the king falls from bias of nature; there's father against child.

Those who revised *Lear*'s ending believed that nothing good comes of reenacting this kind of tragedy—the unnatural kind, featuring fathers against children. No one wanted to see it. No one wanted to know it. I doubt that these revisionists were just squeamish, or simply trying to please the crowd. Consider what Samuel Johnson wrote in the introduction to his 1765 anthology of notes on Shakespeare. Johnson called it "a play in which the wicked prosper, and the virtuous miscarry." Elaborating, he says that while this "may doubtless be good, because it is a just representation of the common events of human life," Cordelia's death so offends "natural ideas of justice" that the human mind will simply choose to "relieve its distress by incredulity."

I am going over the longue durée of Chinese tragedy, looking at what can be set right by art and what cannot. Will the world appreciate what has happened to the Chinese people, its intensity, its scale? Perhaps Johnson was right, that *Lear* is a fundamentally different kind of tragedy.[2] What if seeing *Lear* makes

2. Johnson was notoriously ambivalent about moral economy and orderliness, even as he's known (especially care of Boswell) for loud pronouncements

things *worse*? What if "the audience will not always rise better pleased from the final triumph of persecuted virtue," because *this* account of persecuted virtue will not liberate its audiences, but only drive them to despair or disbelief? What if, in pointing to the thing, the precise mechanism for its intensification is set in motion? After all, "We are not the first," as Cordelia says, "Who with best meaning have incurr'd the worst."

Does *Lear* prevent the harm it depicts or does it, with the best intentions, incur the worst? The play has a running joke on what is the worst and how bad it can get. The worst goes from something that can still be differentiated from wickedness to something whose presence and effects one can no longer be sure of. First, Lear: "When others are more wicked: not being the worst / Stands in some rank of praise." Then, Edgar: "To be worst, The lowest and most dejected thing of fortune, / Stands still in esperance, lives not in fear." And, again from Edgar: "the worst is not / So long as we can say 'This is the worst.'" Then, Cordelia: "we are not the first / who with best meaning have incurred the worst," an idea that introduces the widest gap between good intent and horrific outcomes. Finally we have Edmund, boasting before he dies about outcomes still unseen: "What you have charged me with, that have I done; And more, much more; the time will bring it out."

What will time tell? What will it bring out? Right away it tells us that in this pyrrhic war between good and evil, the reputation of the good will not bear up. As *Lear* shows, some victims

---

about the wrongness, the disorderliness, of the world. Part of what you have to remember is that Johnson's student, David Garrick, is the one responsible for consolidating Shakespeare's reputation as "the bard." Before his canonization, the author function—the sense that you could do wrong by what Shakespeare intended or recover what he really intended—wasn't as strong yet. Things had not yet been apotheosized.

are deeply unlikable—those you wish to shun—because they are poor, infirm, weak, despised, discredited and self-discrediting. Victims are also pariahs. If you do not like Lear the person and would rather not be around him, you're in luck, because you won't have to wait for long. This play replaces the entire set of the unlikable and the lovable with those who are likable because they are unobjectionable.

Does the ending of the play give us hope? Albany and Edgar are eminently likable, in part because they're not paying *that much* attention, though they basically do good. "Run, run, O run," Albany says to the messengers after Edmund commutes Cordelia's execution. On hearing the news of Goneril and Regan's death, he asks for their faces to be covered out of respect (if you do not suspect he's been instrumental in the killing of Goneril, as some people do). Albany's gestures are properly solemn and stately, but what has he really done for anyone? And Edgar, for his part, reacts well, if slowly, to bad news and atrocity. He responds to the gentleman's desperate cry of "Help, help, O, help!" in the last scene of the play by asking for more details—"What kind of help?"—thus causing more delay. "What kind of help?" is the responsible and the tragicomical reply. Albany and Edgar, earnest and blameless, a smidgen pious, a smidgen stupid, but genuinely trying. They are two different people, obviously, but, like almost everyone else in the play, they are locked into a logic of interchangeability. In a pinch, Edgar can be Albany; Albany, Edgar. They speak other's lines across the Folio and Quarto editions, the "survivors" of an unsurvivable play who could also stand in for James I.

Let's look at the play's parting words, sometimes given to Edgar, sometimes to Albany:

> The weight of this sad time we must obey
> Speak what we feel, not what we ought to say.
> The oldest hath borne most. We that are young
> Shall never see so much, nor live so long.

I ask my students if this is the right message to take away. They find it hard to say. In this speech, as in the division of the kingdom, something is not quite right. Verbal flourish causes us to consider what's being said. Have the eldest borne the most? Is it true that we who are young shall never see so much, nor live so long? Is it true of the play? Is it true of the world? Why is someone speechifying? The speech sounds final, but also vague and generic, as if it wasn't quite sure what to learn from what has happened.

Can history recover from betrayals between parents and children? Tragedy answers no. After Maoism provisionally ended in 1979, adaptations of *King Lear* immediately appeared in the Sinophone world. Chinese people told their stories of corporate succession and sibling rivalry, and the strain placed by rapid modernization on Asian filial piety. *Lear* adaptations in China, Taiwan, and Hong Kong avoided the elephant in the room, which is that what had just immediately happened was Learian.

Take this story, for example: Right before he died in a Beijing hospital in 1978, an eighty-five-year-old poet-critic wrote a ditty critiquing the Gang of Four. By any standard it was a terrible poem, saved only by the fact that it was, at least, sincere in its clichés: "let every evil be swept clean away by an iron broom." The poet was Guo Moruo, known in China for many works of literary, cultural, and anthropological scholarship and the mind behind one of the supposedly great works of literature that survived the Cultural Revolution, an epic poem about rebirth and revival called *The Phoenix Rising from Its Ashes*. As a student of Chinese language in the 1990s, you were supposed to look up to Guo Moruo's works, and this one especially, as an exemplary case. He was, in his lifetime, hailed as a Chinese Goethe.

Guo Moruo's second son, Guo Shiying, was killed by Red Guards at the age of twenty-six; his third son, Guo Minying, killed himself at the age of twenty-four. These deaths took place roughly eleven years before Guo Moruo's own death by natural causes. Guo Shiying been subjected to punitive measures for the poetry society he founded at Beijing University, where he was a philosophy major, specifically for the implications of the name of the society, "X": Was it a reference to the cross of Christianity or another taboo topic? Shiying had already done two years of labor reeducation in Henan when the controversy arose. His sister would later learn that after being "tried" and locked away by his classmates, he jumped from the three-story-high window and survived only to be tied up and beaten to death. His younger brother, Minying, had killed himself under similar circumstances the year before, having effectively been turned in by a classmate at the Central Academy of Music for bringing in a record player to listen to in class. The classmate wrote up a report to Mao in 1964 on the "serious problems" (*yanzhong wenti* 严重问题) for class struggle at the school. Mao's reflections on this letter, recorded in *Mao's Manuscripts Since the Founding of the Country* (*Jianguo yilai Mao Zedong Wengao*) would form the beginning of his official statement about "adoration of the West," one that would culminate in the need for it to be addressed immediately "among students and teachers." Although he might not have been named directly, Guo Minying, feeling the stigmatization, would drop university studies a year later and join the army. Two years after that he took his own life.

While all of this was happening, Guo Moruo churned out sycophantic poems for party leaders. One particularly bad one was dedicated to Jiang Qing (Madame Mao). He ostentatiously denounced his own work and the work of his former friends and fellow critics, well ahead of absolute political necessity. In 1969, just a year after his second son's death, Guo Moruo received commendation and praise from the chairman at the 9th National Congress. For the rest of his life, he milked his sinecure as a high-ranking party official, enjoying nearly all of the luxuries and comforts of China's political oligarchy. What he said on his deathbed is unclear. Was he, in fact, remorseful for his slavish and treasonous outliving of his own sons? Did he write one last terrible, honest poem? Or were these really his last words: "I am very grateful for the care of the party. I regret that I have worked too little for the party. After I die, don't keep my ashes, but scatter them in Dazhai to fatten the fields."

Guo Moruo certainly wasn't the only one to outlive his children in this disgraceful way. Liu Shaoqi, the chairman of the party from 1959 to 1968, had abetted many of Mao's worst crimes until they turned savagely on himself. When that happened, he implicated his own son, Liu Yunbin, who had just returned to China from the Soviet Union as an atomic physicist. In 1967, two years before Liu Shaoqi was found with hay in his stomach in a prison in Henan, Liu Yunbin threw himself in front of a train in the suburbs of Baotou. Guo Moruo was only one of countless people who weighed their children against what made them feel important in life and sacrificed the former.

Fast-forward to the present, where history repeats itself without end. The current general party secretary, chairman of the central military commission, and president of the People's Republic of China is still stuck in his own Learian tragedy. Xi Jinping's own half sister, Xi Heping, died during the Cultural Revolution, hanging herself from a shower-curtain rail when student militants ransacked their home. His father, Xi Zhongxun, former propaganda minister and vice premier, was purged in 1962 and subjected to severe persecution. Having once masterminded the party's bloodletting, Xi Zhongxun was now persecuted by everyone, including his own family members. As the teenage son of this ousted official, Xi Jinping, along with his siblings, was first ostracized at school, then denounced and sent to a remote region of Shanxi. His own mother participated in his denunciation ceremony.

The wider world outside of China drew the wrong conclusion from this family/state tragedy. When Xi Jinping succeeded Hu Jintao in 2013 and began to consolidate power, journalists and pundits around the world exhibited an optimism that betrayed their faith in the chastening power of a Learian tragedy. They were so hopeful that it meant a change for the better, because they had assumed that Xi would go out of his way to avoid repeating the circumstances behind his family's persecution during the Cultural Revolution. Surely no one who has experienced that kind of cruelty can endorse such a regime, they thought. What they didn't understand was that the Cultural Revolution came to the Xi family at the end of the end of the end of Maoism. At that point lightning rounds of revenge tragedy were perpetrated by victimizers and victimized alike, all without the satisfaction of real vengeance. From these twisted lessons of childhood Xi learned to keep a low profile, bide his time, and "become redder than red."

Guo Moruo and Xi Jinping are extreme cases of Learian tragedy going all in for more Learian tragedy. Few families broken by Maoism look as broken as these, but still there are more than you could ever imagine.

It is widely known that the Cultural Revolution ruined familial love, kinship ties, and social trust. Look gently inside the homes of some of your Chinese neighbors. You will see Learian tragedies play out between the dearest of the dear. You will see pleas that resemble "unsightly tricks," ugly insults that cannot be repeated. The curses hurled upon mean children and adults are extreme. They rival Lear's curses for his own daughters (to Regan he says: "I would divorce me from thy mother's tomb, / Sepulchring an adultress"—in other words, I will dig her up, retroactively nullify our marriage, and bury her a sinner who bore you out of wedlock). Such verbal abuses betray an elemental resourcelessness.

These are Learian dramas not in the sense of dealing with bungled succession and inheritance, but in the way they play out Lear's understanding of *aftermath*, a conclusion with a hidden history. Even the most ordinary transactions between family members and intimates compulsively replicate the language and psychic structures of "reeducation" and coercive reform.

I have a colleague, also an English professor, whose family member had been caught up in the Cultural Revolution just out of finishing school. That family member saved herself and left her own relatives to die in Shanghai. Another colleague's parents were lower-middle-class peasants who paid for being in that class and spent the better part of the twentieth century in poverty. We crouch in various corners of the world, each one of us still living out these fearsome injuries.

Lear is invoked anytime there's perverse unhappiness between parents and their children, anytime there's a dysfunctional family. It's ordinary stuff, as Cavell says, but the ordinariness creates one more layer of gaslighting. Focus too much on the family, and you lose sight of the actions of the state. All foibles and ugliness become the people's own fault. You stop asking questions about the historical circumstances in the same way that the sublimity of the *Oedipus* trilogy distracts you from asking questions about the play's prehistory—the characters Atreus, Thyestes, and Chrysippus, or the relations between Elis and Thebes, or questions about the even trickier circumstances in Sophocles's own historical moment, the Peloponnesian Wars under way. Tragedy becomes too universal and now abets the erasure of history. At the same time, attention to historical specifics does not seem to help. Blame it all on the state, historicize and contextualize it completely, and you've lost sight of the way in which the state exploited vendettas and weaknesses inside the family for its own maintenance, renewal, and, finally, its cover-up.

Outside of the worst cases the circularity still holds: when the personal becomes political, the most flagrant crimes of the state are folded into dysfunctional family dynamics. Mass psychosis and paranoia confuse cause and effect by definition; if it is inflicted by the state it is very hard to exorcize, since policy and personal conduct have become one.

ↂ

In China, rehabilitation in the 1970s and '80s took place without a change to party rule or an international tribunal. There was a widely publicized trial for the worst perpetrators, the senior Communist Party members Jiang Qing, Zhang Chunqiao, Yao Wenyuan, and Wang Hongwen, known as the Gang of Four. But how do you put mass bullying on trial?

Lear tries to do it when he is in the hovel with Gloucester, Edgar (as Tom O'Bedlam), and the Fool. "It shall be done; I shall arraign them straight," Lear says to Tom, whom he calls his "most learned justicer." Lear puts Goneril and Regan on trial in this make-believe court to "anatomize" their hearts, to see why they did what they did. His wish to "arraign Goneril" is answered by Goneril herself, many scenes later, when she is confronted by Albany with her incriminating letter to Edmund. Her answer: "The laws are mine, not thine: Who can arraign me for 't." Goneril, Regan, and Cornwall are punished extrajudicially because their crimes also fall outside the law, something that has long vacated these lands. Any trial can only seem like a show trial, a mockery of a trial.

In the West, accounting for Maoism got off the wrong foot with Edgar Snow's 1937 *Red Star over China*, a catastrophically naive inside look at the beginnings of Chinese Communism for which Snow's widow seems to have spent the rest of her life atoning. Childlike in its insistence and its monocausality, Mao's grand narrative worked on a West that believed in self-correction. His 1946 statements to Anna Louise Strong and his subsequent 1956 speech "US Imperialism Is a Paper Tiger" exemplified the party's canny awareness of the consensus-generating power of anti-imperialism, which served as its rallying cry around the world even as the People's Republic of China was itself blossoming into an imperial state. Pageantry and lavish junkets were bestowed upon foreign writers disillusioned with their home countries—people like W. E. B. Du Bois and Julia Kristeva—and global Maoisms flowered. Mao's interview with Strong took place at the end of three internecine purges, the first in in 1931, eleven years before Wang Shiwei's public torture in Yan'an.

Even though the last violences of the Cultural Revolution are now roughly sixty years in the past, with numerous small acts of reckoning having taken place in China and abroad, the magnitude and casualness of its suppression is still greatly misunderstood (by the global public, certainly, and in academia, where distortions grow every day). Victims of the regime never found themselves part of a defined identity group with a cause that warranted advocacy from others. There's been so much history and so little reckoning, and so much flagrant revisionism, in one lifetime. It took a long time for the Chinese and the Chinese diaspora to find the language and psychological capacity even to say that something happened to them, and to their parents and grandparents. You cannot rely on diasporic expats to tell the story, even if serious language and cultural barriers have been overcome. It's a simple matter of numbers. Those who did the harming or were completely complicit had far better access to opportunities to live and study elsewhere.

The archaeology of post-Mao cultural production reveals that much was corrected and that it wasn't just unremitting censorship. Books, popular media, films, television, public discourse: all have reckoned with this history, and truths have been told. "Scar literature," the bitter fictional and memoiristic writings about atrocities under Mao's China, was published almost as soon as people were able to do so, in the late 1970s. As a teenager I watched historical reckonings as they appeared in film: *To Live* (1994), *Xiu Xiu the Sent-Down Girl* (1998). Most focused on the traumas of the sent-down youths and delivered biting critiques of communism in China. So much was correctly and bravely represented for the general viewing public, which was almost everyone in China. For a long time the CPC stole credit from the Nationalist Party for the defeat of the Imperial Japanese Army during the occupation. Even this line was being reassessed in the '90s and early aughts. In other words, China has not censored the Cultural Revolution—if it were only so easy as outright suppression. Some acknowledgments of wrongdoing can be more effective at covering up the truth. We enjoyed a period of leniency toward retelling the truth of history of the Cultural Revolution, the Tiananmen Square Massacre, and the decades in between. That leniency has been retracted. These books, films, and TV series have disappeared from the Chinese public sphere and will soon disappear from cultural memory.

The seed of Maoism's revival in China wasn't even planted by Deng Xiaoping's stubborn commitment to the Four Cardinal Principles in 1979. Tragedy tells us the tripwire is always set earlier. Chinese victims of the state couldn't tell their story correctly and consistently without hyperbole and melodrama. This tendency toward inelegant overstating or misstating of the case came of prolonged, unremitting exposure to propaganda and whitewashing. Take a look at what happened to higher education. In the field of psychology: "In the dark days of China's Cultural Revolution, the government closed the nation's psychology departments and research institutes. It banished psychologists to remote areas of the countryside to work the land. It dismissed psychology itself as a bourgeois pseudoscience promoting a false ideology of individual differences."[3] In sociology: "Mao Zedong's new government terminated all sociological programs in 1952. Sociologists became targets of political torture during the antirightist movement and cultural revolution."[4] In anthropology: "cultural anthropology was labeled a 'bourgeois social science' and thus was eliminated as an academic field of study."[5] Literary studies is a hard one to prove because "Chinese literature"

3. Rebecca Clay, "Psychology around the World: 'Seizing an Opportunity' for Development Chinese Psychology Moves from 'Pseudo-science' to an Increasingly Accepted Field," *Monitor on Psychology* 33, no. 3 (March 2002): 64.

4. Yanjie Bian and Lei Zhang, "Sociology in China," *Contexts* 7, no. 3 (Summer 2008): 20–31.

5. Enzheng Tong, "Cultural Anthropology and the Social Reforms in China" (master's thesis, Wesleyan University, 1996).

(or "Department of Literature") was preserved under "Chinese (language)." You could still study in the "Chinese (language)" department during the Cultural Revolution. Foreign language and comparative literature departments were abolished: "From the 1960s to the 1970s, comparative literature is silent: One obvious explanation for this is that the political situation in China during the time permitted no studies of Western literature, and comparative literature, by definition, is concerned with foreign literature, and thus the interregnum. Obviously, the political exclusion of comparative literature was a consequence of Mao's cultural policy and an extension of the establishment of political uniformity in the domain of literary studies."[6]

Unable to get it right, robbed of the tools to get it right, Chinese people left the door open for it all to begin again.

You keep changing the narrative, they keep changing the narrative. Historical whitewashing, accusing testifiers of insanity and conspiracy; and then . . . something worse than all of that.

Lear leaves a complicated legacy of discreditation. Because the past is mostly sealed off to simulate what it might feel like to be inside such a history, because history has to be inferred, everything that motivates the events inside the play becomes subject to the unreliability of any bystander's personal interpretation. *This character is selfish and therefore he does this; that character is withholding and therefore she does this or that.* The story of the play becomes a free-for-all for anyone's armchair psychologizing. A. C. Bradley opens with the fact that *Lear*'s "excessively painful" quality breeds "distaste" in the audience/reader. He saw that anyone could come along and

6. Zhou Xiaoqi and Q. S. Tong, "Comparative Literature in China," in *The Princeton Sourcebook in Comparative Literature*, ed. David Damrosch, Natalie Melas, and Mbongiseni Buthelezi (Princeton University Press, 2009).

call it a disagreeable play, dismiss it on the grounds that it is a flawed play, thinking they've caught plot holes the way you catch continuity errors in TV serials. Those protecting the play from this sideswiping know that they're up against real difficulty if they're serious about their apologia.

The play extends uncertainty to every corner. Take another look at the play's unmarked disguises. Disguises and their unmaskings are everywhere in Shakespeare, but this is a play in which you might never learn all of the disguises. Kent is disguised as Caius; Edgar as Tom O'Bedlam and perhaps again as a soldier. But who is the Gentleman who delivers intelligence to Kent in act 4, scene 2? It's not intelligence that helps them in this battle—not useful military intelligence, in other words—but it's intelligence nonetheless. Through him we learn of the King of France's sudden return. What a strange, sad "war" they're in. How could this gentleman have given eyewitness to Cordelia's reaction to news of Lear's mistreatment at the hands of her sisters, to how exactly her tears fell? What kind of a witness/emissary has he been? If he's been there the entire time, and with such a head as he has, why didn't he intervene? Come to think of it, where were France and Cordelia the whole time? And on and on. . . .

The gaslighting reappears in *Lear*'s offstage deaths, a device that introduces ambiguities that become subject to interpretive abuse. It shouldn't be ambiguous, and yet many have believed that the Fool is hanged offstage because Lear exclaims, "My poor Fool is hung." That uncertainty can easily be resolved (Lear meant Cordelia, not the Fool, though the substitution is remarkable), but it's harder to be sure for the other offstage deaths. Kent likely dies soon, offstage, and his words are rather unambiguous: he will go where the king has gone. But we cannot be *absolutely* certain that it will happen. Gloucester dies offstage of overwhelmed contrition, a broken heart, but you hear this later from Edgar, who gravitates toward gravitas. Regan and Goneril die offstage. Cornwall dies offstage. Their deaths are so wished for you don't even pursue the details. You don't pursue the details because none are given, and also because you do not care about justice for them. Cordelia dies offstage and her executioner dies offstage. Edmund does not succeed in passing her execution off as a suicide, but we still cannot know if she killed herself or not. Offstage deaths are a simple device for fostering doubt. How much can you be sure of in this world, in this play? You cannot even be sure if the reporting of death matches the manner of death. You can lose your mind trying to square the details in this play. Some are so deep in the play's unaccounted details that people—including professors—have developed conspiracies out of whole cloth: for example, that Kent is a double agent, or that Albany is the secret villain who had Goneril killed. Someone at a Shakespeare conference said that Lear expressly wanted to outlive his children. *Where does he say he wants to outlive his children?* I ask. It's implicit, is the response—he does outlive his children; desire is unconscious. You develop paranoia reading the *Tragedy of King Lear*. You become distrustful of everything, you leap to conclusions, things never go your way, you are convinced the world is against you.

In *Lear*, the heartbroken are made insane, their words discredited by being called insane. To top it off, the main character dies literally heartbroken. Students can hastily conclude that Lear deserved what he had coming, and that the daughters and in-laws were justified in their extravagant cruelties. Or else they say, "Lear grows increasingly insane." I can't tell you how many times I've seen or read some version of these words at every level of reading competency. The most succinct version is Henri Fluchère's 1956 reading of the play: "a senile King, derived from Kyd's Hieronimo, who passes from blindness to lucidity by dreadful stages of madness."[7] But where is the smoking gun for

7. Henri Fluchère, *Shakespeare and the Elizabethans*, trans. Guy Hamilton (Hill and Wang, 1956).

clinical insanity? Is Lear not acting his age? Is he not trying his very best to reason at every turn after the first unreason? The first time you see him at Goneril's house he is already contrite, if bursting with "indecency," to use Bradley's word. Just look at how he reasons with Goneril and Regan:

> O, reason not the need: our basest beggars
> Are in the poorest thing superfluous:
> Allow not nature more than nature needs,
> Man's life's as cheap as beast's: thou art a lady;
> If only to go warm were gorgeous,
> Why, nature needs not what thou gorgeous wear'st,
> Which scarcely keeps thee warm. But, for true
> need . . . (2.4.304–11)

Driven to such a state Lear still tries to assess the case, describe the flaying logic of deprivation.

Consider how expediently Edgar teams up with Albany to dismiss Lear's agonized grasping at straws at the end of the play, holding a feather to Cordelia's nose, scanning for any sign of life. They call it "bootless" (i.e., pointless), and that "he knows not what he says." But why should checking his daughter's breath to make sure she is really dead constitute foolishness or insanity? Why do any of the things he says at the end constitute insanity? Any parent would do the same.

Of course, the infuriated are driven to madness. Anger has a privilege, Kent asserts. But only if you're carefully angry. If you're recklessly angry, you lose your privilege. Take a cross-section of Kent's fight with Oswald, the one that leads to his torture. You won't find Oswald in the wrong. The angry are gaslighted not only by others, but by the way things appear at any given moment. Students see the gaslighting as soon as act 2, scene 4 is read out loud. Lear is clearly mistreated by those who gang up on him, his complaints and wishes dismissed as madness or senility. The more they do this, of course, the more senile and broken-minded he actually becomes.

As soon as one gets comfortable discrediting Lear, there's not much to stay one's hand. A ballad is appended to Samuel Johnson's introduction to *Lear*. Like the tales I mentioned earlier, this ballad also wraps up with a lesson: "Thus have you seen the fall of pride, / And disobedient sin." This sits ill with my students who do not see "disobedient sin" in any of the characters. And as for "fall of pride," well, if you really want to accuse someone of pride before the fall, there is almost nothing stopping you. Lear? Prideful. That's often the first insight ventured. Cordelia? Yes, more than anyone, she is called haughty. Kent? People see in his loyalty a sense of self that trumps self-assessment. The Fool? Definitely prideful. He must always have the last word, delivering the punchline even when it's no longer pedagogically useful. Oswald? Yes. Even in dying he must make a grand gesture of fealty to his mistress Goneril. Edmund? Of course. He cuts himself just to get some real attention from his father and, judging by his need to draw attention to it, does so out of pride. Edmund, whose contrition at the end takes the form of an eager do-gooder? Extremely prideful. Albany? Certainly, since his pride recalls the most banal form of male smugness—smugness in one's self-perceived ethical neutrality, in one's (largely untested) goodness. Cornwall is prideful because he makes you pay for not paying too much attention to him at the beginning. *You didn't notice me? Well, look-at-me-now-oh-oops-you-can't.* Is Goneril prideful? Obviously. She would rather die by suicide (if that is what she does) than fall into Albany/Edgar's hands. Edgar may be the only one spared the sin of pridefulness, but we have no guarantee that he will not also be prideful. His final speechifying doesn't give one confidence.

Centuries of tracts on tragedy have created a terrible game of hubris-hunting, as if pointing it out is the whole game. In their simplest acts of will the characters become vulnerable to pedestrian diagnoses of "hubris." We could do this all day.

Hubris is a highly selective judgment. It posits original cause and culpability—in short, justice—when none else can be had.

Even if Maoist totalitarianism can be repeated with variations, we assume we're safe in the knowledge that at least its saddest victims—the best people who were harmed—would not be among the first to clamor for its revival. Surely, one can be safe in that knowledge. *Lear* throws that into question.

The first reason, given the constraints placed on speech, was that even given a real chance to speak up, this type of person could not form the words correctly. Stupid as this victimization was, it seemed to best you at explanation. "Unhappy that I am," says Cordelia, "I cannot heave my heart into my mouth." Besides sadness, "unhappy" can also mean an infelicity: the conditions are not right for truth-telling. If you recount the subtlety of what was done, you downplay its magnitude. If you insist that you were harmed in subtle ways you can't help but sound like the people whose tendency to see themselves as victims even as they victimize, whose proclivity for publicly exaggerating small slights, started the whole thing in the first place. The victims aren't ideal because they have no credibility. Even the playwright has declared interpretive open season on them.

The second reason is worse. The question posed by *Lear*'s basic setup startles me as much now as upon first encounter: What if, in our heart of hearts, with the dearest of the dear, what we want is effectively indistinguishable from propaganda, and nothing, not even the worst punishment, can change this?

In his lecture on *Lear*, Coleridge locates tragedy in the "eager wish to enjoy violent professions" which "the inveterate habits of sovereignty" wish to "convert . . . into claim and positive right, and the incompliance with it into crime and treason." That is as true of the setup and the aftermath of Learian tragedies. Bradley points out that the connubial imprisonment with Cordelia in act 5, scene 2, was not, in fact, Lear's first choice. Even at this late hour, "the disposition from which his first error sprang is still unchanged."

There's no need to guess at what Lear's first choice was because the play wastes no time telling us outright. What Lear *wanted* was to have the daughter he loves profess that love in front of other people. He wanted the person least inclined to flattery to break character. Anything else is second best. Even her intimate expressions of love are just a form of settling, of taking socially and morally acceptable recompense for what the heart desires. That Lear shouldn't have wanted it, or that the wanting issues from somewhere small and contemptible and leads to humiliation and tragedy, doesn't change anything.

Lear is a revenge tragedy—the revenge of the unloved and the undernoticed on those who underlove and undernotice them. You cannot, however, get revenge on those who do not acknowledge you. That was partly Cavell's point. A damaged ego that wants what it cannot have must think like a propagandist, must proceed as if an act of ratification, an act of praise, that has not yet occurred, that has not been earned, has already occurred and has been earned. In *Lear*, one might actually see how difficult it is to denounce propaganda when propaganda becomes indistinguishable from love, when propaganda—the generation of interested, insincere speech—becomes the fabric of relationality itself. Coleridge sees in Lear an "intense desire to be intensely beloved," and concedes that it is "selfish, and yet characteristic of the selfishness of a loving and kindly nature." He might only be fully alive in propaganda, and only makes assertions that no one has any incentive to call out because their reception has been entirely scripted.

Behind victimization is this primal tragedy of unsecurable acknowledgment. Across barren lands, fathers fail to acknowledge their children, sovereigns their lieges, lovers each other. Everyone and no one is prideful, suffering deeply from an extreme deficit of proper pride. *You never see me, you never acknowledge me. I am unlovable and unloved.* There is an inhumane deficit of sincere acknowledgment and kindly attention in this world, because every action in it is backwardly motivated by insecurity and insecurity's inattentiveness. It sounds like psychobabble, but we had no father figures, no mother figures, no one to say: *I see you; I acknowledge you; I give you credit for what you do, how you try, no more, no less.* What happens to a country whose citizens do not receive this kind of acknowledgment from the dearest of the dear? Wickedness, cruelty, endless stretches of suffering. We get naked requests for flattery and the breakdown of the nation: these become each other's chickens and eggs. Parental tyranny leads to childish tyranny leads to state tyranny leads to parental tyranny.

Pingfan 平反 refers to the restorative period from roughly 1979 to 1982, a time when the whole country worked to shed light on injustices and right past wrongs. During this, some human dignity was restored. Some possessions were returned. Some posts were reinstated. Some apologies were issued. It was mostly pathetic, the size of the reversal, the size of reparations, and the size of the interventions that took place. Rehabilitation had too much falseness in it for it to be thorough or lasting. Those who had been victims were required to reenter the space of hyperbolic speech, vacuous banquets, and photo ops with dear leaders. They could be acknowledged, finally, but only if they were willing to recommit to the same propagandistic forms that underwrote their persecution. Younger generations who learned of these atrocities from their parents and inherited from them a basic skepticism about the nation-state often found those same parents going back to defend and even champion ultranationalism, Mao, and now Xi's regime.

It is excessively painful and embarrassing. Reconciling with the party guaranteed that what it took away—the feeling of fundamental worth—was something that only it could give back through the removal of any possible challenge, any calling of bullshit, through entirely scripted interactions. People are often deeply nostalgic for the Mao era, even those who witnessed or bore the worst. What they *needed* they could not get in the China that Mao left—just recognition, credit for their physical and mental labor, acknowledgment of their suffering. What they wanted was children who did not call their bluff when they over-exaggerated or pulled stunts for love, recognition, and witness.

After Maoism ended, and also right before it began, virtuous truth-tellers and meritless flatterers were rewarded equally. By Cavell's lights it makes perfect sense to do what Lear did, using the structure of the most basic meritocratic test to effectively end meritocracy in his kingdom. *Compliments and love only, now*; only the undeserving will clap at your stunts. Avoidance knows what it's doing. From the first warning—"don't embarrass me in front of company"—shame reveals itself to be infinitely resourceful in its self-evasion. A real victim of a broken meritocracy, stripped of dignity, opportunities, and accolades, will, as a matter of survival, stick with those who give only praise. Meritocracy must end for communism to begin, but the fairest redistribution of land and resources, time and attention, is always subject to bias, preference, or, in Chinese, *si xin* (transliterated as "private heart," *selfish interestedness*).

Having survived the opposite of meritocracy, those who suffered the most because they had absolute integrity end up with only half of the integrity they claim to have, and their children know this. The state, which was just other people, has turned them into such people, and such people will be loved and hated for behaviors that obviously reflect what the state has done to them. The wasted generation suffered from the knowledge that their children, if they had any integrity, would be disdainful of their final preferences: I'd rather return to those whom

I know have falsely flattered me, than have nothing at all. In fact, even the "nothing at all" was not really an option: it wasn't Regan and Goneril or nothing at all. It was Regan and Goneril OR being satisfied with Cordelia's answer, which would have meant rescinding the test, which would have meant losing face, which would have meant that Lear knew he had to connive in this way, which would have recursively acknowledged the ego wound that motivated setting up such a situation in the first place, which would've meant he didn't have a single child who loved him and wished to stay with him no matter what, which meant he was already the kind of parent whose child turns them in or betrays them when push comes to shove.

Tragedy inverts cause and effect, before and after, at the deepest level of storytelling and recordkeeping. If it sounds circular, says Freud, it's because shame is circular. The tragedies that spring from shaming sew beforemath to aftermath the way you sew lips shut.

Victims of collective bullying seek no greater justice than to be exonerated through a detailed account of what came before. Surely we can have agreement on objective facts, on the matter of who started it, who was more cruel along the way? Tragedy says no. Airing this history is hard because Pavlovian behavioral modifications are hard to reverse, occlusions and state gaslighting hard to counteract. But even these are not the real barriers, nor is traumatic paralysis the best explanation for the most frustrating silences.

Lear houses one of the deepest insights of psychoanalysis, which is that repression, suppression—whatever one wishes to call it—is perfectly rational in light of certain crimes. Those who become irrationally abusive as a result of calculated abuse see that perhaps they are in the wrong, but to see it fully they have to significantly sharpen their memory of recent events. *What just transpired?*, the victim asks herself. *Who said what first, then what followed?* Memory *is* morality. To go over it again, this person now has to retrace all of the steps.

My grandfather gave a fairly detailed account of the events leading up to his imprisonment and later exoneration. It's an excessively painful achievement of recall. In soberly retracing all of the steps leading up to the worst, you, the memoirist, can come to only one conclusion. People victimized you because you could be victimized, and you victimized others. The body and the mind remember that people around you did this to you, including the dearest of the dear. They always had it in them to do it to you. At school, at work, in your home: you did not play the political game well. If only you had found a way to be clever with minimal sacrifice of integrity, as some others seemed to have done. But that option didn't seem available. You weren't clever enough, and so it happened to you. Suffering only points back to an absolutely individualized mistake. You have no one but yourself to blame.

Bullies also, of course, wish for nothing better than the repression of that "beforemath" because to them it is the aftermath. It is for this reason that they gaslight their survivors. Victims daily remind them that they've wronged someone, or taken part in the wronging of someone. Ask shame what it has done, says Cavell, and shame cannot provide one unshameful example.

Repression thus makes it impossible to proceed with justice if the injustice was intimate humiliation. Freud's concept of repression refers not only to sexual sublimation, but also to a violent classroom scene in which someone, some disruptor, has been singled out for exclusion and humiliation. Here is the rather Learian scene from Freud's *Lectures on Psychoanalysis*, originally given as a talk in the mid-1910s:

> Let us suppose that in this lecture-room and among this audience, whose exemplary quiet and attentiveness I cannot sufficiently commend, there is nevertheless someone who

> is causing a disturbance and whose ill-mannered laughter, chattering and shuffling with his feet are distracting my attention from my task.
>
> I have to announce that I cannot proceed with my lecture; and thereupon three or four of you who are strong men stand up and, after a short struggle, put the interrupter outside the door. So now he is "repressed," and I can continue my lecture. But in order that the interruption shall not be repeated, in case the individual who has been expelled should try to enter the room once more, the gentlemen who have put my will into effect place their chairs up against the door and thus establish a "resistance" after the repression has been accomplished.
>
> If you come to think of it, the removal of the interrupter and the posting of the guardians at the door may not mean the end of the story. It may very well be that the individual who has been expelled, and who has now become embittered and reckless, will cause us further trouble.[8]

Something must be done about this student. He has caused a disturbance. Was the disturbance warranted or unwarranted? Was the expulsion just or unjust? What has happened in the classroom to get to this point is now left to pure conjecture. The classroom decides that it cannot let this student go on as he will inevitably cause us further trouble. Yet this student won't shut up, the disturbance won't abate, and so he or she must be repressed to the point of elimination. "O, that way madness lies; let me shun that; No more of that."

8. Sigmund Freud, "Five Lectures on Psychoanalysis, Leonardo da Vinci and Other Works" (1910), vol. 11 in *The Revised Standard Edition of the Complete Psychological Works of Sigmund Freud*, trans. James Strachey, revised and edited by Mark Solms (Rowman and Littlefield, 2024).

Cordelia has to die. No more. *No more*. Murdering the most innocent would seem to end the cycle of unreliability. Outside of history, Cordelia becomes the archetypal "persecuted heroine," as she was known in the Aarne-Thompson-Uther Index of folkloric types. Anyone could identify with the "persecuted heroine"—and they did. Female victims and female persecutors across twentieth-century China regarded themselves as Cordelia types—the daughters of history who tell the truth no matter what and bear all stoically, an identification that often justified bad behavior and extended the tyranny and abusive love that they recently suffered.

If it does not stop, if the principal actors are not killed off, what follows goes beyond what we learned in the chapter on history. In the legendary line of succession: if Regan had not died, she would have given birth to Cunedagius, one of the nephews who overthrew Cordelia, and he would have sired Gurgustius who would have sired Sisillius who would have sired Kimarcus who would have sired Gorboduc, a queen who was, as William Albion had it, "a most tyrannous mother." *Lear*'s "no mother at all" is followed eventually by a murderous mother. We have another botched division of the kingdom, another collapse of the personal into the political, a monarch whose personal pathologies become the state's. *Gorboduc* is another story that ends in the death of nearly all of the nobility and the start of civil war.[9]

Bradley's deceptively simple observation that Shakespearean tragedy kills its heroes can only be appreciated in light of the unending cycle of psychosis he intuited. Everyone dying *now* prevents the later tragedy from happening: death stops

9. *Gorboduc* is the better-known name of Thomas Norton and Thomas Sackville's late Elizabethan Christmas play, *The Tragedy of Felix and Porrex*. Existential anxiety about Elizabeth's declining years, vivid memories of the bloodletting over Henry VIII's male heir, the upheaval of the Reformation, and, even further in living memory, the history of grafting the Tudors onto the line of succession—all of these real English fears were styled into Senecan tragedies.

reproduction. For Cavell, too, Cordelia *had to* die. For centuries, the surprise of her hasty and meaningless death was seen as the most unjust of *Lear*'s poetic injustices, as if there were no satisfactory explanations.[10] A satisfactory explanation was given in Cavell's essay. Cavell referred to Cordelia's death as a "tracking device." She has to die because only this death, in this manner, tracks something that is happening in the play that nothing else can track. In Cordelia's execution, Cavell writes, "every falsehood, every refusal of acknowledgment, will be tracked down. In the realm of the spirit . . . there is absolute justice."

What Cavell means is this: when Cordelia and Lear are captured by Edmund's army, Lear gets a version of what he wanted. Many have noticed how happy he is at the prospect of imprisonment with Cordelia. Though it means confinement and imminent death, Lear tells Cordelia that they will "live, and pray, and sing, and tell old tales, and laugh at gilded butterflies." In this extended metaphor they are to be holed up together like foxes, impervious to abundance or privation, excess or starvation. Prison guarantees a marriage with his favorite daughter, who is finally prevented from leaving. She can finally be with him, talk to him. They can while away the hours discussing "who loses and who wins; who's in, who's out; And take upon 's the mystery of things, As if we were God's spies."

Under these circumstances, Cordelia's death, its exact timing (before Lear's death), exposes a sub rosa sin on Lear's part that would be far easier, if not more humane, for us to overlook, guilty as he is of far more legible crimes. If she dies now, his wish for marriage-in-incarceration will not come true. Cordelia's execution lifts Lear's last fig leaf. Lear won't be allowed to get away with something for which the soft-hearted believe he should be let off the hook. Out of pity, out of insight into recidivism, the playwright thwarts a wish that, in its essence,

10. See Stephen Greenblatt, *Tyrant: Shakespeare on Politics* (W. W. Norton, 2018), for a recent gloss of this attitude.

had driven most of the tragic events of the play. You want to call Lear out but you won't call him out. This I take to be the saddest wisdom from Cavell's essay "The Avoidance of Love": those who act shamelessly still have one shame in reserve, a real shame that cannot be moved by any intervention or reform, impervious to any kind of future correction. The shame is that you are simply unloved in a situation in which, by your own doing or something that came before you, there is only love or hate. You want to be with the beloved, but that is not her choice. The only solution is insistent delusion. It's too hurtful to get to the bottom of things, but we have to have a mechanism that tells us where the bottom is.

And so Cordelia has to die. No more.[11] She has to die not to convince you of the injustice of a world that could murder such an innocent, or even to halt the endless cycle of the tragedy, as I suggested earlier. She had to die to draw something out, something which would rather remain hidden, and could remain hidden indefinitely. Doing things that resemble conventional forms of parental love and conventional forms of parental tyranny allows Lear to proceed with an infraction for which it's hard to extract a penalty. Cordelia dies to teach someone a lesson, but since the issue is primarily a matter of evading responsibility for a lesson that the kindhearted would never force you to learn, it cannot be properly learned. If she were more flexible and better with words, she might have understood how to prevent this from this start; but she wasn't, and so she won't be able to prevent anything.

11. "No more" recurs in Shakespeare's plays, with the highest number of instances (thirty) in *Cymbeline*. *Lear* falls around the median with twenty-four instances of "no more," but these instances are worth singling out. "We'll no more meet, no more see one another," says Lear in one of his strongly worded weak threats. It cuts itself for every outward cut. "No more" in this play often sounds like the most nastily intoned "shut up."

My grandfather taught me my first palindromic verse, picking playful examples so simple a child could comprehend them. The first example is the plainest Chinese: "Shanghai's municipal water comes from the sea, *shang hai zi lai shui lai zi hai shang* 上海之水来自海上" A true palindrome. This was the pedagogical building block for learning about reversible poems.

Palindromic verses in China have a more pronounced tragic strain. Unlike their alphabetic counterparts, the letters inside words are not reversed; instead, entire verses are reversed. A famous example is the Song-dynasty poet Li Yu's "Husband Longing for Wife," an eight-line poem of seven characters per line that also made sense read in reverse, from the last character to the first. It drives home the point that not much can be read backward, character by character, and still make sense, except senseless, orderless sorrow.

My grandfather loved children and small animals. He wished to care for them, and for others to care for them. He especially liked to paint birds. He painted them about to take off, their wingtips like drooping straight-pointed stars. He painted them as creatures that have sat a long, long time, resting, vigilant, and predatory as only birds of prey are predatory (see figure 7). The crows that he painted are all settling down for a long winter, or perhaps just about to take their leave. There is warmth in this chilled farewell. My grandfather's birds speak farewell without mourning. *No crying now, all will be well.* The solicitude in the eyes of the animals gives away the fundamental kindness of the painter, the way my grandfather imagined all living things to be (see figure 8). He painted animals that his contemporaries had not thought to paint: squirrels, for example, rendered in brush, had a realism and a visual arrangement that matched their European counterparts. He painted hundreds and hundreds of chicks, each different from the other. My grandfather's plum blossoms herald the coming of spring; to see them is to feel that unobtrusive, full-throated blossoming. They are superior to the plum blossoms that hang in museums, exaggerations

FIGURE 7. *Untitled*, 1980. Song Baoluo. Private collection.

FIGURE 8. *Untitled*, 1985. Song Baoluo. Private collection.

of Chinese edginess and chilliness or gaudiness or colorfulness in floral form. My grandfather gave away most of his paintings. He spent years on paintings that he donated to charities for victims of natural catastrophes, beginning with the Tangshan earthquake in 1976. This was just the old practice of *zhenzai* 赈灾—the civic call to materially help peoples of more disaster-prone regions during calamities. Most of the charitable donations ended up in the pockets of the middling officials.

After the *pingfan*, the government "gifted" my grandfather with a ninety-square-meter unit in a five-story building located in a residential neighborhood in the Zhaohui District. These Soviet-style buildings convey the entire emotional truth of that time, the sense of density and desolation, the sunlight falling into the wrong spaces, slogans and phone numbers sprayed on the sides. Dust gathered in the concrete stairwells like ash in ashtrays. Everything was built as if already marked for demolition, a Chinese urban version of the laziest brutalist architecture. People did the best they could, of course, brightening stained concrete balconies with potted plants and colorful bedclothes. And there was color as an accident of industrial taste: green plastic awnings above the caged balcony-kitchens of the first three floors, the blue-and-white enamel placards on the concrete paneling indicating building block and number, a color scheme repeated on the buses, the convenience-stall iceboxes, and popsicles, lain together like enamel cases.

Half a century after his home was raided and confiscated, it was raided and confiscated a second time. My grandfather passed away from heart failure in the fall of 2016. After the funeral, my uncles had stripped the apartment, cut out his paintings from their scrolls, leaving piles of curled silk mats on the floor. They rummaged through his libraries for valuable volumes and autographs, cleared out the drawers of carving stones mined from the counties of Qingtian and Shoushan, white and veined like sheep's fat marbled with trickling blood. They had known exactly what was valuable only because my grandfather had told everyone, separately, where to look, what treasures might be sitting in plain sight, mixed together with the garish junk that he had received as gifts over the years by various dignitaries and opera aficionados—*piaoyou* 票友—that would be completely overlooked by philistines: a dull brass lock, a withered stump of ginseng, a stone the texture and color of liver disease; great treasures if you were a connoisseur. Siblings shouted each other's crimes on the phone; locks were changed several times.

His paintings are beautiful but they fetch no price on the market. Regardless, my uncles cut out the paintings because there is always value, if not in the paintings themselves, then in the gold-flecked rice paper, half a century old, on which they were painted; if not the calligraphic colophons, then the large sheets of UV-resistant glass that encased them. Because their mother, my maternal grandmother, was the child of a business mogul who was sacked in the 1940s, they had long known perverse behaviors in the home. In the early years of Maoist deprivations, when it seemed that they would still be able to keep their house, my grandmother had built false compartments in her wardrobe to hide from her own children imported chocolates and sweets. They learned to break into the cabinetry from the back, and then restore it with the skill of joiners.

In his memoir my grandfather describes how he was dechilded, de-wifed, and then de-childed again. My grandfather's first wife was an affair of the heart, but she, being sterile, was eventually bullied into leaving by the rest of the family. There was no love lost between him and the *fengjian shehui* 封建社会, the "closed and oppressive society" of old China that had assumed different forms under Chiang Kai-shek's regime of militarized feudalism, and in European and Japanese extraterritorialism in China. His replacement wife, my maternal grandmother, bore nine children for the revolutionary cause under an accelerating decline in quality of life. My grandmother embodied China's transition from feudalism to modernity to totalitarianism to capitalism. She began to turn on her own children, turning them into servants, then mortal enemies. When she and my grandfather were finally sent to their cowpens, she shed no tears at parting. Whatever eros there was left in the world of Peking opera superstardom was finally drained away when my grandfather and grandmother were both left bound in the hot sun for six hours every day for a week, in public, Elderly people were lined up in the streets to be hurt and humiliated. Stripped of all dignity, even pain moves to the boring, slow time of Maoist humiliation. A week passes and another "exercise" begins.

Because their livelihoods and chances in the new social system had been taken away, my uncles became good-for-nothings. Hell-raising arguments tore through the family, followed by deadly, creeping silences. My youngest uncle kept getting himself involved in gambling and prostitution houses. Large-scale organized crime was still largely contained in Shanghai, Macau, Fujian, and Hong Kong; there was something lackluster and disorganized, even, about their crimes—a step above petty crime, a step below mafia. My grandfather favored the eldest son, who was given a cloying name: *Xiaobao*, "Little Treasure." This uncle was the one who returned from northern Harbin, the worst of the places to which the family's children had been sent, consumed with frostbite, dyspepsia, and sinister rage. He stayed with my grandfather the longest. They were in each other's clutches till death.

One of the compensations of the last years of my grandfather's life was a bedspread made of an entire water ox hide, a gift from a member of the Chinese People's Political Consultative Conference, of which he himself had been an honorary member in the 1990s, despite hating the government. He'd lain on it for hours, days, years now, only emerging to use the restroom or to check to see if there were visitors. Every once in a while, into that living tomb burst light, heat, clamor, the kind, open, beautiful faces that he wanted to see, saying the things that he wanted to hear, the rare combination of discourse and physiognomy that made him happy. And then it would be all over, and we'd all be leaving again.

Sometimes the cataracts in his eyes shifted, cloudy disproof of all he had seen. He alternated, in his declining years, between those whom he really wanted to see, for whom he'd hurl his heart into time's apertures, and those who ticked down the long hours with him with the forbearance of bureaucrats in state-owned enterprises. Because my eldest uncle stopped counting time, contracted himself to the long haul, he inherited the apartment in Zhaohui. In those last few years when family and visitors gathered in the new flat, he in his paranoia had cameras installed in every corner and would watch the live feed, sometimes from his own home, sometimes in the very next room, on an ancient computer, warning us via WeChat that we ought to be careful, because we were all being watched and recorded.

I tell my grandfather that I'm trying to learn about this past, and that I will tell his story. But this extended hand is rebuffed. He has already written two memoirs. With the exception of the first memoir, my grandfather has never said anything in public, nor published anything, that passes judgment on the Cultural Revolution. In conversations with visitors, opera aficionados, journalists, and writers, he always only expressed mere disapproval—"I don't much care for Mao"—less so that it would pass the censors, and more because he preferred to focus on his life and his legacy.

I tell him how I will try to write about his signature opera, *The Han Emperor Xiandi*. He responds dismissively. *Qie*. He looks out to an area where the children who live in the new development are squabbling over the kiddie rides. When my mother moved him there years ago, she put the staff in the development on notice that my grandfather needed pomp and circumstance. They call him "the longevity sage" and make a big fuss when he enters and leaves the development, a rare event. They hang a blown-up photograph of him in the activities center and seat him outside with a pot of jasmine tea where he can see and be seen. Of his five granddaughters, the two who have stayed in China, living nearby, have joined the party and now wear its insignia. Sharper than a serpent's tooth.

The children of the Cultural Revolution generation assumed that they were quite safe, that their parents were the pitiful ones. *They were destroyed so that we could live.* One needn't be sheepish about saying that tragedy is what's pitiful, that feeling of seeing senseless sacrifice under way. How pitiful it is that the wronged wrong others beyond the minimum understandable amount. How pitiful it is that disfigurement leads to further disfigurement.

Lear is a human sacrifice story and speaks beautifully from its sureness of that fact: Upon such sacrifices, my Cordelia, even the gods themselves throw incense. But what class of sacrifices are these? If we think of a sacrifice as a transaction—this for that—the logic grows even fuzzier. A parent sacrifices for their child so that the child can have a better life. They give up the sweetest portion, parting with that which they cannot bear to part with, so that they might move the gods to pity, *gan dong tian* 感动天 (move the heavens). But when even the gods throw incense upon this sacrifice of yours to appeal to their own god, we have something like an ultimate, mysterious sacrifice. If Lear and Cordelia's imprisonment and deaths are sacrifices, what are they sacrifices for, if not for our edification, if not for the unjust idea that someone else runs a simulation so that we in the present can avoid the same outcome?

When I talk to my mother on the phone I run an old routine: I console her about her generation, the one to have experienced the worst of both worlds—the Cultural Revolution, the miseries of undocumented immigration, and now, the visible decline of the United States, slipping into the hilarious category of downwardly mobile Asians. "Yours was the most unfortunate generation," I say to her in one form or another. "I was very lucky to have come up in the generation that followed yours," I say in one form or another, "to have benefited from your sacrifice." *The oldest hath borne most: we that are young / Shall never see so much, nor live so long.* Except this time my mother has something up her sleeve, too. To my casual schadenfreude she replies, "You're still very young."

My parents' generation and the generation before them call themselves the lost generation, the most unfortunate generation, the one sacrificed to history, and for us. Don't turn out like us, they said. And we more or less took them at their word. *Lear* keeps this disposability in reserve: don't be like Lear. In Higgins's contribution to *Mirror for Magistrates*, the frightful ghost of Cordella recounts her family's downfall so that future magistrates can "avoid and shunne" it. *Lear* would seem to teach by setting an extreme negative example: avoid turning out like this at all costs. Yet perhaps *Lear* revisionists knew that no human being is content to be completely sacrificed.

The year 1980 was the year the one-child policy was rolled out in earnest, the last year that the government gave for women to get on board with abortions for any accidental pregnancies after their first child. Many people had already gotten with the program, as they'd heard rumors, and stopped having more children as early as 1977. A family member of mine terminated a pregnancy at six months in 1980 to avoid the official stigma that was promised would follow: disqualification from public schools—which was then practically all schools—heavy fines, social ostracism at the workplace, relegation to the margins of society. There is no shortage of harrowing accounts of the effects of that policy—for starters, most people born in China between 1978 and 2016 have no siblings, no uncles and aunts for their children—but I think I can safely say that in 1980 most people welcomed this policy. To them, it represented reproductive choice and the end of a teeming world in which everyone fought tooth and nail for very limited resources, the value of their labor reduced to nothing.

A nation of children of the one-child policy accelerated the normality of the sacrifice of the lost generation, but it also turned the sacrifice around. A single child received all the pent-up affection, love, abusiveness, and suppressed superstition. The elderly got on their hands and knees to tie the expensive sneakers of their teenage grandchildren; they laundered their guilt through barely afforded gifts of cars and real estate. All opportunities would be lavished on the child, now thrice cradled, in parental *ni-ai* 溺爱, coddling love. They were coddled in so many ways, allowed to live in the gentler wind of post-Maoist openness, and, even further out, in the rich streams of global capital.

The first major commercial Chinese film adaptation of *King Lear* in 2006 dealt with this last coddling head-on, one slice of a Learian Chinese tragedy in a much larger drama. Set in a future Shanghai, now a leading international center with a bilingual population, Lear is cast as a billionaire Hong Kong businessman, taking up the tragedy of economic liberalization and the exploitative structures set up by foreign investment. The film climaxes in a battle, as in the original, only the location has shifted away from the jagged cliffs of Dover to the heat of the Chinese stock exchange. An unhappy Chinese feudalism meets unhappy capitalism in this *Lear*, and favoritism its most obvious pathology. Only in the film's periphery do we get people who had been prepared by the worst of Maoism to suffer the worst of economic deregulation.

Too much of anything makes it worthless—even a child knows that. How disposable must Chinese people have been to supply in *tian shu* 天数, in astronomical figures, the raw human material, the casualties of some distant people's greed and waste, distant people's thought experiments. There were too many of us. For every one of you, there are six of us. It's comically tragic. We do this quick conversion with currency, dividing a Chinese price tag by six to figure out the cost of things in US dollars. China's population became capitalism's bloody glue, subsidizing, through their labor and the country's resources, the fundamental irresponsibility of the West. Among ourselves, the numbers are too few. And the too many, but also too few, turned on themselves.

Those only children now find themselves with two sets of parents and grandparents, aging uncles and aunts, old family friends, a mortgage, and their own children, who have no aunts and uncles, no cousins. Having only one child further locks the victims of Maoism in their tragedy. There would be no one with whom to compare notes, no one with whom to share the burden. "What happened to our parents?" was a question that was asked in solitude.

Chinese people waited for the government to relax the one-child policy. When that finally happened, many couples decided they didn't want children at all. Why make your life unnecessarily difficult? In response to this disinclination, the government began to social-engineer in the other direction, to once again unnaturally increase population growth. Just two decades ago Chinese citizens were inordinately punished for having a second child. Nowadays, because lavish incentives to have a third child have had little effect, harsher measures have had to be instituted. The government now actively disincentivizes having only one child. Crackdowns on corrupt para-educational industries were widely welcomed because they worked to lower the cost of child-rearing and education. None of these measures have—yet—reversed the rapid depopulation. Senescence dragged down youthfulness, as if the usual yoke of tradition became a yoke of corporeal weight, and the working-class and even privileged youth decided to *tangping* 躺平, to lie down flat. Chinese people call this phenomenon *juan* 卷, or "involution," a senseless competition with no real acknowledgment waiting at the end, a turning in on oneself, a repeat of the old eating the young eating the old.

Lear always seemed to me an everyman's tragedy.[12] In this book I wanted to learn what tales, history, tragedy, comedy, and romance really are. At the core of tragedy is the inability to determine what causes what, no matter how hard you try. So many people have come along to define Tragedy in particular, since on its definition seems to hang the fate of the world. I have always appreciated the fact that Tragedy in *Lear* is excessive meanness and sadness in the home and the state, petty violence, betrayal, and ingratitude. It needed none of the special, theoretical requirements that elevates it above *mere* tragedy. Before the other points of alignment between *Lear* and Chinese history lies this shared belief in the sufficiency of meanness and sadness for world-historical tragedy.

Chinese tragedy holds on to cause and effect as long as possible. Cavell tells us that in Shakespearean tragedy death is always "inflicted," but the infliction itself remains mysterious. You've seen everything with your own eyes, but it's still mysterious. In Chinese imperial tragedy—at least before partial Christianization and other transmissions of the "West Wind," and before the

12. Of these I find George Steiner's in *The Death of Tragedy* (Knopf, 1963) the most rich and convincing. Lamenting the death of tragedy and enumerating its past models, Steiner describes *Lear*'s cultural moment and its peers in this way: "They [the plays] are a result of the concurrence of ancient and complex energies. Beneath the fact of the development of dramatic blank verse, beneath the Senecan spirit of majestic violence, lay a great inheritance of medieval and popular forms. This is the live undergrowth from which the late sixteenth century draws much of its strength. In Shakespeare's sovereign contempt for limitations of space and time, we recognize the spirit of the mystery cycles which took the world of heaven, earth, and hell for their setting, and the history of man for their temporal scale" (22).

onset of full-fledged capitalism—the infliction is not mysterious. We know who did it, and how, but we simply cannot act on that knowledge in time for the victims.

Unlike Greek tragedy, autochthony is not the original sin.[13] Incestuous rape and the sacrifice of children at the altar of the gods do not lie at the cosmological heart of Chinese tragedy. There is instead one of the deepest anxieties over karmic retribution. What if *this* is what always happens in the long run between the individual, the family, and the polity? What if families are always dispersed to the winds of good and evil, and the most righteous are always martyred and persecuted? Like clockwork, and with only ironic variation, some mind-bogglingly severe injustice happens again and again.

Of all the tragic roles my grandfather played, one stands out in the complexity of its tragedy and its compensatory fantasy. The same role, the elderly General Yang (also known as Yang Linggong or Yang Ye) appears in two operettas, often performed together, called *Tuo Zhao* 托兆 and *Peng Bei* 碰碑 [To Ferry a Message through a Dream; Dashing One's Head on a Tombstone]. The operettas come from the same story—based on *The Generals of the Yang Family*—and take place one after the other in time. We're at the northern edge of the Song empire in a battle against the kingdom of Liao (Khitan). One of the armies is led by the loyal and courageous general Yang Ye. By a twist of fortune, the entire imperial army has fallen under the command

13. In his study of mythology, Claude Lévi-Strauss offers a way to make sense of Oedipus's accidental incest. Lévi-Strauss doesn't use the language of tragedy, but he is using its logics: Oedipus is being punished for what? For believing, as we all do, that a child can surely find the escape velocity from a twisted repetition of what already came before. Surely there can be a permissible amount of self-fashioning, some permissible degree of self-mythologizing as someone who not only starts life afresh, out of the shadow of ancestry, but whose life has meaning precisely because one has found that route? Tragedy answers in the negative.

of the villainous Pan Renmei. Acting out of ancient envy and vengeance, and with the aim of destroying the Yang family, Pan abandons General Yang to certain death at the hands of the enemy troops on the Mountain of the Twin Wolves. The operetta *Tuo Zhao* opens with the heartbroken old general taking stock of his predicament. It is twilight, he remarks. Their horses have been slaughtered for food; the tents have been burned for fuel. It is so bitterly cold. As part of a rescue mission, six of his sons have joined him in the mountains and all have perished except for one. His youngest son had ridden out to appeal to Pan to send backup, only to be ignobly executed as a spy for the Liao army. In the operetta, this son returns to the encampment as a murdered ghost, sending his father a message in the form of a dream, letting him know that he had not been betrayed or forsaken. *I want you to know why I didn't come in time.* English has no good equivalent for this thing that happens all the time: *I was targeted for harm and then harmed to death (bei hai si 被害死).* All lines of communication have been cut. Messages can only be conveyed supernaturally. The operetta is a fantasy of explanation that comes in the final hour.

In the next operetta, *Peng Bei* [Dashing One's Head on a Tombstone], also known as *At Li Ling's Tomb* (see figure 9), we find old General Yang ending his life in a way for which English also has no name. The dream message has alerted him to the possibility that he and his sons have been the victims of an elaborate treachery. With the last of his contingent pressing him to move on and seek shelter, the general attempts to kill a bird for food, but his bow breaks. Grief and debility have shaken his manhood thus. At this moment, a Taoist sage crosses his path, leading a single maimed old goat. No words of comfort are offered. Instead, the Taoist sage overtly compares the goat to the general before killing it. The general is then led into a temple erected in honor of the General Li Ling, a famous Han-dynasty "defector" who surrendered to the Xiongnu at the end of a similarly doomed military campaign. Li Ling's ignominy was such that when the grand

FIGURE 9. Song Baoluo as General Yang in *Peng Bei* (also known as *At Li Ling's Tomb*). Private collection.

historian Sima Qian came to his defense in the annals, he himself was punished by imprisonment and castration. In this operetta, one my grandfather performed many times during his life, General Yang realizes the moral of the story after he visits the tomb of the so-called national traitor. He is not the only iteration of this particularly twisted Chinese tragedy, one in which heroes are treated as traitors. Many have come before him; many will come after him. The best he can hope for, and the reason why the Taoist sage has encouraged him to commit suicide in *this* temple, in front of *this* monument, is to die in such a way that lets posterity know that he died in undeserved exile and disgrace. *Ba le*, the general says, *so be it*. He finishes singing and dashes his head on Li Ling's tombstone.

My grandfather once sang this particular opera for Mao, at Mao's behest. In the spring of 1959, he was abruptly summoned to perform for the chairman at the Liu estate in the city of Hangzhou. They chose the "Strategy of the Empty City" from the fourteenth-century epic *Romance of the Three Kingdoms*. Afterward, Mao asked for a private rendition and made a special point of asking for this story of the suicide of the General Yang. My grandfather happily complied.[14]

Sometimes I really do prefer Chinese tragedy's profound grimness even if it is not as primed for theoretical interpretation as its Western counterparts. Chinese tragedy tends not to look into the guts of a family to turn up perverse human foibles that confuse cause and effect. I understand the preference for the latter. Burying the origin of responsibility in circular family dynamics deactivates the aspect of tragedy that is most vulnerable to jingoism. Chinese tragedy can easily slide into ultranationalism. The story of *The Generals of the Yang Family* certainly does not escape this fate. But once tragedy is complicated by psychology, it runs the risk of leaving too much up for debate on the matter of causality. Some things should admit no ambiguity. One would not ask these operas whether those harmed to death actually "brought about their own demise," or if their relationships with their children border on the pathological. One would not wish to lose track of the historical context, or forget the corruption of the Song dynasty. The story of the family of Yang is historically and situationally complex, but morally (causally) straightforward: under negligent and corrupt governance, some very good and capable people are deviously harmed to death, and that's the end of the story.

14. My grandfather recounts this episode in his memoir, *Yihai Chengfu*, 190–91.

CHAPTER FOUR

Comedy

MY FATHER'S BEST friend used to be a Red Guard. It makes no sense, but he really is his best friend, a lifelong defender against bullies and detractors. He's regaling us with stories from his Red Guard days. *Oh, you have no idea how funny it was,* he said. *Let me tell you about the time Chairman Mao held the Last Reception with the Red Guards. Hundreds and thousands of us traveled from Zhejiang Province to Beijing to see him. It was the first time many of us had ridden a train, we were crawling with lice. Absolutely overjoyed. We couldn't sleep. When were we going to see Chairman Mao, when were we going to see Chairman Mao? That was the question on everyone's minds. You had a special pose you were supposed to strike and a special march you had to practice. You did left foot, right foot, left foot like this, and you held your* Little Red Book *facing outward straight in front of you, and you chanted: Long/Live/Chairman Mao, Long/Live/Chairman Mao! It was very rhythmic. Days passed, we were still outside of Beijing, not having seen Chairman Mao. We clamored to do something in the meantime. What can we do? What can we do for Chairman Mao? Well, we were told that every single one of us was responsible for keeping Chairman Mao safe. We had to protect Chairman Mao at all costs! So we searched around for anything that might harm Chairman Mao. What about my belt buckle? someone asked. I don't know, that could harm Chairman Mao. Then I'll take off my belt buckle! What about the aglets on my shoelaces, the shoelaces themselves? someone else asked. Well, I suppose that they, too, could harm Chairman Mao. Off went the shoelaces. What happened then when your shoe fell off? You bound it to your foot with string. It was really amazing what people did.*

In any case, one night, in the middle of the night, we were told that we were finally going to see Chairman Mao. I cannot describe the excitement to you. We were so prepared to see Chairman Mao. It was 2 a.m. We got up, we got dressed, we did the special march with the book held high and the long/live/Chairman Mao. Well, it turns out that was just a drill. Which made sense. You had to rehearse to do a good job. The next time at we were woken up at 4am and told that we were finally going to go see Chairman Mao! We got up, we got dressed, we did the march and the book and long/live/Chairman Mao, long/live/Chairman Mao. Well, that was also a drill. Finally, the big day came. We could tell it was finally the day because Red Guards from other provinces had arrived. We were instructed to refrain from picking up the Little Red Book *if it fell from our hands. Why, you ask? That doesn't make any sense? Well, there were 2.5 million people on Tiananmen Square that day. If you bent down you would be mangled. Hundreds of Red Guards had already been trampled to death in the seven massive receptions that Chairman Mao had already held with the Red Guards since June of that year. And many were trampled on that day! I don't even remember walking; we were all floating.*

Do you remember the date? I asked. *Do I remember the date,* he said. *Of course I remember the date. It was November 26, 1966, Chairman Mao's Eighth and Final Reception with the Red Guards. Oh, it was hilarious then but, you know, many things are hilarious now.*

He has us in stitches, this man. Evil and stupidity need only a jovial and theatrical storyteller, and we abandon Tragedy for Comedy.

⩛

My husband regales me with jokes. *Have you heard the one about the pig on the ship?* he asks me. *No? So, all these animals are on a ship and the ship has sprung a leak and it's slowly sinking. The animals come up with a fair and efficient solution. They would take turns telling a joke. If everyone laughed at your joke, you got to stay on the ship. But if even one animal doesn't laugh, overboard you go. It was cruel but better than no solution at all.*

The monkey goes first. He tells a really funny joke. Everyone laughs. But the pig doesn't laugh. Oh no. Overboard goes the monkey. The tiger goes next. He tells a really funny joke. Everyone laughs. But the pig doesn't laugh. Overboard goes the tiger. Now the donkey gets up there and he tells a joke. It's a terrible joke and no one laughs but the pig, who is in stitches. Why are you laughing? *they asked. And the pig, between breaths: Oh my gosh—that monkey's joke.*

⩛

I have an ongoing *Lear* joke with a friend about how we know when things are at their worst and an ongoing joke about how hard it was to write this chapter. You see, the chapter is supposed to be funny.

No, I see that, she says.

Or, rather, it has to be *funny. Jinx,* she says. She reads it. *Hmm,* she tells me. I rewrite it. She reads it again. *I think this is as funny as it's going to get.*

⩛

Oh, you thought the Cultural Revolution couldn't happen twice? The joke's on you. Maoism is nothing if not relentlessly hilarious, even in its timing.

What were the first signs that things would revert? The inattentive world sat up when extradition laws were passed that effectively ended Hong Kong's sovereignty, when disturbing dispatches came in from the autonomous region of Xinjiang. And then it was, "as quoting Xi Jinping," and then his face everywhere. And finally, *Thoughts of Chairman Xi* in every bookstore, on everyone's shelf. It was *Xi Jingping's Classical Allusions* as a serious topic of study, and it was, finally, the definiteness of his indefinite rule. It came when people started waxing nostalgic about former premier Jiang Zemin, and especially that interview he held with Hong Kong journalists, the one in which he scolded them for being "too simple, sometimes naïve." People missed him dearly, cringe as he was.

But when did it really start? It's so hard to remember—some dumbing-down of dialogue or storyline in television and books, or the banal scripting of the dramas of life. I remember the devices that people began installing in their cars around 2005 that detected street cameras. It would alert you—"can-mah-lah"—but soon after, you could reasonably assume cameras were everywhere. In 2011, a motorcyclist plowed over a two-year-old girl in the street, and eighteen people passed by her before an old woman, collecting rubbish, saw her and rushed her to the hospital, too late. *Chinese people are just like this,* Chinese people said. Goodness and wickedness in such proximity. The use of omnipresent closed-circuit television to capture, and encourage people to be, Good Samaritans, coincided with the "human flesh search" of Chinese netizen/citizen vigilantism. In 2006, netizens found the woman who had killed a kitten by putting the heel of her stiletto through its eye. They got her fired and drove her to near-suicide. Crimes of conscience were indeed hidden in every corner of the world and Chinese people ached to punish them.

The earliest Learian turning point in the last twenty years was probably the Wang Lijun Incident of 2012. The wife of a senior cadre had fatally poisoned her sex partner after their business dealings went sour. The investigation that followed exposed an extensive cover-up. Her husband, the party secretary of Chongqing, was arrested and charged. Once favored to succeed Hu Jintao as chairman/president, Bo Xilai had ambitions as great as Xi Jinping's. This was the man once praised by his own father for kicking him while he was down and breaking his ribs. Bo Xilai's subsequent sacking had seemed like a blessing, because he had been transforming the megacity into a Cultural Revolution theme park, replete with cadre outfits and "red songs" at work and in schools. He and his police chief, Wang Lijun, had been wiretapping senior officials and gathering intelligence. Good riddance, everyone said.

For a long while it wasn't clear which Politburo princeling—the second generation of the CPC brass—would win the power grab, which of the ruthless would prove to be the most ruthless. It became clear in the swiftness of Bo Xilai's elimination. Taking advantage of the momentum behind the public denunciation, Xi Jinping consolidated power, eliminating political rivals in a highly orchestrated, nationwide campaign against graft. Everyone in China appreciated the need to root out corrupt officials fattened on years of liberal leadership. Everyone knew how corrupt Chinese officials could be—after all, Emperor Qianlong's minister He Shen's wealth had amassed to ten times more than the Qing dynasty's entire GDP. The rules of official conduct were being rewritten to curb ridiculous excess—sinfully wasteful banquets, multiple mistresses, billion-dollar mansions, prodigal sons showing off their wealth abroad, and uncountable offshore accounts. This flurry of disciplinary activity seemed not only sensible but mirth-inducing. Let's clean up this ridiculous act.

ɰ

We cannot say whether we saw it coming or did not see it coming. Remember the punchline in Gloucester's blinding? He did not see that one coming. Gloucester's would-be tormentors were staying in his own house, enjoying his hospitality. He really did not see that one coming. But Gloucester could not say with a straight face that his eyeballs did not see it coming. Even the second eyeball literally saw it coming. Those who paid even a speck of attention saw it coming; every step of the way they saw it coming.

Stanley Cavell tells us we should regard Gloucester's blinding as a mercy, because it proves that even evil "cannot bear witness to itself." I ponder this. I take him to be saying something like: plucking out someone's eyes is extremely cruel, but this somehow undermines evil, because it means that evil doesn't want to look or be looked at, wants its act to remain unseen. I think the world of Cavell's "The Avoidance of Love," but this particular take makes no sense. How does Evil not bear witness to itself when someone is blinded? Look here: the blinding of Gloucester works like a "your mama" joke. As in: *Your mama's so fat I swerved to miss her and my car ran out of gas.* As in: *Your mama's so fat that when she sits around the house, she literally sits around the house.* Gloucester's blinding takes hyperbole to its literal meaning in the shortest number of steps (I did not see it coming! Well . . .). That's why it's funny.

Lear has some truly hilarious moments in it. We're almost at the end of the play. At this moment, an honest, intelligent joke appears out of nowhere, piercing the sadness. It's act 5, scene 3. Kent has finally taken off his disguise as Caius. Does Lear recognize him? Well. . . .

KENT: If Fortune brag of two she loved and hated, One of them we behold.

LEAR: This is a dull sight: are you not Kent?

Reconciliation and recognition—oh, it was you all along! It was me, all along—are yearned for in this play. But when they come? Kent's, like, *Ta-da, its'a me, my liege,* and Lear is, like, *The eyes, they're not so good. I can't quite tell if you're Kent or not, to be honest.* My edition suggests that I should not read "dull sight" as an insult—as in, *Kent, you are a dull sight.* You have to admit, though, it sounds like an insult. *Oh wow, you're Kent? You look terrible!* Or: *Jesus, you're wordy.* "If Fortune brag of two she loved and hated, one of them we behold"—*Jesus, stop talking like this. Are you Kent or aren't you Kent?* My edition explains that the language in this last line literally means poor eyesight, as if that didn't make it ten times funnier. *All that effort you put into being Caius? My eyes are not so good. I was never able to tell. Even before, I just couldn't make you out. No, literally, my eyes: they're not good. I have myopia, a serious premodern affliction. My eyes are still better than my friend Gloucester's, though.*

Did you just insult me? Or am I overthinking it? Here's a famous example of this back-and-forth between Lear and his Fool:

> FOOL: That lord that counseled thee
> To give away thy land,
> Come place him here by me;
> Do thou for him stand.
> The sweet and bitter fool
> Will presently appear:
> The one in motley here,
> The other found out there.
> LEAR: Dost thou call me fool, boy? (1.4.138–45)

Are you insulting me? *Yes, but please try to keep up. I'm not just calling you a fool. I'm calling you a sweet* and *bitter fool. I'm calling you a fool and I'm calling you bitter. Don't undercount your follies.*

It's character assassination, these insults. Half of the entries in the "Shakespearean Insults" handouts that English teachers used to distribute to students come from Kent's tirade against Oswald in act 2, scene 2:

> A knave, a rascal, an eater of broken meats; a base, proud, shallow, beggarly, three-suited, hundred-pound, filthy worsted-stocking knave; a lily-livered, action-taking, whoreson, glass-gazing, superserviceable, finical rogue; one-trunk-inheriting slave; one that wouldst be a bawd in way of good service, and art nothing but the composition of a knave, beggar, coward, pander, and the son and heir of a mongrel bitch.

Kent's not done:

> Thou whoreson zed, thou unnecessary letter! My lord, if you will give me leave, I will tread this unbolted villain into mortar and daub the walls of a jakes with him.

And he's still not done. To paraphrase the next sequence: *I don't like his face,* Kent says of Oswald. *It's just as likely you don't like my face,* Cornwall interjects, *or Gloucester's, or Regan's.* "Sir," replies Kent, "'tis my occupation to be plain: I have seen better faces in my time" (act 2, scene 2). Oh!

Just look at the hilarious exchange between the King of France and Lear right after he has divided the kingdom and disowned Cordelia. Asking him to walk back his words are Kent (ineffectual) and France, who phrases his objection in a way that really upbraids:

> This is most strange,
> That she, that even but now was your best object,
> The argument of your praise, balm of your age,
> Most best, most dearest, should in this trice of time
> Commit a thing so monstrous, to dismantle
> So many folds of favour. Sure, her offence
> Must be of such unnatural degree,
> That monsters it, or your fore-vouch'd affection
> Fall'n into taint: which to believe of her,

> Must be a faith that reason without miracle
> Could never plant in me. (1.1.245–56)

This way of calling bullshit is so funny. The King of France is making quick work of the ridiculousness of Lear's reaction: *If she is as monstrous as you now say, and so quickly demoted from most beloved to wretched of the earth, then your prior words will "fall into taint," that is, become worthless. And if they are not worthless, and we are to believe that Cordelia could fall so precipitously from grace by her own doing, well, then you'd have to reduce my faith to pure superstition.*

No wonder the King of England will no longer entertain the King of France at his court. Get rid of her and you get rid of him, too. What a son-in-law to have to keep around if you're bent on being Lear. Get him out of here. It's just too insulting.

People take offense too easily. Have a sense of humor. It's just words, how could they be offended? How wondrous it was when intelligent television shows during the 1990s started to really depict the Cultural Revolution's hilarities. There's one I remember well from 2000, a twenty-episode drama called *Love in the Time of Flying Ice and Snow,* directed by Zhang Hanjie, based on the novel by Han Naiyin called *A Place Far Away from the Sun* [*Yuanli taiyang de difang*]. It understood humor's relationship to tragedy—belly laughs and merriment in almost every episode—and it understood how the deeply, genetically comical can be so laughably far from comedy's solace. A bunch of idealistic students are dispatched to the Great Northern Wilderness. There they develop friendship, courtship, and murderousness in one of the most malignant experiments of the Cultural Revolution. The author and the director painstakingly re-created the reality of this surrealism. Each character is finely articulated, each joke and cruelty assembled with accuracy. Zhang and Han studied more carefully the tragic follies of socialism's cult of personality and the petty corruptions of cadre culture. In one episode, someone used a party newspaper to wrap a chicken and learned how humorless everyone had become. One lesson for the comic is that wit triumphs over everything except self-important meanness. When humor and humorlessness butt heads, the room will suddenly feel very cold. Humorlessness decides what things should be taken lightly and what things should be taken seriously—and punished to the full extent of the law.

In the mistreatment of Lear, humorlessness rendered the perpetrators nonculpable. At best they were guilty of criminal negligence. Humorlessness can sit back and wait for opportunities to take advantage of good humor: all it has to do is insist that the other intended their barbs. It's not as though the victims in *Lear* weren't given fair warning. Lear himself got a reminder in act 1, scene 4, long before the worst had arrived. Take care, the gentleman knight says to Lear, as there has been "a great abatement of kindness." Some things can no longer be taken for granted when there has been a great abatement of kindness. This advice sounds easy to remember, but somehow it's not. The gentleman knight's warning emboldens Lear in the wrong way and knavery ensues. Give someone unkind some rope and they will hang you with it for no good reason. This ongoing joke becomes literalized in Cordelia's death.

But are the murderers and torturers the only humorless ones in the play? Consider the painful ugliness of the Fool's riddles and jokes, the ones that should "outjest [Lear's] heart-struck injuries." People might chuckle at the way he sticks it to Lear, but some of the stuff is downright nasty, from incest to whores to mutilation. To Lear, in act 1, scene 4, he says: "thou madest thy daughters thy mothers; for when thou gavest them the rod and puttest down thine own breeches." And then again, the very next time he speaks, because he is relentless: "Thou hast pared thy wit o' both sides and left nothing i' th'middle." "When thou clovest thy crown i' th' middle and gavest away both parts, thou borest thy ass o' th' back o'er the dirt." The Fool sounds like he has a filthy mind that has worked hard to cut others down. This behavior might either be the result or the cause of Lear's stuntedness. Either way, there's not much gentle, good-humored counsel, no incitement to laughter that doesn't instantly chill.

The Fool joins everyone else to demonstrate that the right to self-deprecating humor disappears in a depreciation game. If you are self-deprecating, others will take your cue and depreciate you further. Lear concedes his own hypersensitivity—"curious for envy," he calls it—but it's foolish to admit weakness when you're outnumbered by the ravenous. Back to that run-in between Kent and Cornwall: Cornwall hears Kent's insults and comes up with this comeback: "These kinds of knaves I know which in this plainness / Harbor more craft and more corrupter ends / Than twenty silly-ducking observants / That stretch their duties nicely."

Among the wicked and unkind, comedy approaches character assassination. There's a joke in Regan's death. "Sick, O, Sick!" she cries after it all comes out between her, Goneril, Albany, and Edmund. She's not expressing revulsion at what's happened—she's literally sick to death. If that's not the poison working, says Goneril in an aside, "I'll never trust medicine." Goneril is making a dumb play on words here. Just as Regan is limited in vocabulary, Goneril is limited in wit. All three sisters have trouble speaking. The ensuing insults that Goneril receives from her husband are hilarious, as is the stupidity of her responses. Albany says to her "See thyself, devil / Proper deformity shows not in the fiend / So horrid as in woman." "O vain fool!" is her response. Seeing this weak comeback, Albany delivers an existential blow: "You are not worth the dust which the rude wind blows in your face." "No more, the text is foolish" is her reply. He's insulted her to nothingness; the only deflection she has at her disposal is sneering: *This whole thing is so stupid.*

Ꮃ

When the Gang of Four were arraigned after Mao died, they complained rightly that they had been subjected to political theater as farce. During their depositions in 1981, only Mao's wife, Madame Jiang Qing, still went on making speeches, still tried to justify her actions. Her performance on the December 12th and December 29th trial dates was erratic and buffoonish. The *Chicago Sun-Times* reported that "with a cold laugh" Jiang Qing had scoffed, "You just want my head." During the hearing she spitefully mocked the judge and prosecutors as a "bunch of vampires" and "dirty vultures," interrupting their speeches with contemptuous comments, making faces, and once simply taking off her earphones and closing her eyes to ignore the prosecutor's attack. Given a chance to make a last statement, Jiang Qing said: "Let the monkey king give me more heads for you to chop off!" Her comeback is stupid, clichés all the way through, but there's ominousness in that, too. *You'll have to kill us all to make sure that there won't be anyone else like me.*

This is a tragicomedy of endless scorn. Samuel Johnson reminds us that the commonsense rule that comedy alleviates tragedy doesn't apply to *Lear*. Here comedy makes things worse. G. Wilson Knight found in *Lear* "a humour that treads the brink of tears, and tragedy which needs but an infinitesimal shift of perspective to disclose the varied riches of comedy." "Craughing" is a recently invented word in English, but in Chinese it has long existed (as *kuxiao bude* 哭笑不得 in Mandarin): unable to decide between laughter and wailing.

Lear inhabits comedy in more ways than one. There once was a group of literary scholars who quantitatively determined that among Shakespeare's tragedies *Othello* came closest to being comedy. What accounts for this, according to their study, is Iago's language of seduction.

Othello may be the closest to comedy by criteria identifiable by simple numerical analysis, but *King Lear* outperforms it not only as perverse humor but also as perverse *comedy*. The most important features of comedy—twins, paired marriages, reconciliation, social reintegration, corrected misunderstandings—are all here. We get two reconciliations between a wronged parent and a wronged child—two larger-than-life attempts to move past atrocity inflicted at close range. After Cordelia and Lear are captured, everyone shows up, and we get one of the largest family reunions in Shakespeare. And let us not forget that there is a three-way marriage in Edmund, Goneril, and Regan ("I was contracted to them both: all three now marry in an instant"), and a passel of comedic twins and other doublings that provide entertaining confusions. We can't fault Nahum Tate for nudging the play just a few steps into the safe space of romantic comedy; it was already so very close.

Traditionally, comedy seeks to repair what's broken by means of marriage, lighthearted wit, slightly questionable form, and lovable pairs. In this sense comedy is "culturally conservative." It has social normativity—harmony, flexibility, things being okay—keyed into its essential movements. In its acts of repair, comedy walks a strict line: it must keep its audiences painfully alert to alternative outcomes while it steers everything toward the happy and the light.

In China, terrible tales were coming out about the sent-down youths who got stuck in those remote regions and the discrepancies between the ones who stayed and those who, through luck or scheming, managed to return home. This great drama of injustice began to evolve into happier pairs: rocky marriages that worked themselves out through Chinese and Western forms of therapy; murderous disharmony and vengeful arguments were replaced by uproarious bickering. Comedy as divorce and remarriage was also quickly introduced to film and television.

Luck, mirth, and mercy: their themes and plot devices were sown in the private and public viewing spheres. The reconciliation of Chinese families and communities in the 1980s, '90s, and early aughts modeled itself on whatever was out there: Ba Jin's novels (*Family*, *Spring*, and *Autumn*; *Fog*, *Rain*, and *Lightning*), Chiung Yao's *Six Dreams*, dynastic historical romances, and global models from post-Soviet Russia, India, Taiwan, and the West. Chinese programming experienced a Renaissance in this late Late Socialism, before the party elite's return of the repressed, before Chinese expression had been reverse-engineered to anticipate the masses' consumerist desires and tastes. Chinese cultural production made grand reconciliations designed for adults and children. Studios on the mainland, Taiwan, and Hong Kong served up dramas that aired many hundreds of episodes; satirical and reparative forms sprung from the country's most ancient wisdoms: metered ballads, the tavern storyteller, solo and duo stand-up humor routines like the *er ren zhuan* 二人转, *xiangsheng* 相声, *xiaoping* 小品, *pingshu* 评书. A *jiemu* 节目, or program, was something to wait for. With only some product placement, and a tasteful amount of borrowing from the West, these dramas had not yet devolved into spectacle and soap opera. All that pent-up love and talent went into the entertainment industry. Directors and producers captured the immediacy and intimacy of sound—what Chinese people sound like—at their cleverest, wittiest, wisest, slowest, dumbest, most naive, most affected, most sincere, most despairing, most joyful, most rancorous, and most triumphantly mute.

If there must be tyrannies, let them be funny ones that we can all laugh off. This was the running joke of antitotalitarian skits and dramas during the restoration. We felt the loosening through humorous subversiveness, singing patriotic red songs with the words swapped out. *And the songs traveled all the way to Beijing Tiananmen, Chairman Mao heard them and was so happpppy; he praised us for our ass-kissing flatterrrry; and such a thorough brain-washinnnng.* Subversion is tried out in the simplest exercises of rhyming. We had comedy and criticism for a long while. A few I remember fondly: *The Remembrances of Happy Incidents in the Ma Family* (2010, directed by Yang Wenjun), *The Trivial Business of ¥6.60* (2013, directed by Zhou Xiaobing), *Happiness Is Like a Flower* (2005, directed by Gao Xixi). People were reunited, or soon to be reunited. Slapstick flourished because we all needed to see a bit of ordinary cruelty, but on the balance we got more good-humored jokes than jokes made at someone else's expense. In this open laughter and celebration, everyone is allowed to exaggerate a little, to enjoy a healthy bit of distension. In the reconciliation after totalitarianism people are permitted light and heavy laughter unrelated to the immediate mandates of the state. People could make fun of the absurdities of Maoism and the cadre culture it left behind.

The *pingshu* storyteller Shan Tianfang had had his teeth pulled out during his reeducation, but speechless complainers like him were slowly learning to speak again. By the early 1990s, Shan Tianfang was performing subversive acts in the Spring Festival Gala. I've rewatched early CCTV Chinese New Year galas from this time—the annual televised extravaganza of song, dance, and national feelings that first aired in 1983 and nowadays gets over a billion viewers. Humorous skits (*xiaoping* 小品) and cross-talks (*xiangshen* 相声) did most of the heavy lifting involved in restoring critical speech. My parents' generation tasted real freedom in the 1988 skit/traditional opera vignette "Turning Off Lights with the Blind," performed by the comedy master Zhao Benshan. It had officially licensed everyone to laugh at the stupidities that were code for Chinese bureaucracy. Comedy masters poured out of the woodwork. Soon after, we had nationally televised skits starring Chen Peisi and Zhu Shimao that made fun of cadres implementing draconian regulations or taking advantage of new state enterprises. In the early days, CCTV programs were magical works of human expression. They modeled social and political subversiveness and genuine patriotism and love—of country, the world, and the people in it. The CCTV New Year's Gala is no longer very watchable, algorithmically populated as it is now by apparatchiks and consumerism.

In those years the story of the country and the people in it felt overall closer to Lear's happy-go-lucky twins: a *Comedy of Errors*, *As You Like It*, or my favorite, *Love's Labor Lost*. Keeping with the motif of twins, these can all be seen as jocular versions of *Lear*. In *As You Like It*, written a few years before *King Lear*, Rosalind flees political and personal persecution by her uncle, who has just usurped the duchy from her father. She has a friend in her uncle's daughter, Celia, and together with the Fool they flee, cross-dressed, into the woods of Arden. There they find both queer and straight love. Things get increasingly complicated after their exile, but these complications promise good outcomes. Lear's terribly sad "Blow, winds, and crack your cheeks" monologue is a wassail in Lord Amiens's "Blow, blow, thou winter wind / Thou are not so unkind." Amiens's role combines Kent and the Fool, but where the Fool disappears and Kent ends his own life, Amiens heralds Christmastime.

Love's Labor's Lost is even closer to *Lear*. There are absurd decrees by princes that sound like the CPC's bloviating three- and five-year plans. There is spying on your fellow man and the devising of elaborate purges and punishments. Shakespeare turns all of this danger into a mirthful business, swerves away from authoritarian catastrophes, from pain, tragic death, and disaster. At the close of the play, the pageant actors sing a canticle of spring and winter. Don Armado wraps up the light-hearted, song-filled political "purge" they've all just experienced with a number: "The words of Mercury are harsh after the songs of Apollo. / You that way: we this way." You that way, we this way. In *Lear* this option—of parting amicably on good-faith promises, of live and let live—is no longer available to you. Comedy is where that still can be had.

A few years ago I came upon the novella *King Lear and Nineteen Seventy-nine,* written by Canadian Chinese writer Xue Yiwei. It tells the story of a family that was split asunder in the Mao era reunited by their efforts to stage a production of *Lear*. The novel is based on the author's own discovery of a copy of Shakespeare in his grandfather's drawer in 1979, two years after Mao's death.

King Lear and Nineteen Seventy-nine mends a treacherous familial betrayal. It works as hard at reconciliation as, say, *The Tempest,* written a few years after *Lear.* Some great harm has been done that's both personal and political. Reversing it means taking things back to the point before the thing had been done—before the Duke of Milan, Prospero, was betrayed by his brother Antonio and exiled from his city-state. When the play begins, the traitor and his collaborator, the King of Naples, find themselves tossed by storm onto the island where Prospero and his daughter have lived for years, and where Prospero has the clear upper hand because he can deploy the weapon of magic, and they're ready to be served their just deserts. What is served is not just deserts, however, but forgiveness, and forgiveness that keeps lowering the threshold for its possibility, so that even the audience's customary applause at the end of the play would count as forgiveness. As *The Tempest* makes clear, that requires nothing less than magic, nothing less than pure creation and colonialism (James I had chartered the Virginia and Plymouth companies in 1606, resulting in the settlement of Jamestown in Virginia and Popham in Maine; the East India Company was founded just six years before that). In *The Tempest,* survivors of an artificial calamity and survivors of a real intent to harm are separated into groups, their treacheries and noble purposes sorted out with game theory and mirth. Justice is restored, people are returned to their rightful offices, a disorderly coup and a well-oiled conspiracy are both suppressed, and the credible threat of a dark reckoning withheld. In this reconciliation, the intent to harm drains out to sea. It is as if we could get back to the start, when my students, colleagues, friends, and family hadn't turned me in, or sold me out, or caused my exile from my home country.[1] It's the work of fairies getting up in the middle of the night to go over stories and texts, tracing the secret pathways between them and the real world. In this true fantasy, a family could get over the hurts of the Cultural Revolution by working together as amateur playwrights and textual scholars on *King Lear.*

We have needed to see these Nahum Tates of *Lear*, too—comedic adaptations, real exercises at mending. These spring from the conviction that some endings are too extreme to be admissible, and that safer outcomes have to be possible. The author who turns Learian tragedy into reconciliation comedy knows his work is fiction—we can probably count on one hand the number of families that were able to repair broken bonds in this way—but what else is there to do?

One finds Learian comedies everywhere in Chinese and Chinese diasporic cinema. One of the most hilarious of these is Ang Lee's film *Pushing Hands*, about a Chinese father who comes to live with his son's family in their big house in America. As soon as the film opens, we know that this elderly father, Mr. Chu, has become a domestic burden. It's as if Ang Lee decided to expand Lear's stint with Goneril and show how parental and filial care realistically wear you down. Alex, the son, lives in a quiet suburban neighborhood. He is a computer science professor. His wife is a Caucasian woman, a writer named Martha, and together they

1. I am indebted to Ben Jeffrey for this reading of *The Tempest* and the broader argument about the material requirements of full reversals in Shakespeare.

have a young son. Mr. Chu finds himself unwanted in their house. Alex isn't home most of the day, and so the living space must be shared with Martha, someone who requires precise, controlled conditions for her work. Mr. Chu is a gentleman-scholar and a tai chi master, so it doesn't seem like he would be a nuisance. And yet, his presence in the house is unwanted. His presence at the dinner table is unwanted. His more-than-mechanical presence, that is. He is welcome to share space and to eat his dinner, but no more than that.

A strong-willed parent who is intentionally or inadvertently passive-aggressive is not easy to have in your house. Everyday matters start to grate. These people cannot share space even though they live in a spacious home. Ang Lee is doing the best he can—what any person can—to normalize the Learian story of Chinese immigration and assimilation among the damaged elderly and their children. He goes out of his way to render cross-cultural encounters as actually abrasive and disruptive, so that his audiences don't romanticize them. Mr. Chu is an annoyance. Although he's mostly very quiet, he also sings Peking opera at his leisure, and each verse sounds like a long whine. If you're not predisposed to liking this music—this cultural experience—you won't like it. You can't even tune it out. The viewer is invited to sympathize with the daughter-in-law: "By day and night he wrongs me; every hour / He flashes into one gross crime or other, / That sets us all at odds: I'll not endure it." Martha complains to her husband, "Alex, it's impossible, he's taken over my workroom, I just don't have the space to think." His angry and heartbroken response: "Not enough space? In China this house is big enough for four families!" This prefigures the expression Mr. Chu uses when he decides to leave them unannounced: "Heaven and earth is so vast, how could there not be a single space that can tolerate me, a single spot where I can live?"

Pushing Hands is a comedy wrapped tightly around crimes of negligence and cross-cultural impasse. This phase of Ang Lee's career used the comedic form to demonstrate more quickly how bad it can get for the immigrant family that's still coping with China's recent past. With an almost caricatured stoicism, Mr. Chu leaves their home to strike out on his own, relieving his son of his financial and emotional responsibilities. The family makes a panicked search for him, but Mr. Chu is nowhere to be found. He has entered the subaltern world of extremely punishing Chinese restaurant jobs, unregulated migrant housing, and interethnic tensions between different kinds of Chinese people. He endures the bullying and exploitation that's unique to this world. Here Ang Lee rolls out a longed-for fantasy of heroic justice, and we get an entire subplot in which Mr. Chu wins over the bullies at work after standing up to their boss. His tai chi skills are displayed, and you learn the power of the martial art of pushing hands.

Pushing Hands has a happy ending. Mr. Chu is reunited with his family, and father and son have a heart-to-heart and come to an understanding. A Cultural Revolution reconciliation story is layered on top of a difficult assimilation/retirement story, and the effect is almost comical. In this scene Alex finds a picture of his dead mother on his father's bed. It is time to mend everything. Referring to the Red Guards who killed his wife, Mr. Chu says: "They knew that they couldn't hurt me. So they took it out on you and your mother. Their tortures only inspired me . . . to perfect my kung fu" (see figure 10).

This scene is very hard for me to watch. I crack up at the very end. Every element in this movie contributes to the fantasy—the fact that this grandfather is a tai chi master, the fact that he can be squatting, martial-arts style, while practicing his brush calligraphy at the same time, the fact that this is what he chooses to do with his free time. It merges these fantasies with the fantasy of the robustness of the community that exists for Chinese immigrants in Chinatown, the way the family gathers in the bathroom after the son returns home from his futile search, the cartoonish villainy of the restaurant owner who employs the grandfather as a dishwasher, and so on, until it has drawn together every scene, every character, every talent someone has, every plot twist, into wish fulfillment.

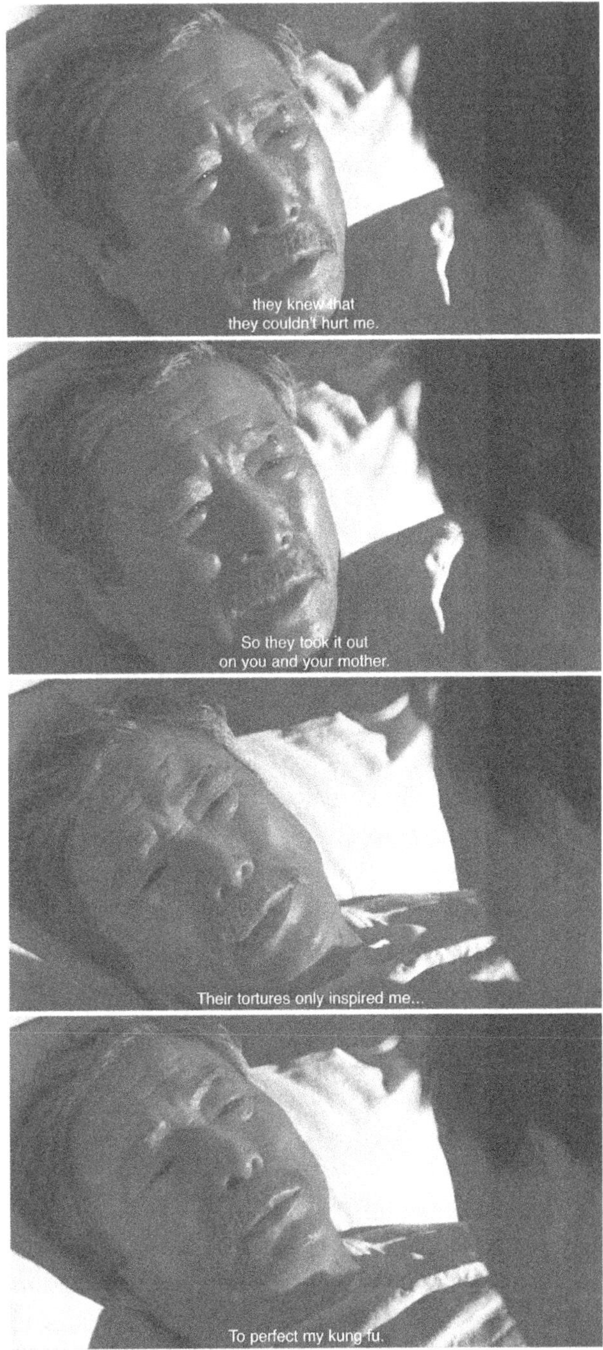

FIGURE 10. Scenes from Ang Lee's *Pushing Hands*, 1991: a) 1:05:15; b) 1:05:17; c) 1:05:56; d) 1:05:59. Film Movement Studio.

Pushing Hands outlines the best-case scenario for such victims of history and circumstance—for that Chinese generation—if the goal is restoration. Even the anecdote of Mr. Chu's wife being beaten to death is an act of wish fulfillment—if only all victimizations were so obviously bad. It, too, is melodramatic, a choice painfully compelled by the nature of the crime. Of course, the Red Guards beat people to death right in front of their family members. Bian Zhongyun, a principal at Beijing Normal University's attached girls' middle school, was the first woman beaten to death by all-female Red Guards. The expression "beaten to death" lies just on the cusp of colloquialism. One could say it casually. It could almost sound funny, like getting your ass whupped in school.

"Beaten to death" is comic relief. People immediately understand how bad it was, one; and two, it sounds like schoolyard shenanigans. Innumerable people were, indeed, beaten to death; however, it's an exaggeration to take the beaten-to-death family member as an emblematic case. After the Cultural Revolution, many people went around telling belligerently childish, belligerently monocausal stories about who the oppressors were, and who the victims were, often exaggerating when they didn't know how to describe the suffering they had endured. Cultural Revolution narratives can be tacky pieces of theater. *Don't exaggerate*, Regan snaps at Lear, after listening to his long complaint, "These are unsightly tricks." Like everyone and everything in *Lear*, Ang Lee has had to exaggerate. *Pushing Hands* has understandably reached for catharsis and its solution as movingly as could be wished for, and as unlikely as they come.

Reconciliation, please, however we can manage it. *Lear* makes impossible requests of Justice, Forgiveness, Correction, and Repair, producing reconciliations that are both too brief and not quite credible. One wonders at how Cordelia and Lear actually managed to meet up, to say nothing about the plausibility of the exchange between Gloucester and Edgar on the cliffs of Dover. Contrived reconciliations do not last; those who complain that revisionist *Lear*s are in poor taste manifest this anxiety. Charles Lamb observed that in changing *Lear* to pure comedy "Tate has put a hook in the nostril of this Leviathan . . . to draw about the beast more easily." Lamb was lodging a deeper misgiving about comedy's intentions, that it dumbs down a problem in order to tame it. The mere fact of being staged makes the play vulnerable to gimmickry, hurting its chances at being taken as seriously as it needs to be taken.

Directors of *Lear* have had to contend with the fact that too many scenes in the play can come off as stupid comedy if they don't get it just right. I've seen it staged hilariously, a winking farce that does not even pause for Cordelia's murder. That's one way to avoid the blunder of staging it straight and having people snicker at the wrong moments. If poorly acted or poorly staged, scenes like the division of the kingdom or the quick succession of deaths at the end can come off as slapstick. In 1709 Nicholas Rowe introduced an interpretation for Lear's frenzied acts in the hovel: "Tearing off his clothes." No stage directions appear for this scene in the 1608 Quarto or 1623 Folio. Until the early twentieth century, the dramaturgical consensus was to have Kent and the Fool restrain Lear from stripping. It's too tricky to stage.

Lear presents a challenge to the dramaturge because of its comedy. The dramaturge has his hardest test, I think, in the fake fall at "Dover." Even under the best conditions, with the best staging, the best acting and lighting, your audience cannot help but laugh. It doesn't seem plausible, the therapeutic solutions they're being shown. It insults one's intelligence to think that it might actually go like this. Let me get this straight: Gloucester, bleeding from his orbits, *walks* to Dover and somehow manages to meet up with Edgar, who actually convinces him that he survived a suicidal fall from the top of a hill or cliff somewhere? These feints are the stuff of fluff dramas, the stuff of comical martial arts/crassly commercial historical romance/rom-com TV. We used to count how many times someone would fall off a cliff only to be saved through some improbable trick. Along with romantic comedy and family comedy, we also got goofy doppelgangers, stupid deaths, and the most ersatz stratagems. Behind these forms, a vehemently earnest hope for the mending of families and the mending of countries.

Bad comedy presages bad times by rushing to fix them. If something goes wrong in a country and in the family, one can always blame it on the fool/critic. We can take the temperature of a country by closely studying those professionally obliged to entertain and speak truth to power.

Like its global counterparts, Chinese opera fool roles run the entire gamut of human types and are accorded "jester's privilege"—that mixed blessing of being able to speak with impunity. The *chou* 丑, the ugly or deformed who become jesters, span the entire gender and moral spectrum and hail from stations of life as far apart as imperial administrators and washerwomen. *Chou* are just one of the many "set" roles in Peking opera. There are also *laodan* 老旦 (elderly woman), *xiaoshen* 小生 (young man), *huadan* 花旦 (young woman), *wen-wu shen* 文武生 (roles that are civic or martial), just to name a few. But *chou* enjoy a unique privilege, which is that they are allowed and even encouraged to improvise their lines in an art form that largely shunned arbitrary, reckless improvisation. To speak truth to power even more penetratingly, the *chou* alone is permitted to break the fourth wall and address the audience and contemporary events. This effect can be jarring if the *chou* actor is feeling especially outlandish. Imagine seeing an actor in a Song-dynasty story turning to the audience and speaking directly to the members of the Politburo. That's how much political power was extended to those playing the *chou*, although most never exercise that privilege anymore.

The *chou* pays for this privilege. My great-grandmother Song Fengyun was Peking opera's first female *chou*. She performed acrobatics and sleights of hand and sang mocking and lighthearted songs. Her face aged faster than other women's because she made thousands of facial expressions every day. The *chou* is the most expressive character. Every thought has to be squeezed out of the physical body, and this takes its toll. What's more, once an actor decides to become a *chou*, he or she is never really able to stand up straight again. That is because the *chou* have to move across the stage on their haunches. They have to maintain this posture even when they perform acrobatic tricks, When they land from their flips, they must land in a squat. They can never sit on tables and chairs but must perch like creatures. In exchange for this hobbling, for the indignity and discomfort of spending most of their lives in a squatting position, the *chou*s are allowed to make penetrating jokes, to have the entire empire under their thumbs.

In late and post-Qing China, the most famous *chou* was Xiao Changhua (figure 11), born in 1878, the third year of the Emperor Guangxu. Xiao Changhua commanded the most classical *chou* figures, performing alongside the great Mei Lanfang for most of his career. Xiao died at the age of eighty-nine, at the beginning of the Cultural Revolution, old enough that no one would bother to inquire how he died, because they could safely assume that his time had come. He's lived a good long life in turbulent times, they might say. His illustrious career bridged the beginning of the end of the Qing empire and the beginning of the end of the Mao era.

But this is how Xiao Changhua died: it just so happened that the most famous role he performed came from a problematic opera. *Silang (the Fourth Son) Visits His Mother*, another story from the Yang family that we saw in the last chapter, was

FIGURE 11. Mei Lanfang (*right*) with Xiao Changhua in a Peking opera. Sovfoto/UIG/Bridgeman Images.

the favorite opera of the number-one enemy of the state at the time (Liu Shaoqi). Hand-calligraphed "big character" posters and "little character" posters denounced capitalist roaders and traitors as "Fourth Son," all because Liu Shaoqi's endorsement of this opera exposed counterrevolutionary subversions in the storyline. All who were involved with the opera suffered the consequences. In 1967, Red Guards doused Xiao Changhua with boiling water until he died, as a joke.

In order not to become a tyrant, the sovereign needs to hear gentle roasting and effective criticism. His jester must play what the philosopher Michel Foucault called the "parrhesiastic game," the tricky dance of correcting the sovereign who keeps the truth-teller alive at their whim.[2] The jester must practice *dazhi ruoyu* 大智若愚 to play the idiot, to strike and then soothe, if only to model a different behavior than that of the tyrant he's critiquing.

So much rests on the Learian Fool. His responsibilities become overwhelming. You can feel the strain in the play's jokes themselves. Lear's fool is able to make so much out of so little, and he always receives so little appreciation. His dazzling spins on the aphoristic form ("Have more than thou showest, Speak less than thou knowest" . . .), for example, are met with scorn instead of acknowledgment. If you don't like my play on words, he quips, it is because "'tis like the breath of an unfee'd lawyer—you gave me nothing for 't." He works so hard for nothing, so underappreciated and unrecognized that he doesn't even get a name.

Come to think of it, where was the Fool in act 1, scene 1, of *Lear*? He's so full of wisdom after the fact. Where was he when a well-timed, well-said, well-intended joke could have saved the day? The least generous reading is that he didn't show up this time because he rarely wanted to exercise his jester's privilege, always had his own skin in mind, or just didn't care. The most generous reading of the Fool's absence from these critical moments, besides tiredness, sickness or age, is that he knew he would only have made things worse. Having spent such a long time with the bighearted, mistake-prone belligerence of his master, the Fool may have become too close, no longer possessed of critical distance. At such proximity, the Fool has absorbed many

2. In the lectures Foucault gave at UC Berkeley in 1983, in English, later compiled into the volume *Fearless Speech*, ed. Joseph Pearson (MIT Press, 2001), he writes: "For, as we shall see, the commitment involved in parrhesia is linked to a certain social situation, to a difference of status between the speaker and his audience, to the fact that the *parrhesiastes* says something which is dangerous to himself and thus involves a risk, and so on" (13), and "If there is a kind of 'proof' of the sincerity of the *parrhesiastes*, it is his courage. The fact that a speaker says something dangerous—different from what the majority believes—is a strong indication that he is *parrhesiastes*" (15).

of Lear's traits. We learn that he pines for Cordelia, and perhaps even clings to her, like Lear. Like Lear in too many ways, the Fool also fails to see correctly *in time*, and lacks faith *at the right moment* to speak eloquently, with the right amount of jolliness, when needed.

Under extreme political pressure the philosopher-fool disappears. I don't know why adaptations of *Lear* have killed off the Fool. It should remain painfully unclear what happens to him. The Fool, as grand entertainer, has to perform a vanishing act. Everything is moving along, and, suddenly, the person responsible for merriment and criticism is not there anymore. We just saw him a moment ago acting out a play with Lear and Edgar in the hovel. He just did a good bit there: *Oh, is that Goneril?* he exclaims: "I took you for a joint-stool." A joint-stool! Har har har. The Fool was in top form, no signs of fading.

It takes a while to notice a disappearance when things are getting bad, but one day you look up and they're gone, the comics and comedians who enlivened your days and cued your witticisms. Comedians grow old and embittered, too, become metacomical and turn into tragic historians of their own art form.

In 2011, a top-billed play called *Sorrows of Comedy* made a very brief and glorious run at the Beijing People's Art Theatre. In it, a comedic playwright wins over a one-eyed Nationalist Party censor during the Japanese occupation. In China, one of the safest ways to complain about censorship under the Communist Party's regime is to set it in the past, in the Nationalist Party's regime. The play wasn't particularly funny and offered a rather standard take on the growing censorship and suppression of the critical arts. Still, Chinese comedians saw *Sorrows of Comedy*

and winced at the danger. China's top comedic filmmaker, Feng Xiaogang, proclaimed later that year that

> The pressure of censorship on filmmakers and creators has been reinforced. The SARFT makes dubious interpretations of everything, and passes judgments on questions of principle. The required revisions have become ridiculous. . . . This stupid system is hampering cinematographic creation and thus damaging it.[3]

Feng spoke out again a couple of years later:

> A lot of times when you receive the order [from the censors], it's so ridiculous that you don't know whether to laugh or cry, especially when you know something is good and you are forced to change it into something bad.[4]

Feng's protestations are heroic and bathetic. Comedy's sorrow is that it will bend under pressure, cave to stupidity. Nothing came of this complaint, and Feng Xiaogang adapted his play to better suit the times.

In *Lear* the Fool takes his leave. He could not deal with it anymore. Let's go back to act 3, scene 6, to see what happened. "Make no noise, make no noise," says Lear to the Fool in their hovel, "Draw the curtains. So, so. We'll go to supper in the morning." This mention of supper reminds us that Lear, the Fool, Kent, and Edgar hadn't eaten anything in a long time. Lear loves his Fool, and so promises that there'll be a meal in the morning. It's an empty promise, but what can you do. "And I'll go to bed at noon," the Fool retorts (i.e., "yeah right, we'll supper in the

3. Zhuang Pinghui, "Filmmaker Rebukes Censorship," *South China Morning Post*, Sept. 1, 2011.

4. Rachel Lu, "Chinese Film Director: 'Censorship Is Torment,'" *The Atlantic*, April 18, 2013.

morning"). Or maybe he didn't say it sarcastically. Maybe it was: "I cannot *not* call out your bullshit but I say it with kindness." Perhaps he takes his job seriously. The Fool must subversively speak truth to power to the end, even if there's no one to correct anymore besides the starving and broken-hearted.

You needn't ask what happens to the Fool. He doesn't come back because his kind effectively becomes extinct by the time we finish the play. There might not be any more Kents in this world, in the short and maybe even long term. But Fools of this kind? They will have disappeared as a category.

CHAPTER FIVE

Romance

A ROMANCE, TO end things. In the conviction that teaching *King Lear* gives real caution, and in other ways, I find myself in the deepest romance of my life.

King Lear could easily be called *The Romance of King Lear*, even though Shakespeare seems to have gone out of his way to remove romance from the play. In the anonymous 1605 *King Leir*, the King of Gallia sees Cordella for the first time and finds himself caught "in such a labyrinth of love / As that I know not which way to get out." I think about this line a lot—a labyrinth of love. Shakespeare walked away from this and many other romantic opportunities in order to leave room for deeper romances.

Romanticists saw how truly romantic the play was. William Hazlitt said this about *Lear*: "The passion which [Shakespeare] has taken as his subject is that which strikes its root deepest into the human heart; of which the bond is the hardest to be unloosed." *Lear* is romantic, then, because it is about the ultimate *fang bu xia* 放不下—the ultimate expression of being unable to set something down or to let something go.

When John Keats wrote "On Sitting Down to Read *King Lear* Once Again," his mind held tight to romance. He wanted to use the poem to say goodbye to it. Goodbye, romance, you "golden-tongued . . . Syren," "shut up thine pages and be mute." Be gone so that the poet can properly take stock of *Lear*, absorb the "bitter-sweet of this Shakespearean fruit." Keats understood that romance somehow gets in the way of important understanding—she seduces and misrepresents—but he still could help it. The first half of the poem sent romance packing; the second half lapsed back into it with the abandonment of an addict.

When through the old oak forest I am gone,
Let me not wander in a barren dream,
But when I am consumed in the fire,
Give me new Phoenix wings to fly at my desire.

Lear is for people for whom love, the trial of death, and desire never die. Meet me at the end of the world, says the romantic. Nothing can part us, or part us from our deepest romances.

Fairness and absolute equality are romantic. Fairness no matter what. So is meritocracy. Meritocracy no matter what. If Marx's work had been disseminated in China alongside *Lear* we would have known that no distribution of property and land can be separated from human wants, and no human wants can be disinterested. There is always favoritism in it, of loving this more than that, which the act of spurning the favorite does nothing to hide.

I am an only child; my husband is an only child. All of our friends growing up were only children. A friend with siblings once shared a secret with me, a way to determine if someone was the favored child growing up. It's a very simple test, she said. If they respond to the question "Did your parents have a favorite?" by saying that their parents didn't play favorites, then you know that they were the favorite child, because they perceive equality as the norm.

Communism was one of China's longest romances. No amount of history or tragedy can change how much people loved this period, felt themselves to be in love. In Fang Lizhi's memoir, *The Most Wanted Man in China*, he described the regime as a discourse of love, a constant incitement to love. Maoism was mixed up with love for the country, for the kindhearted people among the struggling poor who would do anything for you, for the underdog. It championed love of the unfrivolous, of unbelievable conservation and hard work, of songs that moved from "that small matter of love between two people" to "that greater and more devout love."[1] When restaurants became themed in China in the early 2000s, the Cultural Revolution and "red culture"—*Little Red Books*, red songs, Communist outfits—was one of the themes to which people flocked. Those restaurants boomed. Villages started to shape themselves into the past. That was how Bo Xilai, the mayor of Chongqing, rose to power (before he was sacked)—by tapping into people's deepest romances. Maoism was revived in the Red Culture Movement, which encouraged people to "Sing Red songs, read classics, tell stories, spread slogans." One official (Xie Dajun) refused to involve his work unit in the movement and in the end committed suicide. To most other people, however, the campaign was inspiriting, and nostalgic. It brought back all the romantic memories of the past.

Walk through this forest once again through the genre of romance, and one sees how many people stuck with the party despite its abuses, shared in its sadnesses and exulted in its exultations. My paternal grandmother, my *nainai*, never missed a meeting, practically had a child in a field so as to not stop working. How could she, she said, when everyone else was working themselves to the bone? Toward the end, when even people

1. Fang Lizhi, *The Most Wanted Man in China: My Journey from Scientist to Enemy of the State* (Henry Holt, 2016), 64.

like them got into political trouble, my *nainai* and *yeye* spent three months hiding on a covered cot at a relative's house. The kids were not told where they were hidden and looked for their parents for months. When they were finally reunited, sick and weeping, my grandparents happily gave credit to the party for ending their separation. To this day my *nainai* will pat her chest and declare proudly, referring to herself: "If it weren't for the Communist Party there would be no Lou Suqing." Her father was a bricklayer who died young from an injury on the job. Her mother scratched out an existence with five children, subject to all the cruelties of old-world chauvinism and lawlessness. If it weren't for the party they would not have lived, my *nainai* says, nor would she have had a job, more or less equal standing in the household and in society. She poured all of her love and industriousness into the party.

People abroad took up the romance. Guided by ideological zeal, Orientalism, accelerationist fantasies, and genuine mistakes of observation, they turned China into the place where the *real* Communist revolution occurred, one undeterred by violence, mass death, and utter destruction, the place where human suffering doesn't matter that much because Chinese people suffer stoically and beautifully, which was not untrue.[2] In *Red Star over China* Edward Snow paints a rosy picture of soldiers of the

2. Alain Badiou said in an interview, "On the one hand, there is no doubt that two fundamental episodes of Mao's political struggle can be regarded as grave failures, which took a high toll in human lives: the Great Leap Forward and the Great Proletarian Cultural Revolution. And you're right in seeing in both of them a passion for the infinite real movement. But, on the other hand, these two episodes proved Mao's determination to find new ways to really move toward communism. Mao wanted a communist revolution in a socialist state. So he had to keep creating something new, keep forging ahead, keep trying, because communism is precisely the infinite that the finitude of the state, including with its brutality, is incapable of by itself." "Alain Bourdiou: 'Mao Thinks in an Almost Infinite Way,'" *Verso*, May 16, 2016, https://www.versobooks.com/blogs/news/2033-alain-badiou-mao-thinks-in-an-almost-infinite-way.

Red Army, a picture of fairness, heartiness, and diligence that I would not dispute:

> during all my travels in the Red districts I was not to see a single fist fight between Red soldiers. . . . They sang nearly all day on the road, and their supply of song was endless. Their singing was not done at a command, but was spontaneous, and they sang well. Whenever the spirit moved him, or he thought of an appropriate song, one of them would suddenly burst forth, and commanders and men joined in. They sang at night, too, and learned new folk tunes from the peasants, who brought out their Shensi guitars.
>
> What discipline they had seemed almost entirely self-imposed. When we passed wild apricot trees on the hills there was an abrupt dispersal until everyone had filled his pocket, and somebody always brought me back a handful. Then, leaving the trees looking as if a great wind had struck through them, they moved back into order and quick-timed to make up for the loss. But when we passed private orchards, nobody touched the fruit in them, and the grains and vegetables we ate in the villages were paid for in full.[3]

My parents might still be deeply in love in that world. In theory, which is to say in Romance, the women there were heroic, righteous, beautiful, and unvain. The men cared about the rights of women and the rights of men, joined revolutions, stole from the filthy rich and gave to the poor, took down corrupt officials, achieved things against all odds. In that world, love for country, love for equality, and love for one's fellow man joined in everlasting song.

Lear knew going in that distributive equality would have to be forced through a romance. For one thing, actually existing, nonimaginary assets cannot be divided *equally*. The thirds that Lear was giving out could not have been identical. The critic

3. Edward Snow, *Red Star over China* (Grove Press, 1968).

and scholar David Kastan describes the piece of land Lear had intended for Cordelia as "a third more opulent," proving from the other direction that he never intended to be fair, nor could be. There will always be portions that are more desirable. Still, Lear *was* trying to divide his land in a fair way, not everything for the favorite, but a substantial portion for everyone. Failure to produce a male heir has opened up a wonderful opportunity for a history-changing social experiment. Among three daughters we divide this land, the less deserving and more deserving all in it together. Together let's blunt-force solve the problem wherein kings grow old and can no longer govern, if they ever did govern. Let's blunt-force solve the problem where some people are objectively better than others, some far more loved than others, imbued with far more goodness and authority. Fairness is a big ask of Romance; to secure it you need a lot of make-believe, a lot of gracious letting go. The prize is great, especially for those who think of themselves as solutionsists: to secure it means finding a solution to many things all at once, a big achievement of ability and character.

In every thread of *King Lear* someone is desperately in love. It's actually a rare occurrence in Shakespeare's plays, people who are desperately in love. *Lear* is a play for the extreme romantic, then, because these people really cannot be separated.

Kent's loyalty is a solid romance. "Now, banished Kent," he says to himself, "If thou canst serve where thou dost stand condemned, / So may it come thy master, whom thou lov'st, / Shall find thee full of labours." In other words, Kent is asking himself how he can still serve, and be of good to someone, while he is wronged and condemned. He wants his beloved master to see how much he's tried, how much he's still good for. "Prithee heart, break," exclaims Kent at the end. It's not just an expression. He's referring to Lear's heart, willing it to stop: This is heartbreaking for the old man; please literally break and be done with it already. This is what becomes of the brokenhearted.

Another romantic speech: *My Cordelia, let's not cry anymore. Don't give them the pleasure.* These are Lear's parting words to Cordelia. He tells her that the "goodyears" are coming for our tears like beasts at the latch (act 5, scene 3). *Against the wolves of our times let us put on a brave face, Cordelia,* he tells her. *Let them literally devour our eyes before we shed another tear.* You can almost see why Regan goes for the eyes. "I would give my eyes" is one of the most romantic hyperboles.

Cavell takes the view that *Lear* is a literally devastating love story that must destroy the world before it can end. It must do so because so many different kinds of love are compressed into one. Extreme patriotism and fealty are mixed with extreme love of self. There's father-daughter love with a hint of incest thrown in.

As Cavell reminds us, one cannot really separate filial love from romantic love or from love of country in a Learian world. Love is so feared because it's in love's nature to show others who you really are. Love and humiliation sit quite close together. As a result, any part of a play that really puts love to the test will be painfully extreme. Lear's love for Cordelia is and isn't incestuous, says Cavell, is and isn't abusive. Their love differs from all known and accepted forms.

Like any lover, Lear needs proof of this love. He needs assurance that someone still loves him and wants daily to be with him after he's been "unreasonable, despotic, but *fondly loving*, indecent in his own expressions of preference, and blind to the indecency of his appeal for protestations of fondness" his whole life.[4] He cannot just take it on good faith. If you think you're the kind of

4. A. C. Bradley, *Shakespearean Tragedy: Lectures on "Hamlet," "Othello," "King Lear," "Macbeth"* (Macmillan, 1904).

person who doesn't need indications and assurances, try asking your loved one "Do you love me?" and see how you feel if they say, "I already told you last year." There is something wrong with the total absence of expression. Victims of organized humiliation need conspicuous praise for conspicuous feats, conspicuous demonstrations of love. Nothing means anything in private; nothing can remain unsaid.

The Fool *loved* Cordelia, and was bereft when she left. This explains Lear's complaint in act 1, scene 4, that he had not seen the Fool "these two days." Lear is informed that "Since my young lady's going into France"—that is, Cordelia's departure—"the fool hath much pined away." Two people are pining away, loving her for very similar reasons. There just isn't enough of this love to go around. They are grossly outnumbered, the kindhearted. Actually, they're not, if we measure the ratio of good people to bad people in this play. They might be outnumbered by one or two (in which camp do we count the Fool?), but it *feels* like they're greatly outnumbered, a state that greatly intensifies love and the pain of betrayal.

Why do they love Cordelia? Because she is true and kind and hasn't given up. She would seem to answer Lear's empty formality with what looks like coldness. But Lear must understand that his daughter sees through the empty formality, and that she hates it. After all, this is why he loves her. Can you stomach the empty formality to satisfy me, who loves you because you are the kind of person who cannot stomach empty formalities? Can you forgive my stunt and make a onetime exception?

Cordelia sees it, Lear sees that she sees it, everyone sees it. We all know what this is about, we just can't say it. Bradley thus sees Cordelia as every bit ensnared in the tragedy as Lear because she cannot overlook things when they most need to be overlooked:

> At a moment where terrible issues join, Fate makes on her the one demand which she is unable to meet . . . it was a

demand which other heroines of Shakespeare could have met. Without loss of self-respect, and refusing even to appear to compete for a reward, they could have made the unreasonable old King feel that he was fondly loved. Cordelia cannot, because she is Cordelia.

Love and be silent. Rest just a while in the settings favored by romantics: a downpour, a cozy hovel, the white cliffs of Dover. Here, just love and be dumb. Talk if you must, but talk about "nothing." Talk of love—love spurned, love wanted.

In a Learian world, "Love and be silent" is the only thing a person of conscience can do, and yet it is not a real option at all. You're not allowed to love and be silent. At the same time, parents understand how painful it must be if a child never wishes to express their feelings publicly, if the child seems to be withholding, and perhaps really doesn't reciprocate their love quite as deeply as they might have hoped, despite their best efforts. Parents reading *Lear* can imagine what it might feel like, extracting a judgment you'd most like to hear from someone who refuses to compromise on important matters. When the child refuses, she is making a moral judgment that is in effect an aesthetic judgment. *I don't wish to flatter you in front of others, not just because it isn't good and won't lead to good things, but also because it just looks bad. It's tacky.* In almost every rendition of *King Lear* that I've seen, of the three sisters Cordelia is played by the most beautiful actress. The aesthetic judgment is there implicitly.

Not that many people can withstand the Bartleby-esque exercise of absolute free will, the "I prefer not to" that tenders no explanation. Why are you so cold? No explanation. Why do you rebuff my advances? No explanation. Ben Marcus's 2015 short story "Cold Little Bird," about a boy who simply feels nothing for his parents, is a recent literary example of this test of faith.

Shakepeare's Cordelia is not like the boychild from "Cold Little Bird," to whose inexplicable exercise of free will is added the malaises and disaffections of contemporary culture, but she is in his vicinity.[5]

Lear asks for a specific thing and Cordelia cannot give it to him. He has hung his heart on the one person who will not openly express that love at the moment when it is most needed. Whether this is because she does not ultimately love him enough, or whether she knows that no good can come of this exception-making, has no bearing on the adjustment that we, as readers and playgoers, must make. It makes no sense to say that in the course of the play Lear finally learns which daughter is true and faithful, as he knew this all along, just as it makes no sense to believe that seeing what untruth can do will reverse the original desire.

Cordelia does love—Stephen Greenblatt calls hers "a sustaining, generous love"[6]—but what if Lear cannot wait for subsequent actions to demonstrate her fidelity? What if proof is wanted before a calamity, before it has to *come to that*? We want to know if our child, our parent, our friends and lovers will come to our assistance in our most dire moments, when we're at our most pitiful. Instead of indulging these wishes, she rips away this last, tattered fig leaf, leaving us naked before the world's assaults. If others have not begun to openly assault the one spurned but are only contemplating doing so, it is only a matter of time. Everyone now knows that that person is, for all intents

5. So much hangs on the way that Cordelia says her "nothing." I've never seen a performance or an adaptation in which Cordelia says it petulantly; the consensus seems to be that quiet restraint is best. But there's a gradation even in kind and quiet restraint. The child who does not wish to cause trouble for others says "nothing" in response to solicitude and concern ("What happened to you?" / "Nothing"). The child who risks appearing to be sullen to prevent further questioning also says nothing ("Anything interesting happen at school?" / "Nothing"). Do you have anything to say to me? I have nothing to say to you. Is everything okay? It's fine, it's nothing.

6. Notes to *The Norton Shakespeare*, 3rd edition, ed. Stephen Greenblatt.

and purposes, unloved in the way they wished to be loved. The vulnerability of love is now dead weight. "People capable of such love," writes Cavell,

> could have removed mountains; instead it has caved in upon them. One moral of such events is obvious: if you would avoid tragedy, avoid love; if you cannot avoid love, avoid integrity; if you cannot avoid integrity, avoid the world; if you cannot avoid the world, destroy it.

The life of the romantic is lived on the slipperiest of slopes. Cavell's own slippery slopes captures the all-or-nothing thinking that subtends all romance.

Cordelia is, of course, also asking for a onetime exception, for something romantic. Without losing self-respect, and without proceeding with his stupid little plans, could her parent finally be reasonable, for a change? Unreasonableness and foolishness tend to show up in those capable of excessive love, and it is extremely nice to be excessively loved. We all know that. It is extremely not nice to existentially embarrass your parents or your country, especially in front of company. Go down this path, and it becomes a public flogging of your parents and children, stripped for the act. Still, in Cordelia's mind, one must set a threshold that cannot be crossed, must self-differentiate before it is too late. And so one might as well time that defiance to the perfectly natural and ordinary departure of a daughter from the household through marriage. Not this time, says Cordelia to her father, and *especially* not in public. She, too, gives the romantics' ultimatum: Change your ways or forever goodbye.

What is romantic? A play about love shown at Christmastime. A story of mistreatment around which two people might gather, as before a fire in winter.

Someone I loved dearly once told me a story while we were in New York during a terrible snowstorm. The temperature had dropped to ten degrees below zero, making it physically impossible to walk the length of a block. Cars slid on the streets like slabs of ice. In the story, someone he knew had coordinated an excursion with several family friends to go open-water swimming in the dead of winter. They had brought along a teenage daughter, who was encouraged to join in, and who struggled alongside the adults in the icy water. When they finally emerged, the adults were clapping her on the back and encouraging her to jump in again. The girl was clearly traumatized, my friend related, and maybe even went into shock. The adults were congratulating themselves for having crafted a grown-up adventure that was not for the faint of heart, but in actuality something terrible was happening. Someone should have taken note of the girl's distress, he said, and wrapped a blanket around her.

I have a wonderful colleague whose mother died too young of cancer and whose father speedily remarried. The significantly younger stepmother made her father rid the house of everything that belonged to, or was reminiscent of, the dead mother. One day my colleague told me that she had received in the mail a boxful of her childhood awards, notebooks, and artwork. How awful, I said, that the stepmother won this battle and was able to purge the house of their memories, but how lucky that she was able at least to get back some of her possessions for safekeeping. My colleague winced and said, *Well, no, because the only meaning these things have is that there's someone who treasures them that's not you.*

She has a connection to *A Winter's Tale*, this colleague of mine. When she was twenty-one years old she was "interviewed" for an article in *Time* magazine on the life-changing experience of watching *A Winter's Tale* in the reconstructed Globe.[7] Words were put into her mouth. "I was so close I felt I was part of the action," she is supposed to have said. My colleague would never

7. Barry Hillenbrand, "Theater: A Long-Overdue Encore," *Time*, June 1997.

have said anything so aggressively banal. She took something else from *A Winter's Tale*—how twisted redemption can be for the irredeemable.

A Winter's Tale, she tells me, reworks *Lear* into the category of "late romance." The story is simple enough. A king has severely wronged his wife and children. When he realizes what he has done, Leontes sets about making amends. But it is winter. He is in the winter of his life, the winter of his mind. The king hasn't enough physical or cognitive energy left for a redemption without gross shortcuts. And so we get a bold-faced rewriting of what is possible. The wife he has murdered out of paranoia and stupidity comes back to life, as does the daughter he left for dead at infancy. They forgive him for what he's done, despite the stretches of years, the hardship and exile, and a dead son. For one person's redemption, others must abandon realism entirely. From *Lear* we walk into a fireside tale.

What is romantic is the belief that it will not have been for nothing that such things happened. That someone is watching, keeping score. That someone has been there all along and will quietly look out for everyone. A servant finally speaks up when Cornwall moves to pluck out Gloucester's second eye: "Hold your hand, my lord: / I have served you ever since I was a child, / But better service have I never done you / Than now to bid you hold." This servant goes on to kill Cornwall, but at the cost of his own life. A gentleman appears out of the blue during the storm in act 3, scene 1 to inform Kent of Lear's present circumstances. Kent, recognizing this man without naming him to us, shares critical intelligence with him: "From France there comes a power into this scattered kingdom, who already, wise in our negligence, have secret feet in some of our best ports and are at point to show their open banner." Kent informs him of the rivalry between Albany and Cornwall, who employ servant-spies who are also

French spies in disguise. He informs him of France's imminent invasion of England and orders the gentleman to go to Dover, where he will meet up with others who will take up the righteous cause. "I am a gentleman of blood and breeding," Kent tells this gentleman, and will count on his gentlemanly behavior. Another gentleman, or perhaps servant or knight, cries "Help! Help!" for Cordelia, and yet another verifies Lear's claim that he had indeed avenged her.

> LEAR: I killed the slave that was a-hanging thee.
> SECOND CAPTAIN (OR GENTLEMAN): 'Tis true, my lords, he did.

As befitting a romance, we have gentlemen to spare. This underpopulated play had not one but two gentlemen (or captains). Could this last one have witnessed Lear's killing of the guard who hung Cordelia? Or is he being careful not to extinguish all hope and so chooses to lie?

The mystery continues into Lear's last lines—"Look there, look there! He dies." Who is he referring to? A number of critical guides help explain the terrible ambiguity that the Folio, being different from the Quarto, introduces, especially for these lines. I think that Lear is trying to convince us that he delivered justice to his daughter's executioner, that he "kill'd the slave who was a-hanging [Cordelia]," and insists on it to the end. "Look there, look there! He dies" seems like a last romance.

Hope needs very little to go on and is itself a bluff. Activist-journalist Dai Qing closed out her introduction to *Wang Shiwei and "Wild Lilies"* with a very romantic fantasy:

> Probably, on some day in the future a little girl in Shiyan will be honored for her outstanding performance in dancing or singing. Upon receiving a certificate of merit, she will come

> across the name of a man whose life and death and the struggle after his death will be unknown to her. In actuality, that was the ugliest nightmare in human history—the smothering of dignity and freedom of thought in the name of revolution. The nightmare started when Wang Shiwei, the stranger, was persecuted; the announcement of his wrongful persecution could be the beginning of the end of this nightmare.

I keep these lines close. Dai Qing wrote this in 1992, one year after her imprisonment for her involvement in the Tiananmen Square protests, something in which she involved herself after she was radicalized by her reporting on the Three Gorges Dam. I am moved by her fantasy that such a little girl exists, that such a school exists, and that it would award such a prize to her. In this fantasy of future reparations, meritocracy works. Symbolic gestures—a trophy, an award—will help us find our way back to historical truth. It's Dai Qing's equivalent of Cordelia's bluff. "Time shall unfold what plighted cunning hides. / Who cover faults, at last shame them derides."

Romantics believe that the arc of time bends toward justice, that people of the future will see the letters we've sent to them and make things right.

In the month that I was born, the city of Hangzhou had just entered *xiaoxue* 小雪, the twentieth segment of the twenty-four solar terms. There's *shuangjiang* 霜降, "hoar-frost"; *lidong* 立冬, "the instatement of winter"; *xiaoxue* 小雪, "light snow"; *daxue* 大雪, "heavy snow"; *dongzhi* 冬至, "winter solstice"; *xiaohan* 小寒, "slight chill." The solar term "light snow" never corresponded with the onset of snow, at least not south of the Yangtze, and there was always plenty of time before the "great chill."

My first memory of a movie theater in China was going to see a Taiwanese film called *Mama, Love Me Once Again*, later released under the English title *My Beloved*. In it, a young mother has to give up a child that she has out of wedlock. At first she is left alone to raise the boy, which she does beautifully, despite great hardship. Soon enough, the family that rejected this woman because of her class status learns that their new daughter-in-law is sterile. They resort to material then psychological bribery to gain custody of the boy, and they succeed. The boy is wrenched from his mother. Only five or six years old, he travels the length of Taipei to return to her, is sent back, and chances it again. The boy is inconsolable. He refuses to be assimilated by his new family members, who are loving only as a function of leading a very comfortable life, but he is a good boy, so he eats the delicious foods that his well-dressed grandpa and grandma place into his bowl. He looks at his bowl of rice like a bowl of snow.

We stepped into that movie, my mother and I, into its skies of tungsten and drizzle, its view cameras and woolens, its 1980s hair and giant stuffed animals, and children and mothers getting down on their hands and knees to beg adults for permission to keep the things that belonged to them. Just that summer we had to prostrate ourselves because my uncle—my mother's eldest brother—had rifled through our papers and hidden our documents, thus freezing our US visa applications. She had grabbed his sleeve, tearing it at the cuff. People hid things from each other all the time: a piece of clothing that a husband didn't like his wife to wear, a present from another relative. Above all, they went after each other's papers.

Less than a punishment or a retaliation, these incidents were born out of a perverse commitment to behavioral conditioning, in the belief that by repeatedly deforming other people's reality, getting them to think *I know I put it here* at all hours of the day—they might get them to finally concede that they don't know what's best for themselves. We begged each other in this blindness of the years, the children stupidly repeating the parents' wheedling for exceptions and for clemency. In the movie, the son is reunited with his mother years later, too late, in a home for the insane. She is still clutching his toy panda, her love so great that we wince.

Every person in China knew the lyrics to the theme song in *Mama, Love Me Once Again* and the simple choreography that went with it. Kids put up their thumbs for the lines "in all of the world only Mama is best" and held themselves in an embrace for the line "to be in her arms again." Besides my cousin, my mother was my abiding love in those years right before we emigrated, the person into whom I threw almost all of my energy and enterprise, the city of Hangzhou just a pretext for our daily life together.

It was a love "incapable of being chilled by injury," her own or others'. My mother made a "broadcasting station" in the corner of our room from where I was to practice being a news anchor or a diplomat in the UN. She daily balked at anything that combined old callousness with the obsequious transactionalism of the new era. She would ask me: Why should the peach seller be held responsible for the flavor of his fruit and ask for the forgiveness of the customer, as it often came to pass in China, as though he were morally reprehensible if it turned out not to be sweet enough, if the skin wasn't thin enough, or if it bruised too easily? I remember being taken by my mother to see the ice carvings at Wulin Square during "Major Chill," the coldest of the twenty-four Chinese solar divisions, with yesteryear's cotton quilts stitched inside new jackets. Students wore blue-and-white uniforms and Communist red neckerchiefs, crowding around the Soviet-style plaster sculptures of Chinese maidens in the music fountain. I remember the brightness of the square and the traffic of bicycles and automobiles in all directions. My mother told me how far the ice had to travel to reach our southern city, how it was lifted out of the slowest-moving parts of a tributary of the Amur River, cut from where the frozen water is densest and clearest, the sediments having sifted down to the riverbed, and that in our enthusiasms we may have overlooked someone in the darkest quarters of life.

In the colorless buildings of the No. 14 High School, where she taught, and in our sunless living quarters, she was always doing something fun and important, instilling in everyone a sense of high adventure and romance. Her students, each having chosen literary English names like Silas, Kent, or Tess, would rush up the stairwells to salute the snow-gray of the morning. My mother reformed them all: the boy who set fire to his classmate's hair, the boy who filled boxes of raisins with dried boogers, the girls who cornered each other in the lavatories. She deconditioned the maliciousness that cinched them like a noose and got everyone singing Karen Carpenter's "The End of the World." I remember the class in unison. In singing, we kept our appointments with loved ones in a long and tasseled dream.

Though *Lear* deliberately kept romantic love out, as if to control for something, its deepest layers overlap with Shakespeare's most famous romance.

Romeo and Juliet was likely the first Shakespeare play fully translated and performed in China, probably the second or third story I'd ever heard. It appealed to our penchant for fanatic love and poetic self-killing. My mother loved it, as she loved the idea that people could die for romantic love. Dying for romantic love was a reprieve from dying for ideological love.

Like *Lear*, *Romeo and Juliet* is a romance of human sacrifice. What will it take to resolve the problem we have on our hands? We have two houses, alike in dignity, in fair Verona, where we lay our scene. Alike in dignity is the key stipulation; otherwise, the problem would be far easier to solve. It has to be solved and it needs to be solved now, in the span of one generation, without the aid of the supernatural, without divine intervention. There is a friar in *Romeo and Juliet*, but no mention of heaven or hell, or any state after death. Everything that happens must happen on earth. You must work with what you have.

Romeo and Juliet takes the pagan belief that only human sacrifice will assuage intractable curses and turns it into a civic lesson. The management of the city-state of Verona requires the death of a young boy and of a young girl. This is an ancient formula for the absolution of sins, a paganism that the play passes off as free love. *Lear* makes even more pagan sacrifices—it outromanticizes *Romeo Juliet* on this score: if something truly precious is laid waste, maybe you will all learn a lesson. Upon such sacrifices even the gods themselves throw incense.

As a rather romantic person, I am taken aback by how many people default to romantically nihilistic readings of *Lear*—that it all means nothing, and the gods just kill us for their sport. It's true that everything that happens in the play happens in a pre-Christian England, a time that is traditionally seen in the West as one awaiting salvation. The play's overlap in words with the book of Job and the Gospel of Luke locks its sufferers in both the horror of the Old Testament and the horror of the New. Sinners are subjected to the hands of an angry Old Testament God, someone who, in his blind anger, acts too indiscriminately or too severely. To make matters worse, the landscape distinctly registers the empty chill of the New Testament world. These characters are alone and endangered in a Christlike way, moving strangely between the city outskirts and the seat of a bloodthirsty and punitive state power. It feels like a human sacrifice caught between two systems of signification, one ancient, one postmodern. As such, every crisis of faith has been rolled into one, and we get a deep, deep romance.

In Lear's last romance, hope can seem like it comes down to virtue's malleability. If Cordelia is a Christ figure, she is, like Christ himself, too cryptically withholding, too gnomic in her speech, wishing to say no more than what needs to be said. The romance of pliancy is, of course, that Cordelia may change a little, mend her speech but a little, stop emulating Christ, just a little.

It's easy to get carried away by a romantic thought. A student's paper reminds me it's simply not true that Cordelia does not budge. She is asked to mend her speech. She does mend her speech, lest she "mar" her fortunes. She does not wish to mar her fortunes any more than you wish to mar your fortunes, or I to mar mine, but that is not why she mends her speech. She tries again: *Let me find another way to reason with you, as I cannot give you up.* This is even more romantic than the idea of feminine flexibility: the idea here, more stubbornly planted, is that no insanity and cruelty can be completely closed off to reason, that something can always be coaxed back from the point of no return.

We're in a schoolroom, faced with one of the simplest pedagogical diagrams—a pie chart. *Lear* is the wrong way to learn what thirds are. After the upset, what was once supposed to be divided into thirds is now halved; each half retains an extra sixth of the original whole, a sixth to which they are not entitled. A bit involved but not difficult, math-wise. A child can see how it works and follow along. If this kid can see the concept of "thirds" in fractions, a cognitive step above halves, then he can begin to learn the more complicated relations between things. He can advance.

A math problem that doesn't quite work out is still a math problem. I cannot help but look at things practically. If we have a clear explanation of what happened, step by step, we can have a solution, and no matter how childish or politically naive the idea of a real solution or satifying explanation sounds in our postmodern times. The wrongly accused first say, "Let me explain [myself]." Upon realizing that they're being targeted for persecution, and that explanation doesn't matter at all, they still say, "Let me explain [the world]."

The most romantic part of this story is literary-critical: The child believes that she can figure it out for herself, sift irreparable damages from reparative ones, rescue love from nastiness. Let's say that your parent, your state, your sovereign, is being abusive. They falsely accuse you or others of inane offenses, or they force you to accept objectively foolish and illogical accounts and plans. They ask you to accept wrong as right, to pretend to love when you really do love. They overpower your protestations with their truly frightening rage—a rage that's maddeningly shy of sublime. We assess the pageantries of false praise and demanded acknowledgment, the casual cruelties of abandoning people outside to their own devices, the mistreated animals, the failed pet projects, and try to be as equanimous as possible, rendering blame unto the right parties, including ourselves and truly superhuman forces, so that at least we can secure a fair distribution of blame.

Some parents and states are, of course, truly abusive—Gonerils and Regans who profess boundless love but give no real time or attention, merely hiding inside clichés. Your treasures are worthless to them. Why throw away just one thing? Why not ten? Or twenty? Put a child in solitary confinement for an hour? Why not four? Or eight? One cannot ever hope to *show* these parents because, alas, they have already shown you. On the other hand there is the parent who has placed the onus of fixing the world on their children, who has, to the best of their abilities, set up the conditions of that forbearance, who is a flawed and pitiable teacher struggling with trying to live decently in a wrong and junk-littered world: these parents cause real suffering, too, but there is a world of difference.

In their gut, the child already knows this dilemma: How much should I reason with this abuse? Love causes her to hesitate. She cannot figure out if drawing attention to the illogical part of it all is even the right thing to do. Sensing that the parent's violent action betrays some fatal disproportion, some beseeching ridiculousness, she makes a judgment call. Letting it go is not right, and calling the authorities is not right. She can't explain what happened. Sometimes it's only minutes, just a few exchanges, and yet the fast-paced illogicality and compression of history, the whiplash of rage, prevent any kind of real reconstruction. She is, therefore, reassessing the situation—with assistance. She is replaying it in her head by rereading it on the page. There's something glitchy here, something *Lear*-like, something unmethodical. Foolish and extreme at the same time, the parent, the teacher, the institution, the country have all given themselves no easy way out, no face-saving way to retract a statement or stay their hand. This is what raises your awareness in the first instance.

It's not hard math. In the simplest, most straightforward layers of this abuse—in the one, two, threes, as it were—there's something goofy going on. You weren't the brightest child, perhaps, but you paid attention to some goofy things and not other goofy things. And most of all, you paid attention to the clues that let you know that, even amid endless wrongness, some summaries of wrongnesses raise enough questions to merit a second pass.

Let's look at Edgar's (or Albany's) final pronouncement again.

> The weight of this sad time we must obey
> Speak what we feel, not what we ought to say.
> The oldest hath borne most. We that are young
> Shall never see so much, nor live so long.

These verses are truly very lovely, like a doleful wind that sweeps the fields. The second line of this parting speech interrupts the singsongy iambic pentameter with somber dactyls. Meter tells us about the soul of the speaker, and Edgar is true. When he makes a speech or gives instruction, it comes from the heart. The speech gives credit where credit is due, even if the accomplishment is the accomplishment of bearing the worst. Take heart and have pity because the worst really is over. The elderly did absorb that blow on our behalf.

Pedagogy needs romance to work, and yet it also has to work against romance, to make the most romantic lessons about suffering curious upon reflection. Edgar's last lines should be read straight, even if they don't quite check out: The weight of this sad time we must obey. I don't know what it means to obey a weight, even figuratively, but I obey as a child obeys. Something should feel burdensome in sad times. We should speak what we feel, not what we ought to say. What we feel is not just feelings, of course, but what we really ought to say. I think it's true that *the oldest hath borne most*, and *we that are young shall never see so much*, or will have to live so long, to have to experience life as something that will not end.

Edgar wants what I want, what every romantic wants: for things to end beautifully, first to last. From Wang Shiwei's first suspicion that something was wrong to this moment in time. Edgar (or Albany) and I would like to make a speech to the few who are left. It is a bad speech, but it's also a profoundly good one, because it makes us go back and check. This is Romance's romantic self-redemption. Having gotten to the play's vespers, to the part that we hear before we say good night, we see that we must rouse ourselves and go over it again. In this small but lasting kindness, romance leads us back to loyal-hearted skepticism, to reason's first morning.

ACKNOWLEDGMENTS

NOT QUITE IN the order in which gifts were received:

To my grandfather, for writing his book, and for his staggering memory. To my parents, for their integrity. To my godparents, for their great and unexpected love.

To Jesse Landers, the chair of the department at the University of Notre Dame at the time when I started this project, for putting up with me and for pointing me in the right direction, *Lear*-wise. To my colleague Peter Holland for his *Lear* and for our discussions of Kozintsev. To Ian Newman for Edgar's "What kind of help?" and other ingenious observations and much-needed levity. To Kate Marshall for the warmth of her friendship and her long winter's tale. To Hye-jin Juhn, then East Asian librarian at the University of Notre Dame, for helping me and helping me again. To Alan Thomas, who pointed me to the best sources on Holinshed, Coleridge, and tragedy. To Tom Howard, for the first read-through, and for bringing home the idea that inarticulacy is a fate worse than death, and Matt Hunter, for the second read-through, and for again bringing home the idea that inarticulacy is a fate worse than death. To Emily Howard for teaching me how to fallow the field and understand literature and love. To Rachel Feder, who saw this story first, and who always got to things first, a kind and intelligent Goneril for a Regan to copy. To Jane Hu, who sat with me in the stocks and provided life-saving humor and criticism throughout. To Rebecca Porte for her incomparable grasp of Cordelia's predicament. To Jennifer Lyons for reading and encouraging the manuscript and Anne Savarese for the painstaking edits. To James Collier, Natalie Baan, Susan Clark, Kathleen Strattan, Chris Ferrante, and anonymous readers for Princeton

University Press, and to my copyeditor, Anne Cherry, who worked the penultimate miracles, and whose sign-off, the cerise heart of "A. Cherry," is the best possible sign-off for a book on *Lear*.

BIBLIOGRAPHY

CHINESE HISTORY AND *King Lear* each brings a thicket of citations. I am not a textual scholar or a historian. There is nothing in textual scholarship like the "text" of *King Lear*, nothing in historiography like contemporary Chinese history. Among Shakespeare's plays *King Lear*'s various versions have generated academic high jinks and intense animosity. People have lost their minds and careers over *Lear*'s irreconcilable versions. Half the time we'll have to place our hopes on Albany, and half the time on Edgar, as if they were actually interchangeable? Wrapping up this play the playwright remembers the way a particularly cruel comedian remembers. The readers are dropped into act 1, scene 1, in the middle of a ridiculous predicament—not knowing the difference between an Albany and a Cornwall. Because of the ridiculous discrepancies of the text the readers are forced to accept a similar predicament at the end, permanently.

Aside from all of the discrepant versions I discuss in "Tales" and "History," there is also the matter of the discrepancy itself. How to describe what's different between Quarto and Folio and the Conflated version? The introduction to the Arden *King Lear* explains it best, but even it cannot say it succinctly. The Quarto and the Folio each has lines that the other does not and makes cuts that do not quite accord with those added lines. And that's not all: the Quarto has two versions, Q1 and Q2, and contemporary scholars have assembled a combined text, which also introduces troubling ambiguities (see Gary Taylor and Michael Warren, *The Division of the Kingdoms: Shakespeare's Two Versions of "King Lear"* [Clarendon Press, 1983], Brian Vickers, *The One "King Lear"* [Harvard University Press, 2016], Grace Ippolo, *Revising Shakespeare* [Harvard University Press, 1992], Steven Urkowitz, *Shakespeare's Revision of "King Lear"* [Princeton

University Press, 2014]). Which version of *Lear* should you stage or read or use to teach or conduct scholarship? Each difference contains significant information and so at no point is it safe to assume that what needs to be seen would be seen by *everyone*. Discrepant versions are inherently disconcerting, but it feels even more so for this play, where so much hangs on the smallest evidence. A safe outcome can always be reversed, and things are always open to revisionism.

The Chinese government practices a variety of revisionisms, each more complicated than the one before it. Still, it is not true that the average young person in China doesn't know about the Cultural Revolution, or Tiananmen Square, or Xinjiang, or that there are as many instances of file deletion, image alteration, or changing the record as people think. There is a huge volume of extant critical data and recordkeeping, and I have endeavored to point to major works here.

The following are bibliographic notes. Two obvious disclaimers: there is historically significant *Lear* scholarship that I have not mentioned here, such as Charlotte Lennox, "The Fable of the *Tragedy of King Lear*"; G. Wilson Knight, *The Wheel of Fire*; Northrop Frye, "'King Lear,'" in *Northrop Frye on Shakespeare*; Kenneth Muir's introductory essay for the 1986 Penguin Critical Edition of *Lear*; William Empson's discussions of *Lear* in *Seven Types of Ambiguity* and *The Structure of Complex Words*; W. H. Auden, *Lectures on Shakespeare*; and the 1982 volume of essays *On "King Lear,"* edited by Lawrence Danson.

China and *Lear* have been treated in Dongshin Chang and Alexa Alice Joubin, "A Confucian *King Lear* in Shanghai, 1995," in *Sinophone Adaptations of Shakespeare: An Anthology 1987–2007* (2022); Emily Sun, *Succeeding "King Lear": Literature, Exposure, and the Possibility of Politics* (2010); Xiao Yang Zhang, "The Chinese Vision of Shakespeare (1950–1990): Marxism and Socialism," collected in *Shakespeare in the World of Communism and Socialism*, ed. Irena Makaryk and Joseph G. Price (University of Toronto Press, 2006); Shuhua Wang, "From Maoism to (Post) Maoism: Hamlet in Communist China," in Makaryk and Price, eds., *Shakespeare in the World of Communism and Socialism*; Qi-Xin He, "China's Shakespeare," *Shakespeare Quarterly* 37, no. 2 (July 1986):149–59.

1. Tales

This author recommends both of Stephen Orgel's introductory essays in the Pelican *King Lear* (Combined Text); Stephen Greenblatt's introduction to *King Lear* in *The Norton Shakespeare*; and David Bevington and David Scott Kastan's introduction to *King Lear* in their *Four Tragedies: Hamlet, Prince of Denmark, Othello, the Moor of Venice, King Lear, Macbeth* (Bantam, 1980; reissued 2005) to get started. These essays combine commentary on plot and character with relevant contextual historical information; they also give a solid overview of the differences between the Quarto and Folio versions.

Samuel Taylor Coleridge makes his observation about the division of the kingdom in his *Essays and Lectures on Shakespeare and Some Other Old Poets and Dramatists*, given around 1818, published in 1907 (Turnbull and Spears, Edinburgh).

> It was not without forethought, nor is it without its due significance, that the division of Lear's kingdom is in the first six lines of the play stated as a thing already determined in all its particulars, previously to the trial of professions, as the relative rewards of which the daughters were to be made to consider their several portions . . . [these facts] let us know that the trial is but a trick: and that the grossness of the old king's rage is in part the natural result of a silly trick suddenly and most unexpectedly baffled and disappointed.

The corroborating lines from A. C. Bradley's *Shakespearean Tragedy: Lectures on "Hamlet," "Othello," "King Lear," "Macbeth"* (London, Macmillan, 1904):

> The very first words of the drama, as Coleridge pointed out, tell us that the division of the kingdom is already settled in all its details, so that only the public announcement of it remains. Later we find that the lines of division have already been drawn on the map of Britain (l. 38) and again that Cordelia's share, which is her dowry, is perfectly well known to Burgundy, if not to France (ll. 197, 245). That then which is censured as absurd, the dependence of the division on the speeches on the daughters, was in Lear's intention a mere form, devised as a childish scheme to gratify his love of absolute power and his hunger for assurances of devotion.

Stanley Cavell's line that Cordelia is asked to pretend to love when she does love appears in the essay "The Avoidance of Love: A reading of *King Lear*," collected in *Must We Mean What We Say* (Cambridge University Press, 1969) and again in *Disowning Knowledge in Seven Plays by Shakespeare* (Cambridge University Press, 1987). The Samuel Johnson remarks on Lear that appear in this book are from his notes to his edition of *Lear* and from his *Preface to Shakespeare*, published in 1765. Sigmund Freud's essay "The Theme of the Three Caskets" is published in *The Standard Edition of the Complete Psychological Works of Sigmund Freud*, trans. James Strachey, Vol. 12 (Hogarth Press, 1958).

On the Chinese tradition of the *juemingci* (suicide poem) and, more broadly, the tradition of writing lyrics in exile, see David R. Knechtges and Taiping Wang, *Ancient and Early Medieval Chinese Literature, A Reference Guide* (Vol. 3. has an entry for Xifu Gong and the first *juemingci*) (Brill, 2014) and François Cheng, *Chinese Poetic Writing* (Indiana University Press translation, 1982).

Shakespeare's arrival in China has to be pieced together. The best resource is a Chinese-language article by Luo Xi 罗昕 writing for the magazine *Peng Pai* 澎湃 called "晚清民国时期的莎士比亚中文版都长啥样? [What Did Late Qing Chinese Versions of Shakespeare Look Like?]" (https://www.thepaper.cn

/newsDetail_forward_1458861, 4-20-2016). *Lamb's Tales from Shakespeare* produced two early Chinese adaptations. *Xiewai qitan* 澥外奇譚 was published anonymously in 1903 by Shanghai's Dawen Publishing House. In 1904 Shanghai Commercial Press published Lin Shu and Wei Yi's 吟邊燕語 [An English Poet Reciting from Afar]. Eighteen years later they published a more direct translation of Charles and Mary Lamb's *Tales*. Shakespeare's journey to China before and after the Civil War is surveyed in Emily Sun, "Shakespearean Retellings and the Question of the Common Reader: Charles and Mary Lamb's *Tales from Shakespeare* and Lin Shu's *Yinbian Yanyu*," chap. 2 in Sun's *On the Horizon of World Literature: Forms of Modernity in Romantic England and Republican China* (Fordham University Press, 2022); and Yun-Fang Dai, "'I should like to have my name talked of in China': Charles Lamb, China, and Shakespeare," *Multicultural Shakespeare: Translation, Appropriation and Performance* 20, no. 35 (2019): 83–97. Lin Shu and Wei Yi's *Yinbian Yanyu* isn't available in translation, but English readers can consult Alexa Alice Joubin, *Chinese Shakespeares: Two Centuries of Cultural Exchange* (Columbia University Press, 2009) and Michael Gibbs Hill, *Lin Shu, Inc.: Translation and the Making of Modern Chinese Culture* (Oxford University Press, 2012). On the translation practices and lives of early-twentieth-century Chinese Shakespeare scholars Sun Dayu, Zhu Shenghao, Bian Zhilin, Liang Zongdai, and others, see: Andrew Dickson, *Worlds Elsewhere: Journeys around Shakespeare's Globe* (Henry Holt and Co., 2015); Xiaoyang Zhang, *Shakespeare in China: A Comparative Study of Two Traditions and Cultures* (University of Delaware Press, 1996); Murray J. Levith, *Shakespeare in China* (Bloomsbury, 2015); Ruru Li, *Shashibiaya: Staging Shakespeare in China* (Hong Kong University Press, 2003); Qi-Xin He, "China's Shakespeare," *Shakespeare Quarterly* 37, no. 2, (July 1986): 149–59; Tonglin Lu, "Zhu Shenghao: Shakespeare Translator and a Shakespearean Tragic Hero in Wartime China," *Comparative*

Literature Studies 49, no. 4 (December 2012): 521–36; Hsiao-yen Peng, *Modern China and the West: Translation and Cultural Mediation* (Brill, 2014); Xu Tian, "The Lonely Bian Zhilin (徐天, "寂寞卞之琳")," *News China* (中国新闻周刊), June 27, 2022 (Issue 1049); Yuenian Huang (黃岳年), 弱水讀書記: 當代書林擷英 [Weak Water Reading: Essence from Contemporary Books] (秀威出版 Qiu Wei chubanshe, 2009); Renfang Tang, "Chinese Shakespeares: An Intercultural Study of Adaptations across Performance Genres," PhD dissertation, University of Hull, 2016; Xueying Kong, "Change and Un-change: Bian Zhilin's Struggles in the War Time, 1937–1958" (master's thesis, The Ohio State University, 2016). On the life of Sun Dayu, the most persecuted of the Shakespearean scholars: The cancellation of Shakespeare under Maoism can be found in many of the sources on Shakespeare in China and more specifically in Robert Guillain's *When China Wakes* (Walker Press, 1966).

2. History

For critical and scholarly overviews of *Lear*'s relationship to its historical sources (Geoffrey Monmouth's *History of the Kings of Britain*, John Higgins's *Mirror for Magistrates*, Raphael Holinshed's *Chronicles of England, Scotland, and Ireland*, Philip Sidney's *Arcadia*, and the anonymous 1605 play, *The True Chronicle History of King Leir, and his three daughters, Gonoril, Ragan, and Cordella*, and others): Wilfrid Perrett, *The Story of "King Lear" from Geoffrey Monmouth to Shakespeare* (Mayer and Müller, 1904); Harriet Archer, *Unperfect Histories: The "Mirror for Magistrates": 1559–1610* (Oxford University Press, 2017); Scott C. Lucas's introduction in *"Mirror for Magistrates": A Modernized and Annotated Edition* (Cambridge University Press, 2019); Annabel Patterson, *Reading Holinshed's "Chronicles"* (University of Chicago Press, 1994); Philip Schwyzer, *Literature, Nationalism, and Memory in Early Modern England and Wales* (Cambridge University Press, 2004); Lynne Bradley, *Adapting Shakespeare for the Stage* (Taylor and Francis, 2016);

Helen Cooper, *The English Romance in Time: Transforming Motifs from Geoffrey of Monmouth to the Death of Shakespeare* (Oxford University Press, 2014); Lloyd Edward Kermode's essay "*King Leir* within the Thicket: Gender, Place, and Power," *Renaissance and Reformation/Renaissance et Réforme* 35, no. 1 (Winter 2012): 65–84; John E. Curran Jr., "Geoffrey of Monmouth in Renaissance Drama: Imagining Non-History," *Modern Philology* 97, no. 1 (August 1999): 1–20. Internet Shakespeare Editions (https://internetshakespeare.uvic.ca/Library/Texts/Lr/index.html) provides full texts of *Lear*'s sources and some adaptations, such as Nahum Tate's version. Songs and rhymes inspired by *Lear* can be found in the University of California at Santa Barbara's English Broadside Ballad Archive (https://ebba.english.ucsb.edu/). David Kastan, *Shakespeare and the Shapes of Time* (Palgrave Macmillan, 1982) offers a sharp meditation on *Lear* and the representational logics of historiography.

Readings of *Lear* in its own historical milieu (James I, the Plague, and the English Civil War): James Shapiro, *1606: Shakespeare and the Year of "Lear"* (Faber and Faber, 2016), from which this book greatly benefits; Christopher Wortham, "Shakespeare, James I and the Matter of Britain," *English: Journal of the English Association* 45, no. 182 (Summer 1996): 97–122; Gary Taylor, "Forms of Opposition: Shakespeare and Middleton," *English Literary Renaissance* 24, no. 2, Studies in Shakespeare (Spring 1994): 283–314; *"King Lear" and Its Afterlife*, ed. Peter Holland (Cambridge University Press, 2002); and *A Routledge Literary Sourcebook on William Shakespeare's "King Lear,"* ed. Grace Ippolo (Routledge, 2003). On *Lear* and other totalitarianisms and relevant political/ideological readings of *Lear*: Peter Holbrook, "The Left and *King Lear*," *Textual Practice* 14, no. 2 (2000): 343–62; Tiffany Ann Conroy Moore, *Kozintsev's Shakespeare Films: Russian Political Protest in "Hamlet" and "King Lear"* (McFarland, 2012); the chapter entitled "The Birth of the Totalitarian State in the Tragedy of King Lear," in Ava Zilberfain, *Stealing the Story: Shakespeare's Self-Conscious Use of the*

Mimetic Tradition in the Tragedies (Bloomsbury, 2007); Richard Ashby, *"King Lear" "after" Auschwitz: Shakespeare, Appropriation and Theatres of Catastrophe in Post-war British Drama* (Edinburgh University Press, 2020); Leah S. Marcus, "Retrospective: *King Lear* on St. Stephen's Night, 1606" in *Puzzling Shakespeare: Local Reading and Its Discontents* (University of California Press, 1988); Stephen Greenblatt, "Shakespeare and the Exorcists" in *Literary Theory: an Anthology*, ed. Julie Rivkin and Michael Ryan (Blackwell, 1998).

For a comprehensive history of twentieth-century China and Maoism, I recommend Frank Dikötter, *A People's Trilogy 1962–1976: Mao's Great Famine, The Tragedy of Liberation*, and *The Cultural Revolution.* Histories I consulted include: Roderick MacFarquhar and Michael Schoenhals, *Mao's Last Revolution* (Harvard University Press, 2008); Song Yongyi, *Mao Zedong he Wenhua Dageming: Zhengzhi xinli yu wenhua jiyin de xinchanshi* [Mao Zedong and the Cultural Revolution: A New Interpretation from Perspectives of Political Psychology and Cultural Gene] (Lianjing chubanshe, 2021) and his "Chronology of Mass Killings during the Chinese Cultural Revolution (1966–1976)," *Mass Violence and Résistance* (SciencesPo, 2011); Chang-tai Hung, *Politics of Control: Creating Red Culture in the Early People's Republic of China* (University of Hawaii Press, 2021); Ma Jisen, *Wai jiao bu wen ge jishi* [The Cultural Revolution in the Foreign Ministry] (The Chinese University Press, 2005); Tania Branigan, *Red Memory: Living, Remembering and Forgetting China's Cultural Revolution* (Faber and Faber, 2023); Stanley Karnow, *Mao and China: A Legacy of Turmoil* (Penguin, 1990); Yang Jisheng, *Tombstone: The Great Chinese Famine, 1958–1962* and his *The World Turned Upside Down: A History of the Chinese Cultural Revolution*, both translated by Stacy Mosher and Guo Jian and edited by Edward Friedman (Farrar, Straus and Giroux, 2013, 2021); Jie Li, *Utopian Ruins: A Memorial Museum of the Mao Era* (Duke University Press, 2020); Lingchei Letty Chen, *Great Leap Backwards: Forgetting and Representing the Mao Years* (Cambria, 2020); Helen Zia, *Last Boat Out of Shanghai: The Epic Story of the Chinese Who Fled Mao's Revolution* (Ballatine, 2020); Gao Hua, *How the Red Sun Rose: The Origin and Development of the Yan'an Rectification Movement, 1930–1945*, trans. Stacy Mosher and Guo Jian (Chinese University of Hong Kong Press, 2019); Jung Chang and Jon Halliday, *Mao: The Unknown Story* (Anchor, 2011); Lian Xi, *Blood Letters: The Untold Story of Lin Zhao, a Martyr in Mao's China* (Basic Books, 2018). Gregory Benton's newly released translation of Wang Fanzhi's *Mao Zedong Thought* and his edited volume *Prophets Unarmed: Chinese Trotskyists in Revolution, War, Jail, and the Return from Limbo* (Brill, 2015) detail the purge of early Communist leaders like Chen Duxiu who were branded Trotskyites. Chen Duxiu's life is chronicled in Lee Feigon, *Chen Duxiu, Founder of the Chinese Communist Party* (Princeton University Press, 1983); and Xiaomei Chen, "Fifty Years of Staging a Founding Father: Political Theater, Dramatic History and the Question of Representation," in *Representing the Past: Essays on Performance Historiography*, ed. Charlotte M. Canning and Thomas Postlewait (University of Iowa Press, 2010). See also Gregory Benton, *Chen Duxiu's Last Articles and Letters, 1937–1942* (University of Hawaii Press, 1998) and Israel Epstein, *Woman in World History: Soong Ching Ling* (Foreign Language Press, 2004).

Intimate historical overviews can be found in Ji Xianlin, *The Cowshed: Memories of the Chinese Cultural Revolution*, trans. Chenxin Jiang (NYRB 2016); Zhang Yihe, *Wangshi bing buru yan* [Past Events Do Not Vanish Like Smoke] (Shi Bao Press, 2004); Ma Bo, *Blood Red Sunset: A Memoir of the Chinese Cultural Revolution*, trans. Howard Goldblatt (Viking, 1995); Ai Weiwei, *1000 Years of Joys and Sorrows*, trans. Allan H. Barr (Crown, 2021); Jung Chang, *Wild Swans: Three Daughters of China* (Simon and Schuster, 2003); Jan Wong, *Politics of Control: Creating Red Culture in the Early People's Republic of China* (Anchor, 1997); Nien Cheng's *Life and Death in Shanghai*

(Grove, 2010); Joshua Zhang and James D. Wright, *Violence, Periodization and Definition of the Cultural Revolution: A Case Study of Two Deaths by the Red Guards* (Brill, 2017). The story of Zhang Hongbing and his atonement for his mother's death is told in *The Guardian* and many other newspapers in 2013, and again in the *Global Times China* in March of 2016.

On the lead-up to and the aftermath of the pro-democracy student protests and Tiananmen Square Massacre: Perry Link and Wu Dazhi, *I Have No Enemies: The Life and Legacy of Liu Xiaobo* (Columbia University Press, 2023); Julian Gerwitz, *Never Turn Back: China and the Forbidden History of the 1980s* (Harvard University Press, 2022); Margaret Hillenbrand, *Negative Exposures: Knowing What Not to Know in Contemporary China* (Duke University Press, 2020); Yiyang Ding, *Chinese Democracy after Tiananmen* (Columbia University Press, 2002); Jeremy Brown, *June Fourth: The Tiananmen Protests and the Beijing Massacre of 1989* (Cambridge University Press, 2021); Liao Yiwu, *Bullets and Opium: Real-Life Stories of China after the Tiananmen Square Massacre*, trans. David Cowhig, Jessie Cowhig, and Ross Perlin (One Signal, 2020). See Jeffrey Wasserstrom's discussion of *Lear*'s role in the student protests and their aftermaths in "History, Myth, and the Tales of Tiananmen," in *Popular Protest and Political Culture in Modern China*, ed. Jeffrey Wasserstrom and Elizabeth Perry (Taylor and Francis, 2018). I drew the most from Louisa Lim, *People's Republic of Amnesia: Tiananmen Revisited* (Oxford University Press 2014); and Guoxiang Wang, "Beida mingzhu yundong yishi [Documenting the Democratic Movement at Peking University]," in *Yuanshang cao: jiyi zhong de fanyoupai yundong*, ed. Niu Han and Deng Jiuping. The best depiction of trauma and suppression in the years leading up to the pro-Democracy movement is a work of fiction—Yiyun Li's *The Vagrants* (Random House, 2009).

On Maoism's origins in the mobilization and infrastructure of mass health campaigns: the Four Pests campaign—its origins and death toll—see Judith Rae Shapiro, *Mao's War against Nature: Politics and the Environment in Revolutionary China* (Cambridge University Press, 2001); on snail fever, see Ruth Rogaski, "Nature, Annihilation, and Modernity: China's Korean War Germ-Warfare Experience Reconsidered," *The Journal of Asian Studies* 61, no 2 (2002): 381–415; Miriam Gross, *Farewell to the God of Plague: Chairman Mao's Campaign to Deworm China* (University of California Press, 2016); and Lien-teh Wu, *Plague Fighter: The Autobiography of a Modern Chinese Physician* (Cambridge: W. Heffer & Sons Ltd, 1959).

One of the goals of this book is to reverse the public opinion of the literary figures Wang Shiwei and Guo Moruo. The latter has been the subject of many adulatory biographies, whereas there is almost no writing on the former, a person practically unknown to the West and excluded from most literary biographies of contemporary China. David E. Apter and Timothy Cheek's introduction to Dai Qing, *Wang Shiwei and "Wild Lilies": Rectification and Purges in the Chinese Communist Party 1942–1944* (Routledge, 2020) can be paired with the chapter "Rectification" in Margaret Hillenbrand and Chloë Starr, eds., *Documenting China* (University of Washington Press, 2014). The video documentary *The Buried Writer: Wang Shiwei* (RHTK production company, 2010) is available with English subtitles. Chinese-language biographies/edited collections of Wang Shiwei include *Lixue Danxin: Wang Shiwei*, ed. Li Jialing and Chen Siyu (Henan University Press 2012); Jun Zhang, *Wang Shiwei quan zhuan: Ye bai he Xia de yuan hun* (Jilin wenshi Press, 2020); and S. Louisa Wei, *Wang Shiwei: wen yi zheng feng yu si xiang gai zao* (City of Hong Kong University Press, 2016). Guo Moruo's actions have to be pieced together. A short biography can be found in Xiaobing Li, *Modern China* (ABC-CLIO, 2016), and a longer, albeit still adulatory one in Xiaoming Chen, *From the May Fourth Movement to Communist Revolution: Guo Moruo and the Chinese path to Communism* (State University of New York Press, 2007). The deaths of his sons Guo Shiying and Guo Minying are described in Feng Xigang, *Guo Moruo de Wannian Suiyue* (Zhongyang wenxian Press, 2004).

On the party's world-facing propaganda campaigns: In the late 1950s the party started invoking anti-imperialism, while anti-imperialism as a concept, at least, was introduced by the party in the '20s: "The spread of the concept of imperialism in China reached its initial climax during the 1920s when the Chinese Communist Party first introduced the term 'anti-imperialism' and during the large scale nationalist movements" (Jianwei Wang, "The Chinese Interpretation of the Concept of Imperialism in the Anti-imperialist Context of the 1920s," *Journal of Modern Chinese History* 6, no. 2 [2012]: 164–81). See also Edward Friedman, "Reconstructing China's National Identity: A Southern Alternative to Mao-Era Anti-Imperialist Nationalism," *The Journal of Asian Studies* 53, no. 1 (February 1994): 67–91. On Mao's making light of Japanese atrocities in China for political appeal to Japanese leftists, see Justin Jacobs, "Preparing the People for Mass Clemency: The 1956 Japanese War Crimes Trials in Shenyang and Taiyuan," *China Quarterly* 205 (March 2011): 152–72. For insight into Mao's PR campaign directed at disaffected American intellectuals and the Black Liberation Movement, see Yunxiang Gao,"W. E. B. and Shirley Graham Du Bois in Maoist China," *Du Bois Review: Social Science Research on Race* 10, no. 1 (Spring 2013): 59–85, and her book *Arise Africa, Roar China* (The University of North Carolina Press, 2021). See also chapter 5 of Reiland Rebaka, *Du Bois: A Critical Introduction* (Polity Press, 2021) and Robeson Taj Frazier, "Maoism and the Sinification of Black Political Struggle," in *The East Is Black: Cold War China in the Black Radical Imagination* (Duke University Press, 2015). Rana Mitter, *China's Good War* (Harvard University Press, 2020) offers a good overview of the political reasons behind early suppression of the facts of the Japanese occupation of China during WWII.

On Scar Literature, reform, and antiparty writings during Maoism, see: *A Companion to Modern Chinese Literature*, ed. Yingjin Zhang (Wiley, 2015); Merle Goldman, *Literary Dissent in Communist China* (Harvard University Press, 1967), Perry Link, *Roses and Thorns: The Second Blooming of the Hundred Flowers in Chinese Fiction, 1979–80* (University of California Press, 1984) and his *The Uses of Literature: Life in the Socialist Chinese Literary System* (Princeton University Press, 2021). Wang Rongfen's letter of dissent and her writings from prison, "Wo zai yu zhong de rizi [My Days in Prison]," can be found at www.secretchina.com/news/gb/2017/03/20/817410.html.

For more on Professor Chen Hongguo's teahouse *Lear* and other work by contemporary Chinese historian-critics, see Ian Johnson, *Sparks: China's Underground Historians and Their Battle for Their Future* (Oxford University Press, 2023).

The student referenced on page XXX is Luisana Gonzalez DiTillio, cited with permission.

3. Tragedy

Coleridge's lecture on *Lear* is collected in *Essays and Lectures on Shakespeare and Some Other Old Poets and Dramatists* (Turnbull and Spears, 1907). On *King Lear* as Tragedy, and the essence of tragedy, see: Stephen Booth, *"King Lear," "Macbeth," Indefinition, and Tragedy* (1993); Rhodri Lewis, *Shakespeare's Tragic Art* (Princeton University Press, 2024); and Devin Byker, "Promised Ends: The 'Exceeding Torments and Strange Behaviors' of *King Lear*" (Exemplaria, 2021).

For Hannah Arendt on Maoism and theories of totalitarianism, see P. Baehr, "China the Anomaly: Hannah Arendt, Totalitarianism, and the Maoist Regime," *European Journal of Political Theory* 9, no. 3 (2010): 267–86. Arendt's phrase "mass organizations of atomized, isolated individuals" and her assessments of China both come from *The Origins of Totalitarianism* (Harcourt Brace, 1973). The essay "Thinking and Moral Considerations" is collected in *Responsibility and Judgment* (Schocken

Books, 2003). Masha Gessen's application of Juan José Linz's clarification of the difference between authoritarianism and totalitarianism can be found in her interview with Eric Black in *MinnPost*, Sept. 25, 2020. Gessen's extended descriptions of life under Stalinist totalitarianism can be found in *The Future Is History: How Totalitarianism Reclaimed Russia* (Penguin, 2018) and conversation on the *Los Angeles Review of Books* podcast ("Masha Gessen on Russia's Evolution from Soviet Socialism to Putinism," Dec. 29, 2017).

For contemporary Chinese history, including biographies of Xi Jinping, Bo Xilai, and the second-generation CPC princelings: Ezra F. Vogel, *Deng Xiaoping and the Transformation of China* (Harvard University Press, 2011); Alfred L. Chan, *Xi Jinping: Political Career, Governance, and Leadership, 1953–2018* (Oxford University Press, 2022); Desmond Shum, *Red Roulette: An Insider's Story of Wealth, Power, Corruption, and Vengeance in Today's China* (Scribner, 2021); Pin Ho and Wenguang Huang, *A Death in the Lucky Holiday Hotel: Murder, Money, and an Epic Power Struggle in China* (*Public Affairs*, 2013). On Xi Jinping's descent into autocracy I strongly recommend the eight-episode series "The Prince" produced by *The Economist*: https://www.economist.com/theprincepod.

Film, photography, and other visual sources: Marc Riboud's photographs taken in China were published in 1966 in *The Three Banners of China* (Magnum Photos) and can also be found on Artstor. Wang Bing's documentary, *Dead Souls*, was released in 2018 through Grasshopper Films. At the time of this writing it is available for screening in its entirety on YouTube under its Chinese title, 死灵魂. Michelangelo Antonioni's documentary film *Chung Kuo—Cina* (1972) is also available for screening in two parts on YouTube. On the censorship of Antonioni's film and the international Maoist campaign against him, see Lucy O'Meara, "Barthes and Antonioni in China: The Muffling of Criticism," *Textual Practice* 30, no. 2 (2016): 267–86; and Stefano Bona, "Italian Film-makers in China and Changing Cultural

Perceptions: Comparing *Chung Kuo—China* (Michelangelo Antonioni, 1972) and *La stella che non c'è/The Missing Star* (Gianni Amelio, 2006)," *Journal of Italian Cinema and Media Studies* 2, no. 1 (March 2014): 41–58. The story of Selma Vos is from Nakao Eki Pacidal's Chinese-language translation (published in Taiwan in 2023, under the title 色爾瑪：逃離希特勒魔掌，卻成毛澤東囚徒) of Carolijn Visser's Dutch-language biography, *Selma: Aan Hitler ontsnapt, gevangene van Mao* [Selma: Escaped from Hitler, a Prisoner of Mao] (Atlas Contact, 2016).

Glenda Jackson's *Lear*, directed by Sam Gold and produced by Scott Rudin, ran at the Cort Theater in New York in the spring of 2019. Contemporary Chinese book, film, and stage Chinese *Lear*s include Sun-Shine Wang's 1968 *King Lear* and her subsequent collaboration with Simon Shan-chun Hong in their 1974 *King Lear*, starring W. T. Fu and Joseph Wang, both performed at the National Taiwan Arts Education Center; Li Liuyi's 2018 adaptation of Gregory Doran's English production of *King Lear*, translated by Daniel Yang and starring Pu Cunxin, Lu Fang, Zhao Lin, and Luo Wei, which ran in the National Centre for the Performing Arts in Beijing. Wu Hsing-kuo's 2001 *Lier zai ci* [Lear Is Here], starring the director himself in all the roles, was performed at the Novel Hall for Performing Arts; David Tse's 2006 futuristic adaptation of *King Lear*, starring Zhou Yemang and David Yip, can be found on MIT's Global Shakespeare's website (https://globalshakespeares.mit.edu/king-lear-tse-david-2006/). Daniel S. P. Yang, "*King Lear* in Beijing and Hong Kong," *Asian Theatre Journal* 28, no. 1 (Spring 2011): 184–98, compares his own adaptation for the Hong Kong Repertory Theater in 1993 to Sun Jiaxiu's version for the Central Academy of Drama in Beijing in 1986. On Nanjing University's aborted production of *Lear* by Professor Chen Jia and his students, see Wang Kaihao, "Golden Jubilee of the Bard's May Night," *China Daily*, May 2014, and Cong Cong's chapter "The 1964 Shakespeare Jubilee in China, Its Aftermath and Its

Echoes," in *Shakespeare Jubilees, 1769–2014*, ed. Christa Jansohn and Dieter Mehl (LIT Verlag, 2015).

On Peking opera, drama, and the Cultural Revolution: Byung-Joon Ahn, "The Politics of Peking Opera, 1962–1965," *Asian Survey* 12, no. 12 (Dec. 1972): 1066–81, and "An Interview with Ch'en Pi-lan on the Cultural Revolution," *World Outlook*, July 14, 1967, https://www.marxists.org/archive/chen/chenongpcr.htm; Walter J. Meserve and Ruth I. Meserve, "China's Persecuted Playwrights: The Theater in Communist China's Current Cultural Revolution," *Journal of Asian and African Studies* 5 (1970): 209–15; *Rethinking Chinese Socialist Theaters of Reform: Performance Practice and Debate in the Mao Era*, ed. Siyuan Liu, Tarryn Li-Min Chun, and Xiaomei Chen (University of Michigan Press, 2021); Douwei Wessel Fokkema, "Maoist Ideology and Its Exemplification in the New Peking Opera," *Current Scene* X, no. 15 (1972) 13-20; Joe He, *A Historical Study on the "Eight Revolutionary Model Operas" in China's Great Cultural Revolution* (University of Nevada Press, 1992). On the cataclysm of Wu Han's play *Hai Rui*: Tom Fisher, "'The Play's the Thing': Wu Han and Hai Rui Revisited," *The Australian Journal of Chinese Affairs* 7 (Jan. 1982): 1–35; Yan Jiaqi and Gao Gao, *Turbulent Decade: A History of the Cultural Revolution*, trans. and ed. D.W.Y. Kwok (University of Hawai'i Press, 1996); and Mary G. Mazur, *Wu Han, Historian: Son of China's Times* (Lexington Press, 2009). The most comprehensive account of the suffering of Peking opera artists during the Cultural Revolution is only available in Chinese: Zhang Yihe, *Lingren Wangshi* [Past Stories of Peking Opera Stars] (Hunan Literature and Art Press, 2006), since removed from the list on account of censorship. An excerpt has been translated into English by Alice Xin Liu for Words Without Borders ("Last of the Aristocrats," wordswithoutborders.org, November 1, 2012).

Chen Hongguo's performances of *Lear* are reviewed in Ian Johnson, "China: A Small Bit of Shelter," *New York Review of Books*, April 2019, and his subsequent interview with Chen, "'One Seed Can Make an Impact,'" in the following issue of

NYRB, May 2019. Other essays on Chen Hongguo: Abby Liu, "Chinese University Professor Quits to Seek Academic Freedom," *Global Voices*, December 2013; and Jun Mai, "How University Interfered with Chen Hongguo's Education," *South China Morning Post*, July 2016.

TRANSCRIPTS OF DOCUMENTS

1. Barbara Walters's interview with Jiang Zemin: "Jiang Zemin Interviewed by Barbara Walters about Tank-man," YouTube, archived by Menschenrechte für China e.V.
2. Deng Xiaoping's "Four Cardinal Principles" can be found in *Selected Works of Deng Xiaoping, 1975–1982* (Foreign Languages Press, 1984).
3. Kuang Huan Fan, *The Chinese Cultural Revolution: Selected Documents* (Grove Press, 1968).
4. *The Tiananmen Papers*, compiled by Zhang Liang, ed. Andrew J. Nathan and Perry Link (Perseus Books 2001).
5. Mao's "Talks at the Yan'an Forum on Art and Literature" can be found in a 1960 edition issued by the Foreign Press in Beijing and *Chairman Mao's Talks to the People*, ed. Stuart Schram, trans. John Chinnery and Tieyun (Pantheon, 1974). His speeches, including the July 14, 1956, speech "US Imperialism Is a Paper Tiger," can be found in the nine-volume *Selected Works of Mao Tse-Tung* (Vols. 1–5 published by the Foreign Language Press in Beijing; Vols. 6–9 published in India by Kranti Publications). See also *Mao Tse-tung on Art and Literature* (Beijing University Press, 1960).

English translations and summaries of the operas *Tuo Zhao* and *Peng Bei* from *The Generals of the Yang Family* can be found in Keith Stevens and Jennifer Welch, "'The Yang Family of Generals': Yang Chia Chiang 楊家將," *Journal of the Hong Kong Branch of the Royal Asiatic Society* 37 (1998): 39–61; Wilt L.

Idema and Stephen H. West, *The Generals of the Yang Family: Four Early Plays* (World Century, 2013); and Jin Fu, *Chinese Theater* (Cambridge University Press, 2012). On the operas *Xiaoyao Ford* and *Shoushan Altar* from the history of the abdication of Han dynasty emperor Xian: David Rolston, *Inscribing Jingju/Peking Opera: Textualization and Performance, Authorship and Censorship of the "National Drama" of China from the Late Qing to the Present* (Brill, 2021); and *The Beating of the Dragon Robe: A Repertoire of Beijing Opera Synopses of 100 Most Popular Pieces*, ed. Nianpei Li (Joint Publishing Company, 1988). The injustice of Dou E is covered in Rudolf G. Wagner, *The Contemporary Chinese Historical Drama: Four Studies* (University of California Press, 2022) and Ni He, *Chinese Criminal Trials: A Comprehensive Empirical Inquiry* (Springer, 2013). Francis Ya-Chu Cowhig's adaptation of the story, *Snow in June*, premiered at the Oregon Shakespeare Festival in 2018 (a print edition was published by Bloomsbury in 2018). For an introduction to the role of petition in premodern Chinese civil society, see Martin Powers, *China and England: The Preindustrial Struggle for Justice in Word and Image* (Routledge, 1990).

4 and 5. Comedy and Romance

On readings of comedy in *Lear*: G. Wilson Knight, "*King Lear* and the Comedy of the Grotesque" in *Twentieth Century Interpretations of "King Lear": A Collection of Critical Essays*, ed. Janet Adelman (Prentice Hall, 1978); Julian Markels, "Shakespeare's Confluence of Tragedy and Comedy: *Twelfth Night* and *King Lear*" (*Shakespeare Quarterly*, 1964); Stephen Book, "Likenesses and Differences between *Love's Labor Lost* and *King Lear*, Comedy and Tragedy," in *"King Lear," "Macbeth," Indefinition, and Tragedy* (Yale University Press, 1983); Robert S. Miola, "New Comedy in *King Lear*," *Philological Quarterly* 73 (Summer 1994), 329–46; Susan Snyder, *The Comix Matrix of Shakespeare's Tragedies* (Princeton University Press 2019). For readings of the Learian fool in particular: George Orwell's essay "Lear, Tolstoy, and the Fool," in *The Orwell Reader: Fictions, Essays, and Reportage* (Harcourt, 1934); R. A. Zimbardo, "The King and The Fool: *King Lear* as Self-Deconstructing Text," *Criticism* 32, no. 1 (1990): 1–29; Robert B. Hornback, "The Fool in Quarto and Folio *King Lear*" (*English Literary Renaissance*, 2004). Edgar in the design of reconciliation: Simon Palfrey, *Poor Tom: Living "King Lear"* (University of Chicago Press, 2014); Russell A. Peck, "Edgar's Pilgrimage: High Comedy in *King Lear*," *Studies in English Literature, 1500–1900* 7, no. 2, "Elizabethan and Jacobean Drama" (Spring, 1967): 219–37. Charles Lamb's comment on Nahum Tate's comedic resolution ("can draw about the beast more easily") comes from his essay "On the Tragedies of Shakespeare," in *Lamb's Criticism* (Cambridge University Press, 1923).

Overviews of the role of the "chou/fool" in Peking opera, and especially the bodily cost of his truth-telling: Xu Chengbei, *Peking Opera* (Cambridge University Press, 2010); Ashley Thorpe, *The Role of the Chou "Clown" in Traditional Chinese Drama: Comedy, Criticism, and Cosmology on the Chinese Stage* (Edwin Mellen Press, 2007); Colin Mackerras, *Chinese Theater from Its Origins to the Present Day* (University of Hawai'i Press, 1983); Wang Shouzhi, *Yuan Zaju Xiju Yishu* [Yuan Dynasty Zaju's Comic Art] (Anhui Art and Literature Press, 1985); Wang Chuansong, *Chou Zhong Mei: Wang Chuansong Tanyi Lu* [The Beauty in the "Ugly": Wang Chuansong on Theater Art] (Taipei, Yuanzhi Press, 1992).

On Chinese dramas in the 1980s and '90s, and their comedic cultural forms: Ying Zhu, *Television in Post-Reform China: Serial Dramas, Confucian Leadership and the Global Television Market* (Routledge, 2008); Yuzhen Guo and Lin Zhang, "The Comedy Narrative of Contemporary Family Drama and Its Motivation Analysis" in *Proceedings of the 4th International Conference on Contemporary Education, Social Sciences and Humanities* (Atlantis Press, 2019). On comedians under Maoism: see the obituary for Shan Tianfang in *Economist* (September 27, 2018) and on the *BBC World News* (September 23, 2018). Colin Mackerras's *Chinese Theater* is also a source for understanding the Chinese street and teahouse comedic forms (*er ren zhuan, xiang shen, xiaopings, pingshu*) that appear in the "Comedy" chapter. See also the *Handbook of Chinese Popular Culture*, ed. Patrick Murphy and Dingbo Wu (Greenwood, 1994); *TV Drama in China*, ed. Michael Keane, Ruoyun Bai, and Ying Zhu (Hong Kong University Press, 2008); Ying Zhu, *Chinese Cinema During the Era of Reform: The Ingenuity of the System* (Praeger, 2003), and her *Television in Post-Reform China: Serial Dramas, Confucian Leadership and the Global Television Market* (Taylor and Francis, 2013); *Not Just a Laughing Matter: Interdisciplinary Approaches to Political Humor in China*, ed. King-fai Tam and Sharon R. Wesoky (Springer, 2017). Xue Yiwei's *King Lear and 1979* was published in the magazine *Zuo Jia* (作家) in three parts (Issues 613, 614, and 614) in 2020. It is not yet available in English translation, but summaries can be found in Lin Gang, "Xue Yiwei's *King Lear*," trans. Stephen Nashaf, *Chinese Literature Today* 10, no. 2 (2021): 39–45; and Jeff Wasserstrom's interview with the author, "Xue Yiwei: In Search of Universal Values," *Los Angeles Review of Books–China Channel*, April 2020.

On *Romeo and Juliet* and its adaptation and reception in China: Ramie Targoff, "Mortal Love: Shakespeare's *Romeo and Juliet* and the Practice of Joint Burial," *Representations* 120, no. 1 (2012): 17–38; *Shakespeare in China*, ed. Shakespeare Association of China (Shanghai Art and Literature Press, 1987); Xiaoyang Zhang's *Shakespeare in China: A Comparative Study of Two Traditions and Cultures* (University of Delaware Press, 1996). Hazlitt on *Lear* appears in *Characters of Shakespeare's Plays* (London, C. H. Reynell, 1817); Frederick Burwick, *Poetic Madness and the Romantic Imagination* (University Park, PA: Penn State University Press, 1996); Emily Sun, *Succeeding "King Lear"* (New York: Fordham University Press, 2010); Mark Sandy, *Romanticism, Memory, Mourning* (Oxfordshire, UK: Routledge, 2013); see John Mulrooney on Keats's "On Sitting Down to Read *King Lear* Once Again": "Keats in the Company of Kean," *Studies in Romanticism* 42, no. 2 (Summer 2003): 227–50.

INDEX

Page numbers in *italics* denote illustrations.